America Faces Russia

Books by Thomas A. Bailey

Theodore Roosevelt and the Japanese-American Crises (1934)

A Diplomatic History of the American People (1940; 4th ed., 1950)

The Policy of the United States toward the Neutrals, 1917–1918 (1942)

America's Foreign Policies: Past and Present (1943)

Woodrow Wilson and the Lost Peace (1944)

Woodrow Wilson and the Great Betrayal (1945)

Wilson and the Peacemakers (1947), combining both Wilson books

The Man in the Street (1948)

America Faces Russia (1950)

RUSSIANS BEING EXILED TO SIBERIA
(From George Kennan, *Siberia and the Exile System*, 1891.)

America Faces Russia

RUSSIAN - AMERICAN RELATIONS

FROM EARLY TIMES TO OUR DAY

Thomas A. Bailey

STANFORD UNIVERSITY

GLOUCESTER, MASS.
PETER SMITH
1964

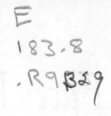

Preface

SEVERAL years ago an American diplomat who had recently returned from Moscow remarked that the more he read of Russia's past the less he found new in her present. This challenging thought lay behind my decision to write a book on Russian-American relations. There are few if any subjects more important today than our dealings with the Soviet Union, and there are few if any comparable problems about which there exists as much popular misunderstanding. It is to be hoped that a clearer comprehension of our relationships with the Russians in the past will enable us to deal more intelligently with them in the future.

In essence this book is a broad survey of Russian-American relations from earliest contacts to recent times. The story is largely concerned with diplomatic problems, and the emphasis, in line with the theme that I have developed in other public opinion studies, is on the American attitudes toward such problems. Some slight attention is paid to the influence of Russian literature on the American mind, but none at all to Russian music, ballet, opera, and theater. The latter have been culturally influential, but they either were relatively unimportant in shaping public attitudes toward Russia or they came so late that those attitudes were already definitely shaped by other factors.

Many of the stereotypes that we as a people formed about the regimes of both Czars and Communists were not well founded in fact. A disquieting amount of the information that we received about Russia was one-sided, warped, or completely false. My primary purpose is to discover what we thought on the basis of what we learned, not what we would have thought had we secured full and accurate information. This is why—and some of my readers will never be able to understand this—I repeat a good many lurid reports that were palpably untrue, without always going out of my way to emphasize their falsity. In a democracy like ours, where public opinion is such a powerful force, the truth is often less important than what the people think is the truth.

Since I am a student of American history, and disclaim any pretense to being an authority on Russia, I have written this book from the point of view of the United States, and have limited the Russian background to such bare essentials as are necessary for an understanding of American reactions. No attempt is made to develop in any detail the evolution of Russian opinion toward the United States. Perhaps one day, when all the extant materials become available, some scholar will write a book on this subject. I wish him luck. It is difficult enough to assess public opinion in a democracy where discussion in the newspapers is reasonably free and unfettered. It is vastly more difficult where the press operates under iron censorship.

I have deliberately chosen to devote more space to the era of the Czars than to that of the Communists. Much of the more recent period is reasonably familiar to prospective readers, and the unavailability of relevant documents militates against writing with satisfying finality. As a historian I am concerned largely with the roots of present relations and attitudes, especially those having to do with national character, and I have found it rewarding to stress the years before 1917, particularly where I have chanced upon virgin materials. Because I am attempting to cover the enormous sweep of nearly two centuries, and because I limited myself for various reasons to a book of this length, I deemed it desirable—not to say unavoidable—to appeal to the general reader through broad interpretation and judicious generalization rather than to the specialist through extensive documentation and elaborate detail.

Two of my colleagues in the History Department who are specialists on Russian or Near Eastern affairs helpfully criticized the manuscript. They are Professor Anatole G. Mazour and Professor Wayne S. Vucinich. Dr. Fritz T. Epstein, Research Associate and Curator of Slavic Collections, Hoover Institute and Library, and Mr. Nicholas I. Rokitiansky and Mr. Robert P. Browder, Slavic Fellows in the Hoover Institute and Library, rendered a similar service. I here record my indebtedness, while advising the reader that they and my other critics do not in all instances approve of either my approach or my conclusions. Others who read the manuscript critically are Professor Edith R. Mirrielees, a former teacher and now editor of the *Pacific Spectator*; Dr. Arthur L. Dean, my father-in-law; and Sylvia Dean Bailey, my wife. Mrs. James Madison Wood, Jr., and Mr. Stuart G. Cross served efficiently as research assistants. The staffs of the Department of State, of the National Archives, of the Library of Congress, and of the Stanford libraries were, as usual, highly cooperative. Scores of United States army and foreign service officers whom I interviewed in Europe during 1947—particularly in Germany, Austria, and Czechoslovakia—provided much off-the-record information as to their dealings with the Soviets near or within the iron curtain. Several hundred of my students—whether in dissertations, theses, or term papers—have broken ground or explored bypaths in a way that has proved useful. Their taskmaster will always feel a keen sense of obligation.

THOMAS A. BAILEY

Department of History
Stanford University, California

Contents

I	The Legend of the Cordial Catherine	1
II	The Era of the Amiable Alexander	12
III	A Muscovite Menace	22
IV	Rifts in the Friendship	35
V	The Calm of Despotism	45
VI	Ferment in the Fifties	56
VII	Fires of Civil Conflict	70
VIII	The Russian Fleet Myth	81
IX	The Purchase of Alaska	95
X	Cracks in the Ancient Friendship	108
XI	Pogroms and Prisons	121
XII	Despotism at Home and Dominance Abroad	136
XIII	Malnutrition and Extradition	150
XIV	The Sunset of the Century	161
XV	A Parting of the Ways	176
XVI	The Russo-Japanese Debacle	185
XVII	Berated Are the Peacemakers	198
XVIII	Battling for Principle	209
XIX	Days That Shook the World	228
XX	The Red Specter of Bolshevism	239
XXI	Reds Become Pinker	251
XXII	The Right Hand of Recognition	262
XXIII	A Descent into the Abyss	274
XXIV	The Strange Alliance	289
XXV	Forks in the Road	304
XXVI	The Shadow of the Hammer and Sickle	319
XXVII	The Cold War	335
XXVIII	A Long View	347
	Bibliography	357
	Index	369

List of Illustrations

Russians Being Exiled to Siberia   *Frontispiece*

Bruin Become Mediator or Negociation [*sic*] for Peace   17

"Brother, Brother, We're Both in the Wrong!"   43

Turkey in Danger   54

Bursting of the Russian Bubble   68

Extremes Meet   74

John Bull and Louis Napoleon Descry upon the Horizon a Cloud
about the Size of Two Big Men's Hands   90

"The Big Thing"   103

The Grand Duke's Reception   109

"No You Don't!"   145

Paderewski's Span Not in It with Alex's   167

The Performer—"It was unintentional!"   181

Russia—"Never will I compromise my dignity for the sake of securing peace"   194

The Edge of the Precipice   207

The Advance of Civilization   226

Breaking into the Big League   231

Svengali   237

What's the Difference?   240

The Government of Russia   245

On the Threshold!   249

Hard to Help   255

The Russian Workmen's Government   260

Aren't We Having Enough Trouble with the Machinery?   263

Just Another Customer   269

Grinding It Out   286

The Three Musketeers . . .   309

"I'm Here to Stay, Too"   321

A Question of Geography   339

An Impossible Trail?   352

America Faces Russia

I

The Legend of
the Cordial Catherine

"What right have I, after all, to interfere in a quarrel
[in America] foreign to my own concerns, on a subject
I am not supposed to understand, and with Courts at
such a distance from me?"—Catherine the Great, 1779

I

I AM so glad to see you here," declared Czar Alexander I as
he advanced graciously across the floor of the Imperial Palace
toward John Quincy Adams, recently arrived in St. Petersburg as the first minister of the United States in Russia.

Thus officially began, on a chill November day in 1809, that
curious and incongruous friendship between the two great nations. It was destined to persist, with numerous ups and downs,
for over a century, and ultimately became an indestructible part
of our folklore. So much misunderstanding exists regarding it that
certain basic explanations must be made at the outset.

One fruitful source of confusion has been a failure on the part
of the American public to perceive that an international friendship is something quite different from a personal friendship. A
personal friend is one to whom we are drawn by respect, esteem,
or even affection. He is usually one with whom we have much
in common, and we seek and enjoy his company. We take pleasure in assisting him in time of trouble, as he does us, not because

of any selfish advantage, but because we derive inner satisfactions from helping those whom we like.

International relationships rest on an entirely different foundation. By Websterian definition, a "friendly state" is simply one that is "not hostile or antagonistic."

In the light of such a definition the traditional Russian-American amity of the nineteenth century was real, even though somewhat hollow. The two systems of government were antipathetic in the highest degree; the two peoples saw practically nothing of one another; and the Czar, as was perfectly natural, exploited us openly in promoting his own ambitions. The most significant bond that the mismated nations had in common was a hatred of England, and out of hatred grew friendship. There is an adage to the effect that the enemies of our enemies are our friends—whether we like them or not.

These are the elemental facts of international intercourse. But the phrase "historic friendship" was mouthed so frequently in the era of the Czars that the undiscerning American, not recognizing the niceties of diplomatic terminology, ascribed to despotic Russia the unselfishness of a personal friend. When the day of disillusionment finally dawned, we revealed a tendency, no less illogical, to write off the whole attachment as completely spurious.

In personal friendships motives are all-important; in international friendships they are not. The results are what count. Motives in the international sphere may be completely selfish, as they commonly and properly are. This was essentially true of Russian-American accord under the Czars, but whatever its motivation the attachment at times seemed very real and occasionally exerted a powerful influence on the course of events.

2

Legends about international relationships are most apt to be born in times of great stress, and under the spell of intensely wishful thinking. Such legends endure tenaciously because they have been burned into the national consciousness by the hot iron of events. This is notably true of our oldest friendship, that with France, whose aid was indispensable to us in our war for independence. Countless millions of Americans, under the spell of the Lafayette tradition, have swallowed the myth that the French monarchy helped us because it admired our revolutionary new democracy, and not because it wanted to achieve its own ends by hamstringing Britain.

Our next oldest traditional friend is Russia. She was on our side, or appeared to be, not only during the War of Independence but also during the hardly less critical years of the War of 1812 and the great Civil War. Little wonder that the legend of Czarist affection for the new republic took a deep hold.

The first of these hoary myths sprang up about the person of Catherine II, better known as Catherine the Great. Generations of our people were brought up to believe that the Czarina was the "Mother of Independence," for presumably out of love for the gallant American revolutionists she spurned a request of George III for the hire of some 20,000 Russian soldiers to crush his rebellious subjects.

It is a fact that in 1775 the British monarch applied to his fellow sovereign for hirelings. It is also a fact that Catherine II refused the royal request. But there seems to be no basis for the belief that she did so out of any sentimental regard for the quarrelsome colonials. In her reply to the king, she pointed out that she had just finished an exhausting war with the Turks, and that for various reasons she deemed it unwise to send 20,000 troops so far away, where they would be out of touch with their Empress. She nevertheless assured His Britannic Majesty that he could count on her good will and her readiness to be useful to him.

The reasons listed by the cautious Catherine may not have been the real ones, but they certainly were good ones. This was an era when certain autocratic courts found it fashionable to toy with advanced ideas, and the unwary have been misled by Catherine's dabbling in liberalism, through Voltaire and others, into thinking that she cherished real affection for rebellious subjects. Her later castigation of the French revolutionists as a "gang of criminals" betrayed her fundamental convictions.

Rebuffed by Catherine II, George III struck a bargain with certain small German states, and ultimately employed some 30,000 so-called Hessians, whose plunderings and blunderings in the new world brought their name into execration. The tradition of Russian-American cordiality almost certainly would never have taken hold if Cossacks rather than Hessians had been turned loose upon the sons and daughters of liberty.[1]

This incident was remembered in a curious context more than a hundred years later. The Bolsheviks were defending the soil of Russia against foreign intervention, including that by United States troops in Siberia and North Russia. Many American liberals and other friends of the new Bolshevist regime protested against our participation. They argued that since Catherine II had generously declined to send Cossacks to America during our war for independence, we should repay this debt by refusing to send doughboys to Russia during her war for survival.

3

In 1780, during the later stages of the American Revolutionary War, Catherine II took the lead in organizing the neutral nations of Europe into what was known as the Armed Neutrality. Her purposes of course were purely selfish. Among other things she hoped to force the British—who were then beset by Spain, France, and The Netherlands—to acknowledge the rights of neutral shippers and thus benefit Russian commerce. She also planned to compel the beleaguered British to accept a mediation

---

[1] A variant of the legend is that Catherine *offered* her Cossacks to George III, but Frederick the Great of Prussia ruined the transaction by refusing to permit them to cross his territory (*Outlook*, LXXVI, 617 [March 5, 1904]). Frederick had nothing to do with such an incident, but the story perhaps has its basis in the fact that he declined to allow certain Hessian troops to pass through his country (P. L. Haworth, "Frederick the Great and the American Revolution," *American Historical Review*, IX, 469 [April, 1904]).

proposal which she was sponsoring in the hope of establishing herself as arbiter of the destinies of Europe.

The news of the anti-British League of Neutrals, which ultimately included most of nonbelligerent Europe, reached America during one of the darkest periods of the Revolution, just after the disastrous defeats at Charleston and Camden. The good tidings gave a lift to our drooping morale, and may have contributed materially to our determination to fight on to Yorktown and beyond. The British were correspondingly depressed. But it does not follow, as many Americans assumed then and later, that Catherine II formed the League out of sympathy for us.

The bare facts are that the Armed Neutrality was a league of *neutrals*, and the United States, as a belligerent, was not eligible to membership. Catherine invited other neutrals to join, but not the revolutionary American republic. Yet because we stood for the same principles of a free sea as the League of Neutrals, we naturally but ill-advisedly tried to push our way in. This is perhaps the only time in the long history of American isolationism, at least until 1948, that we actively sought admission into a European political organization.

An offshoot from the original legend, less widely held, is that the Armed Neutrality won the war for the embattled colonials. "The surrender of Cornwallis at Yorktown," declared a writer for *Harper's Weekly* in 1905, "did not bend the inflexible will of George III; what broke the King's stubborn heart was the adhesion of Catherine II to the League of Neutrals, by which British commerce was exposed to a process of strangulation." [2]

This is manifestly an exaggeration. The League did force the Mistress of the Seas to modify her maritime practices to some extent, but not cripplingly so. It did help bring the British to a fuller realization that the entire world was against them, and that they would be well advised to salvage what they could from the debacle. But the truth is that the Armed Neutrality was not firmly united, and that the scattered forces of its members were not

[2] XLIX, 1368 (Sept. 23, 1905).

formidable. Catherine II in fact ultimately sneered at her own brain child as the "Armed Nullity," and turned her attention to the Turkish problem. After all, why not let the two camps of belligerents waste each other's strength, while Russian power and influence increased proportionately? This was undeniably prudent policy.

Catherine II actually missed an opportunity to become the "Little Mother" of the Great American Republic, had that been her wish. In the dark days before and after Yorktown, the naval strength of Britain was precariously balanced with that of her foes. If Catherine had marshaled the total power of the Armed Neutrality, and had thrown it vigorously into the scales, she might have been able to force the British to terms. John Adams, then the American envoy in The Netherlands, pointed out again and again that in pursuing such a course lay Catherine's certain road to "glory," and he was both surprised and disgusted when she took another path. But the Czarina would never have earned the title "Great" if she had placed the interests of others above those of the nation whose destinies were entrusted to her hands.

4

The strange mission of Francis Dana, who cooled his heels in St. Petersburg from 1781 to 1783, further confuses the Catherine legend.

A new government, like that of the fledgling United States in 1776, does not ordinarily send diplomatic envoys to foreign courts until some hint is dropped that they will be welcome. No such intimation was forthcoming from Catherine II's capital, but so desperate was our need for allies that we decided to pocket our pride and send an emissary anyhow.

Dana was instructed by Congress to secure recognition, assistance, admission to the Armed Neutrality, and a commercial treaty. This would have been an ambitious program for even a welcomed envoy, which the American decidedly was not. The formal reception of an agent from a rebelling state constitutes official recognition, and if accorded prematurely is regarded as a legitimate cause of war by the mother country. The calculating Catherine II, who enjoyed the balancing and mediatory role of a powerful neutral, had no stomach for a clash with Great Britain.[3]

The uninvited guest, who was poorly supplied with funds, took up unpretentious quarters in the Russian capital, and his enforced frugality cost him both prestige and valuable contacts. Dana was a strait-laced Puritan, and neither he nor his secretary and French translator, the precocious "Master Johnny" Adams (John Quincy Adams), then fifteen years of age, found himself at home in the atmosphere of the somewhat dissolute St. Petersburg society.

Dana's reiterated complaints, whether well founded or not, are of unusual interest because many of them were repeated time and again by his successors down to recent times. He was annoyed by the surveillance of the secret police; by the opening of his mail by postal authorities; by the favoritism and blackmail at court (of which he caught only a faint glimpse); by the necessity of having to pay the four principal Russian ministers a bribe of 6,000 rubles apiece, if he hoped to negotiate a commercial treaty; by flagrant graft (the officers of one regiment sold all the horses and pocketed the proceeds); by delays in getting appointments, complicated by humiliating rebuffs; by subterfuges and evasions (the Russian vice-chancellor refused to put his commitments in writing); by empty professions; by the dissimulation of Catherine II; and by the futility of honest purpose and high-minded argument.

Some of these objectionable practices, one should note, were to be found in other European courts, though perhaps not to such

---

[3] Benjamin Franklin, then representing the United States in Paris, through an oversight received a card of visit from the son of the Empress, and acknowledged the honor by signing the callers' list at the house of the Russian ambassador. Fearful lest England take offense, the Russians in great perturbation persuaded Franklin to burn the card and to allow his name to be erased (Francis Wharton, ed., *The Revolutionary Diplomatic Correspondence of the United States* [Washington, 1889], V, 558 [July 1, 1782]).

a pronounced degree. Valuable presents in the form of bribes were common in eighteenth-century diplomacy, and in Russia they may have been a heritage from the days when the Muscovites had paid tribute to their Tartar overlords.

At any rate the long-suffering Dana endured the miseries of the St. Petersburg climate for almost two years. Catherine II had definitely made up her mind not to recognize our independence until Britain did, and since we wanted Russian help so as to achieve that independence, we finally decided that the game was not worth the candle. Dana packed up his belongings and came home, declaring that "the life of a Boston truckman" was preferable to the diplomatic glories of St. Petersburg.

This unhappy experience did much to offset the conception in America of a friendly Catherine II, and gave some currency to a much less widely held counterlegend that the Empress was actually an open enemy of our people. More than a century later, in the 1920's, when uninvited and unwanted agents of the Bolsheviks came to the United States, seeking recognition and assistance, certain American conservatives alleged that in giving them the cold shoulder we were merely following the example of Catherine II in her dealings with Dana.

In all fairness one must conclude that no particular blame attaches to the Czarina. We were far more at fault in attempting to force our selfish attentions upon her than she was in refusing to accept them. It is true that she might have clarified the atmosphere by making known her position to Dana in unequivocal Anglo-Saxon terms, but that was not her way or the Russian way of doing things.

5

During the critical years of Dana's mission St. Petersburg seethed with intrigue. The resourceful British ambassador plotted to offset the influence of his nation's enemies, particularly of France, whose envoy, despite the recent alliance, dealt deviously and highhandedly with Dana. The frustrated American complained to John Adams at The Hague, and through Adams—and even directly—laid his troubles before the men in Congress who were in charge of our statecraft. It is not farfetched to assume that young John Quincy Adams, who later had a large hand in aiming the Monroe Doctrine at Russia, was not immune from the searing impact of youthful impressions. The sum total of these disappointments near Catherine II's court further opened American eyes to the dangers lurking in balances of power and the machinations of European monarchs.

Catherine II did not find it to her advantage to welcome us into the Armed Neutrality, or to recognize us, or to make a treaty of alliance or commerce with us. So she did not. She saved us from these troublesome entanglements in spite of ourselves, and in this sense she may properly be spoken of as the godmother of American isolation.

6

The unfavorable picture of Catherine II already forming in the American mind was further darkened by the part that she played in mutilating the independent kingdom of Poland, and then erasing it from the map.

The first partition of Poland—among Frederick the Great of Prussia, Maria Theresa of Austria, and Catherine the Great of Russia—had taken place in 1772, before our own War of Independence and before we were deeply concerned with the fate of other peoples fighting for freedom.

But the second partition of Poland—between Catherine and Prussia—came in 1793 after we had won our independence. Our sympathies were profoundly stirred by this sorry tale of intrigue and greed, even though the contemporaneous wars of the French revolution stole the spotlight. We showed considerable enthusiasm when the valiant Kosciuszko, widely known in America for his participation in our own War of Independence, raised the standard of revolt in 1794 against Prussia and Russia, only to fall wounded on the battlefield and suffer incarceration in a Russian prison.

Kosciuszko was wishfully hailed in America, especially by his former comrades-in-arms, as the future "Washington of Poland." A popular toast drunk at a banquet in Philadelphia ran: "The brave Kosciuszko and his band of Patriots—May the Polish cavalry ride roughshod over the slaves of the Northern She-Bear. Three cheers." [4] When in 1797 the vanquished hero, after two years of imprisonment, made a triumphal tour of America, the people of Philadelphia unhitched the horses from his carriage and drew him to his lodging themselves.

The final partition of Poland in 1795—among Austria, Prussia, and Russia—wiped the ancient kingdom completely from the map.

It would be a mistake to assume that American resentment against this blow to liberty was directed solely at Catherine II and her Cossacks. Austria and especially Prussia shared the opprobrium, and at times Prussia was more roundly berated. American sentiment on the whole seems to have been pro-Pole, proliberty, and antityranny, rather than anti-Russian. But the Russians were commonly described as servile, treacherous, rapacious, savage, brutal, and bloodthirsty.

Catherine the Great, who personalized Russian ruthlessness and tyranny, received her full share of condemnation in American poems, sermons, toasts, and editorials. The "haughty" "Ruler of the North," the "Imperious Czarina," the "female despot," was a "she wolf" or a "ravenous she bear." One toast enthusiastically drunk at Baltimore in 1795 called for "Execration to the abominable tyrant—May the blood of Poland crying from the dust, bring down Heaven's vengeance on her."

Catherine II died in 1796, the year after the final partition of Poland. Philip Freneau, "the poet of the American revolution,"

---

[4] Miecislaus Haiman, *The Fall of Poland in Contemporary American Opinion* (Chicago, 1935), p. 136.

celebrated her demise by giving a reverse twist to the legend of
the Czarina's denial of her troops to George III:

> She would have sent her Tartar bands
> To waste and ravage gallic lands,
> She would have sent her legions o'er,
> Columbia! to invade your shore! [5]

---

[5] Fred L. Pattee, ed., *The Poems of Philip Freneau* (Princeton, 1907), III, 136.
Quoted by permission of the Princeton University Library.

II

The Era of the
Amiable Alexander

"Our attachment to the United States is obstinate—
more obstinate than you are aware of."—Remark of
Alexander I to John Quincy Adams, 1810

I

THE unfavorable public reaction in America to the rape of
Poland was but an interlude. Except for this one unhappy
episode, relations between the adolescent republic and
the ancient despotism continued virtually unrippled for more
than three decades. The flow of commerce was hardly more than
a rivulet, and there were only a few minor instances of friction,
such as poaching by American fur traders on Russian preserves
in what is now Alaska. Both nations were at loggerheads with
France in 1798, and the Russians, now the suitors, sought to have
us join a coalition against the French. But we were wisely unwilling to forsake the nonentanglement precepts of the Founding
Fathers.

In 1801 Thomas Jefferson mounted to the presidential chair
over the moribund body of the Federalist party. In the same year
Czar Alexander I mounted to the imperial throne over the murdered body of his insane father, in whose death he was strongly
suspected of having had a hand. From his youth onward Alexander had shown a sincere interest in the government of the United
States and a deepening admiration for Jefferson. Following the

Czar's efforts to secure the release of the crew of the United States frigate *Philadelphia*, captured in 1803 by Tripolitan pirates, Jefferson struck up an interesting correspondence with the Emperor, and furthered the instruction of his autocratic compeer by sending him books on the American constitution. It is somewhat amusing to note that when Jefferson established the two-term tradition by spurning a third term, the dictatorial Czar and his ministers expressed regret.[1]

All of this pleasant epistolary interchange took place during the years when Russia and America had not yet established formal diplomatic relations with each other, although the United States consul at St. Petersburg served as a medium of communication. The basic reason for the absence of official intercourse was that neither nation loomed sufficiently large in the other's eyes to warrant more than a consular establishment. Ideological differences had little if anything to do with the delay, as was definitely not true more than a century later following the Bolshevik revolution.

The story of Russian recognition of the United States in 1809 is charged with drama. Alexander I, who had been fighting on the side of Britain against France, was severely defeated in 1807 by Napoleon. The two foemen met on a raft in the Niemen River, near Tilsit, and after prolonged discussions the Czar agreed to change sides and join his adversary. (This shift was hardly less momentous than that of Stalin in 1939, when he turned against the western Allies and made his ill-starred treaty with Hitler.)

As a result of his pact with Napoleon, Alexander I soon found himself at war with the British, who proceeded to cut off seaborne trade with Russia. The Czar, who had hitherto been dependent on English shipping for his maritime outlets, was forced to look elsewhere for a carrier nation, and his eye naturally fell upon the mushrooming merchant marine of the United States. Russia's hitherto friendly toleration of the transatlantic republic suddenly gave way to a warm and persistent courtship.

---

[1] John C. Hildt, *Early Diplomatic Negotiations of the United States with Russia* (Baltimore, 1906), p. 37.

But Alexander I and his advisers looked upon America as much more than a carrier nation. Russia, as well as the other weaker maritime powers, had long suffered from the arbitrary practices of the British navy. A rival must be raised up to challenge "The Tyrant of the Seas"; Russia, landlocked and ice-clogged, could never hope to do so herself. The United States was the logical contender. The lusty young democracy had all the physical and geographical potentialities; besides, it was happily so far away that when it became strong it would not stand in the way of Russia's expansive designs. The basis of Czarist cordiality toward America during the nineteenth century was a determination to cultivate our power and friendship so that we could be used as a counterweight against the naval strength of Great Britain.

The United States grasped the outstretched paw of the Russian bear with understandable enthusiasm. If the Russians needed help against England's maritime might, so did we. This was the period when, shortly after the outrageous British attack on the United States frigate *Chesapeake,* we had turned to the self-crucifying embargo in an attempt to enforce our rights against Great Britain. Thus it came about that St. Petersburg and Washington formally exchanged ministers in 1809, twenty-six years after the recognition of our independence by the Mother Country.

By a singular coincidence the United States waited sixteen years before recognizing the new Bolshevist government in 1933. As in 1809, each nation was willing to enter into formal relations because each felt that it had some definite advantage to gain.

2

By a curious turn of the wheel of chance, the first minister selected for the American outpost in St. Petersburg was the same John Quincy Adams who, as the "Master Johnny" of Dana's days, had received a disillusioning introduction to the Russian Empire. It is regrettable that all subsequent envoys sent to Russia were not so well equipped for their duties, by training and previous contacts, as this rugged chip off old Plymouth Rock.

After a wearisome journey of nearly eighty days on a sailing ship, Adams reached his post. His primary responsibility was to safeguard American commerce, which during these years of blockades and counterblockades was receiving a manhandling from the two sets of belligerents. Fortunately, he was more than ordinarily successful in discharging his disagreeable duties.

Adams was greeted with every show of cordiality at the Russian court. The phrases with which the Emperor and his ministers avowed their friendship for the United States quickly became stereotyped and were repeated, like a well-learned ritual but with every evidence of sincerity, on ceremonial occasions for over a century. Duplicity has often been ascribed to Russian character, but in this instance the St. Petersburg officials were quite frank in avowing their motives. They made no bones about their primary desire to build up the United States as a counterpoise against the British navy and thus defend the rights of weaker maritime neutrals, including first of all the Russian Empire.

The new American envoy had a reasonably happy stay, despite the excessive cold, the long and gloomy winter nights, and the debilitating social functions, which rasped his Puritanical conscience as a waste of time. He described in a voluminous diary his daily walks about the capital; and some of his most delightful passages have to do with meeting Alexander I, similarly engaged in informal strolls, and the subsequent discussions between the two. There can be no doubt that the Emperor still retained his friendly interest in the United States. On one occasion Adams undertook to explain how we had come to seize a portion of West Florida from Spain in 1810 by highhanded methods. The Czar, perhaps thinking of the current reshaping of the map of Europe, smiled and said pleasantly, in the French of the educated classes, "On s'agrandit toujours un peu, dans ce monde." (Everyone always grows a little in this world.) [2]

Adams discoursed lengthily in his diary on the mechanical

---

[2] C. F. Adams, ed., *Memoirs of John Quincy Adams* (Philadelphia, 1874–1877), II, 261.

nature of the Greek Orthodox worship; on the self-crossings, the prostrations, and the kissings of the floor. He described the jewels of the women and the stars and ribbons of the overdecorated men. He stressed the jealousy and suspicion of the Russian officials, whose prying forced him to send his most confidential reports in cipher. He further complained of the delays in connection with passports, and of the generally dilatory nature of the Russian officials, many of whose promises and apologies proved completely empty. This in general was the same picture that etched itself in the memory of Francis Dana, and it is one that was described again and again, with varying shades, by subsequent American ministers.

3

Smarting from maritime outrages and other grievances, the United States rashly declared war on England, June 18, 1812, and prepared to invade Canada. Four days later, and by another strange coincidence, Napoleon even more rashly unleashed an attack on Russia. Among other things, he was exasperated by the refusal of his uneasy Slavic yokefellow to enforce the French restrictions against foreign shipping. By an even more extraordinary coincidence, France opened warfare 129 years to the day before Hitler launched his similarly disastrous assault upon his ally Joseph Stalin. Napoleon got to Moscow, which Hitler never did, but he might as well not have arrived, for the city was partially burned out from under him. The American invasion of Canada likewise backfired, though without Napoleon's initial successes or his frightful losses.

About a week after the fall of Moscow, when Russian fortunes were at low ebb, the Czar proposed to mediate between the United States and Britain, once again his ally. The formal proposal reached Washington early in 1813 when American fortunes were likewise at low ebb, following our failure to conquer Canada, and the Madison administration grasped at this opportunity to

BRUIN BECOME MEDIATOR OR NEGOCIATION [*sic*] FOR PEACE

The Russian bear mediates between John Bull and America. Actually, Russia rather than England took the initiative. The *Wasp* and the *Hornet* were United States ships that had recently defeated British adversaries. An American cartoon. (Courtesy of The New-York Historical Society, New York City.)

withdraw from a war that might prove disastrous. Without even waiting to learn whether London was favorable to mediation, President Madison dispatched two envoys to St. Petersburg. But the British for various reasons declined the good offices of Alexander I, and the whole scheme fell to the ground.

The legend grew rapidly among unthinking Americans that the Emperor attempted to mediate, *primarily* because he was a devoted friend of the United States and wanted to help us out of our difficulties. What are the facts?

It is now clear that Alexander I quite logically tried to intervene, not out of regard for America, but out of regard for Russia. He was in a critical plight following the fall of Moscow. If Britain sent her regular troops to fight in America, she would probably withdraw them from the Peninsular War in Spain, thus releasing French soldiers for the Russian front. By breaking with Napoleon, Alexander had made himself eligible for English shipping, and he was distressed to find his plans ruined by the ill-timed clash between the Mother Country and Daughter Country. He needed our commerce to supplement and compete with that of Britain; and the attacks of American privateers on English merchantmen interrupted his supplies from the outside world. Moreover, if the conflict continued, France and America, which were fighting on the same side against Britain, might by the force of events be driven into an alliance, and this would be harmful to Russia.

The Russian statesmen presumably perceived also that it did not square with long-run Russian policy to see America wasting her strength in a premature and one-sided conflict with the British. The events thus far in the Anglo-American war had strengthened the Russians in their determination to back America as a naval rival against England. The ill-trained armies of the United States had done poorly, but the contemptible "fir-built frigates" and sloops had, in a series of single-ship engagements, deflated the pride of the Mistress of the Seas. Thereafter the Russian court strove more actively to woo the United States, even to the extent of hoping ultimately for an alliance.[3]

4

Two myths have sprung from the major myth that the Czar attempted to mediate because of his love for the United States. One is that by intervening in the nick of time Alexander I brought us and the British together, thereby rescuing us from imminent disaster and securing a satisfactory peace. The other is that the American people universally recognized the Emperor's contribution and expressed gratitude for it.

It is true that although no direct results flowed from the attempted mediation, the American and British negotiators were brought together at Ghent, prematurely as the event proved. Nothing was decided by these emissaries until news from the battlefield indicated that the war had reached a stalemate, and then peace was rather speedily concluded. The probabilities are good that a similar result would have been achieved if Alexander I had never stepped in.

As for American gratitude, there were two schools of thought. On the one hand, considerable praise of the Czar was heard in Federalist New England. The people of this section were generally pro-British, and they vehemently opposed a war in support of the "anti-Christ" Napoleon against Great Britain, whose "fast-anchored isle" was the last important bulwark of constitutional government in Europe. The Russians were fighting against France on the side of Old England, and the New England Federalists naturally rejoiced over their victories. On the other hand, the Democratic-Republicans, who then controlled the government in Washington, applauded the successes of the French and belittled those of the Russians. The administration readily perceived that

---

[3] "How happens it," remarked Count Romanzoff to Adams, "that you are constantly beating at sea the English, who beat all the rest of the world, and that on land, where you ought to be the strongest, the English *do what they please?*" (Adams, *Memoirs*, II, 467).

while Napoleon was winning battles against the British he was pinning down redcoats who might otherwise be used to invade the United States, and who in fact later burned the capital.

When Napoleon's drive toward Moscow began with great momentum, the loyal supporters of President Madison cheered lustily. Then followed the icy retreat, and the New England Federalists gave vent to their joy. The freezing to death of tens of thousands of Frenchmen was celebrated by orations and processions, much to the disgust of the Democratic-Republicans. At an entertainment given in Boston to the Russian consul, glasses were raised in honor of "Alexander the Deliverer." "Cossack" festivals were held and toasts were drunk to the Cossack Platov, who had offered his daughter with a large dowry to anyone who would assassinate Napoleon—a salacious tale that was later proved false.[4]

The enthusiasm of the Federalists for the Czar was loudly condemned by the Democratic-Republicans. He had aroused great expectations in the United States by his mediatory overture, so great in fact as to inspire the fear that it was all a rumor. When he failed to follow through and press the British sufficiently, there was bitter disappointment. Once the fortunes of battle had turned against Napoleon, Alexander I was kept busy in the field, and he seems to have lost interest in his original proposal. The anti-Federalist *Niles' Weekly Register* sneered at the Federalists for having ceased to toast "Alexander the Mediator" and for having substituted "Alexander the Deliverer."

The vitriolic Hezekiah Niles, whose *Weekly Register* was the most influential journal of its kind in America, continued to pillory the "Tartars," and he helped implant in the public mind certain unflattering and not too accurate stereotypes. Alexander I, he declared, was a parricide, having connived at the murder of his father; Catherine the Great had not only murdered her husband but had lived in "open whoredom" with "a regiment of

---

[4] *Niles' Weekly Register*, VI, 144, 145 (April 30, 1814); XXIX, 115 (Oct. 22, 1825).

male prostitutes," whom she rewarded with gifts of some 150,000 slaves. The Cossacks were brave but bloodthirsty, cruel, savage, and unjust, "in their general manners, but little milder than some of the Indians of North America." Russia had produced a "few splendid characters," but the great mass were sodden serfs, subject to the caprice and lust of their masters and hardly above the level of our despised Negroes. The Russian Empire consisted "of *conquered* countries, *usurped* provinces and *ravaged* territories," and "Alexander the Deliverer" continued to hold vast numbers of subject peoples in slavery. "God help the world," cried Niles, "when *religion, order,* and *law* are to be supported by *Russians.*" [5] Yet this violent anti-Federalist and antimonarchist editor freely conceded that Alexander I, bad though he was, was still the best of the European crowned heads.

Such was the general picture that Hezekiah Niles hammered in upon his readers for over twenty years.

---

[5] *Ibid.,* VI, 145 (April 30, 1814).

III

A Muscovite Menace

> "*The powers of Europe*—The removal of *one* tyrant [Napoleon], has transferred the *sceptre* to the hands of *many* [The Holy Alliance]"—Fourth of July toast, 1816, at Augusta, Georgia

I

THE Russian Empire, despite costly sacrifices, emerged from the Napoleonic wars with relatively great power. Like the United States in 1917 and again in 1941, the northern giant had entered the conflict comparatively late, and at a time when both enemies and allies had wasted much of their strength. Alexander I was by far the ablest leader among the monarchs of Europe, and with the balance of power in dangerous imbalance, owing to the exhaustion of potential rivals, he was in a position to dominate the continent. His ascendancy was roughly analogous to that of Stalin in 1945.

The Russian armies, as was later true in World War II, had made an impressive record. They had shown defensive skill in eviscerating Napoleon's magnificent force; and then, spiking rumors of inept generalship and poor fighting quality, had assumed the offensive and expelled the remnants of the invader, though not without heavy losses to themselves. The reputation of Russian military prowess generally remained at a high level until deflated by the Crimean War.

The Czar's troops constituted a substantial part of the Allied juggernaut that rolled into France and crushed Napoleon. Tales of Russian atrocities, many of them no doubt exaggerated or false, found their way into the American press. The "Cossacks" were reported to have pillaged and plundered, robbed and raped, murdered and massacred. In one place they were said to have entered a hospital on horseback and to have despoiled and butchered all whom they found. At Fontainebleau the outraged French peasants killed some of their oppressors, and, according to one news report, many of the dead Russian looters "were found to have eight or ten watches." [1] (All of this is suggestive of the passion for wrist watches and other gadgets which the Russian invader of eastern Europe later revealed during 1945.)

Uneasiness was expressed in the British and American press over the size of the Russian army, which until its collapse in World War I was the largest of any European power. In 1816 the total strength of the Empire's military force was placed at 1,100,000; and there were the now familiar complaints that Alexander I, instead of demobilizing his soldiers, as the other Allies were doing, had increased their number. (Yet it should be noted that figures regarding the striking power of the Russian army during the nineteenth century are illusory. Disproportionately large numbers of soldiers were needed, many of them for police and garrison work, because the Czar had a disproportionately large domain to protect.)

There is also something surprisingly modern about the reports in the early 1820's that Russia was waging what is now called a war of nerves on Persia and Turkey. In 1821, 54,000 Russian troops were said to be mobilized on the Persian frontier, and the next year the Czar was allegedly massing 200,000 men on the Turkish border. The Turks were desperately bestirring themselves to put their country in the best possible state of defense.

The rumor also gained currency that the Russian troops who had been to France were, upon their return home, segregated

---

[1] *Niles' Weekly Register*, VI, 144 (April 30, 1814).

from the "lower orders" of the people. The government presumably feared that these soldiers, having been exposed to the liberal virus of the French Revolution, might exercise a contaminating influence. (This report parallels accounts after World War II that the Moscow regime put its troops who had been outside Soviet borders through an ideological "delousing.")

Just as the overthrow of Hitler in 1945 brought into the ascendancy a Communist power which to many people seemed no less a menace to our civilization than the Nazis, so the downfall of Napoleon and the dominance of Alexander I gave birth to similar misgivings. In the American press reference was made to an alleged remark of Napoleon—likewise paralleling Hitler's propaganda—that the Allies had made a great mistake in not fighting on France's side against the Cossack menace; in another generation all Europe would either be Russian or republican. The Marquis of Wellesley was reported to have said that the victory over Napoleon at Waterloo was unfortunate for England; having put down a power that she might have controlled, she had raised up a power that she would be unable to control.

2

While tales of Russian rapists were drifting into America from France, the Russian consul general in Philadelphia, one Koslov, was arrested in 1815 on the charge of raping a twelve-year-old girl employed in his household as a servant. The accused dignitary was thrown into prison.

The local authorities finally dismissed the case, even though one reputable historian asserts that Koslov was undoubtedly guilty. Only the federal courts could take cognizance of a crime committed by a consular official, and they did not assume jurisdiction in this instance because rape was a common-law offense. The Russian minister in Washington, Andrei Dashkov, after unsuccessfully attempting to secure both monetary reparation and a restitution of Koslov's character, abruptly broke off diplomatic relations on his own responsibility. Then, as now, the Russians did not appreciate the perplexities of Anglo-Saxon jurisprudence.

The imperial court in St. Petersburg was displeased by the cavalier treatment accorded the Czar's consular representative, and for some while thereafter the American minister was conscious of a frigid atmosphere. But upon more mature consideration Alexander I abandoned the high ground that his officials had taken, and normal relations were restored. The influential Washington *National Intelligencer* forthwith praised the magnanimity and flexibility of the Emperor. Minister Dashkov, who had succeeded in making himself thoroughly disagreeable, was recalled in response to American desires.

The whole unhappy affair was scarcely more than a tempest in a samovar. But it demolishes the legend that all was sweetness and light in our early diplomatic dealings with Russia, and that there had never been, as often alleged, any rupture of relations prior to the time of the Bolsheviks. The incident further focused attention on the fact that the Czar had not been sending a high class of representatives to America, as was also true of other European rulers, who did not regard the United States as of primary importance. Henceforth abler diplomatic and consular officials were generally chosen to represent their august master.

3

Alexander I, who had more energy and vision than other despots of his day, took the lead in drawing up a strange document known as the Holy Alliance. In broad terms it bound the signatory sovereigns to govern their subjects in accordance with the principles of the Christian religion. The rulers of Austria and Prussia signed with some reluctance, and possibly out of a desire to humor their powerful fellow monarch.

The Holy Alliance, as such, accomplished nothing of real consequence. But the term "Holy Alliance" was popularly though erroneously applied to the Quadruple Alliance, consisting of the three charter members of the Holy Alliance (Russia, Austria, and

Prussia), with the addition of Britain. If the Holy Alliance was visionary and not to be feared, the Quadruple Alliance was power politics and greatly to be dreaded.

Democratic Americans, nurtured as they were on the anti-monarchical and antialliance tradition, could hardly have been expected to greet the Holy Alliance with unrestrained enthusiasm. But surprisingly enough, it was received with considerable sympathy, especially in New England, which since 1812 had held Alexander I in grateful memory as a mediator and then a deliverer. Nor could Puritan New England take violent exception to any scheme, however meaningless, that was based upon the Christian religion. Despite the nonentanglement precepts of George Washington and the other Founding Fathers, some little agitation developed in favor of our adhering to the Holy Alliance. The Massachusetts Peace Society even entered into correspondence with Alexander I, who replied in cordial terms.[2] But one Baltimore editor probably echoed a more popular sentiment when he branded the whole scheme as a mask "to blind the misguided multitude."

After earlier feelers, the Russian government in 1819 formally invited the United States to join the Holy Alliance. Alexander I was parting company with Great Britain, his late ally in the war against Napoleon, and he returned instinctively to his old policy of cultivating good relations with the transatlantic republic. Almost automatically during the nineteenth century when England and Russia drifted apart, Russia and America drew closer together. Actually, the Russians in 1819 were looking toward ultimate alliance with the United States in support of mutual aims.

"Master Johnny" Adams was now Secretary of State, and with his rich years of experience in St. Petersburg was not to be entrapped by Russian wiles. While praising the righteous aims of the Holy Alliance, he made it clear that the United States was

---

[2] Merle E. Curti, *The American Peace Crusade, 1815–1860* (Durham, N.C., 1929), p. 27.

determined to keep entirely aloof from the political systems of Europe.

American tolerance of the Holy Alliance underwent a sharp change in 1820, when an epidemic of revolutions in Spain, Naples, and Portugal challenged the monarchical principle. The autocrats of Russia, Austria, and Prussia were alarmed by the outburst in Naples. Conferring together either in person or through their representatives at two conferences, one at Troppau and the other at Laibach, they took steps that led to the stamping out of the Neapolitan revolt. Although the crushing was done by Austrian troops, Alexander I had been present at both conferences, and the rumor spread that he had expressed a willingness to ravage Naples with thousands of Cossacks if the Austrians could not do the job.

Red-blooded American republicans were shocked by the snuffing out of the Neapolitan uprising. We instinctively sided with the oppressed rather than the oppressors, all the more so since we were devotees of liberty, beneficiaries of one of the great democratic revolutions of modern times, and sympathizers with the then embattled patriots of Spanish America. By mid-1821 the Russian minister in Washington reported that the American newspapers were "outspoken" against the Allied powers, and he refused to attend a Fourth of July banquet because "some one would be sure to attack the Holy Alliance." A popular contemporary toast was: "The Holy Alliance and the Devil: May the friends of liberty check their career, and compel them to dissolve partnership." [3]

Even the peace society enthusiasts of New England had by now cooled off, and many former friends of the "magnanimous Alexander," when he had been fighting Napoleon, had turned into critics. The Holy Alliance was clearly an unholy enterprise, and the Czar, as its leader, was thought to be more villain than saint, regardless of his high-sounding principles and his former benevolence toward the United States.

---

[3] Washington *National Intelligencer*, June 2, 1821.

4

While American eyes were focused on the repressive menace of Czarism in Europe, signs of a more imminent menace began to appear on what was destined to be our Pacific frontage.

Late in the eighteenth century adventuresome Russian pioneers had established trading posts in what is now Alaska, thus extending the vanguard of empire beyond the frozen wastes of Siberia into a third continent. Pushing down the northwest coast, they built Fort Ross in Spanish California, north of present San Francisco and near the mouth of the Russian River. A few other place names, such as Mount St. Helena, still bear silent testimony to their enterprise.

The preoccupied American was not unduly aroused by rumors of Russian penetration into faraway California. A few discerning citizens perceived that some day we would need a window on the Pacific, presumably San Francisco and its environs. But this all lay in the womb of the future, and in the meantime the scattered Spanish and Indian inhabitants were harmless caretakers.

The St. Louis *Enquirer* complained in 1819 that to its knowledge only one writer had mentioned Russian trespassing on the North American continent. This journal was distressed to note that while our people viewed with "astonishment" the progress of the Russian colossus in Europe and Asia, "they have not thought of looking to the west to see this giant power already mounting upon their own backs." The *Enquirer* had learned by roundabout reports through fur traders, both American and Russian, that the Czar planned to take over not only the gulf and peninsula of California but also Spanish claims to the western coast of North America. The *Democratic Press* reported late in the same year (1819) that the Russians had two or more warships cruising from below the coast of California to above the Columbia River. Most fantastic of all was the rumor, by way of a Russian frigate in Canton, that Spain had ceded California to the Czar in payment for forthcoming assistance in crushing the Spanish

American rebels.[4] But all of these tales caused little stir in a land-surfeited United States.

American indifference was rudely jarred in 1821, when Alexander I issued a ukase or decree forbidding foreign ships to venture within one hundred Italian miles of the coast of present-day Alaska, north of 51 degrees. Legend to the contrary, the decree was not intended as a hostile act. It was not evidence of new imperialistic dreams, but a rather hasty and ill-considered device to protect the monopoly of the Russian-American Company against foreign intruders. Yankee fur traders, among others, had penetrated this region and had not only cut into Russian profits but had debauched the Indians with alcohol. Such encroachments made more difficult local control of the natives and also led to disagreeable incidents which threatened to dampen Russo-American amity.

The American public quickly read into Alexander's manifesto a good deal more than was intended. By unfortunate timing, the document was issued only a few months after the Congress of Laibach, which had been dominated by the Czar and which had sounded the death knell of the Neapolitan revolt. In pushing the Russian sphere of interest well down the Pacific coast into the Oregon Country, Alexander I seemed to be revealing voracious designs on our future bailiwick. We had already cast covetous eyes upon it ourselves, and in the treaty that we had concluded with Britain only three years earlier, we had been admitted to temporary joint occupancy.

The ukase was not only a startling claim to sovereignty over one hundred miles of the open ocean, but it was an inconsistent claim as well. During most of the nineteenth century, and even earlier, both Russia and the United States were leading champions of a free sea against the pretensions of Britain. This was one of the few conspicuous occasions during those years when St. Petersburg temporarily turned its back upon the principle of freedom of the seas.

4 *Niles' Weekly Register*, XVI, 361 (July 24, 1819); XVII, 232 (Dec. 11, 1819).

5

The implications of the ukase were alarming, but American opinion, while generally unfavorable, was surprisingly calm. The newspaper editors seem to have been much more concerned about Russian designs on Austria, Greece, and Turkey. The northwest coast of North America was too far away; the line of 51 degrees established by Alexander I was several hundred miles north of the present boundary of the United States; there was plenty of elbowroom in this vast area for everyone; and the number of American fur traders affected was too few. Even so, more concern seems to have been expressed over our trading interests, especially by mercantile Massachusetts, than over the possible fate of the territory. There was even a little talk in Congress of protecting our commercial stake with fortifications on the Columbia River. *Niles' Weekly Register* sneered at the offensive decree of the "magnanimous Alexander" and suspected that it might mean war, but other spokesmen were inclined to poke fun at the greed of a sovereign who already controlled one sixth of the earth. Some months later a rhymster expressed his views in whimsical verse:

> Old Neptune one morning was seen on the rocks,
> Shedding tears by the pailful, and tearing his locks;
> He cried, a *Land Lubber* has stole, on this day,
> Full four thousand miles of my ocean away;
> He swallows the *earth*, (he exclaimed with emotion),
> And then, to quench appetite, *slap* goes the *ocean;*
> Brother Jove must look out for his skies, let me tell ye,
> Or the Russian will bury them all in his belly.[5]

The Department of State, which is better equipped than the public to perceive far-off dangers, betrayed much more anxiety and made vigorous representations to St. Petersburg, as did the British. The Russian Foreign Office, recognizing that the ukase

---

[5] *Ibid.*, XXIV, 146 (May 10, 1823).

had gone much further than was intended, quickly backed down on Russian claims to the high seas. For various reasons Alexander I decided to contract his overextended holdings and withdraw up the coast past 51° to 54° 40', the present southern tip of Alaska. He formalized this retreat by treaties with the United States (1824) and Great Britain (1825).

Recent scholarship has revealed that the Russian policy of withdrawal was motivated partly by a desire to avoid friction with the United States and Great Britain, so that the Foreign Office would have a freer hand to press for an outlet at the Dardanelles. Why push America into the arms of Great Britain over an issue involving a wilderness of questionable value to land-sated Russia? American friendship in the long run could be worth vastly more than a few cargoes of smelly furs.

6

Alexander I, as a ringleader of reaction, was eager to assist his fellow monarch, Ferdinand VII of Spain, in restoring the yoke of absolutism to the necks of the newly born Spanish American republics. In 1817 he sold to his brother monarch a half-dozen or so rotting warships, which, so the rumor ran, would be used against the South American revolutionaries. In return Russia would allegedly receive the Mediterranean island of Minorca as a naval base, plus the two Californias.

The Spanish revolutionary upheaval of 1820 diverted the attention of Alexander I to dangers nearer home. In 1821 the report spread in America that the Czar was eager to send a large number of his liberty-trampling troops into Spain.[6] Similar tales persisted until 1823, when French troops, acting as the hatchet men for the European sovereigns, did the job themselves in a thoroughgoing fashion. The fear was prevalent that they would next attack Spain's rebellious colonies.

---

[6] The Czar in 1822 had in mind 150,000 troops, but his allies did not welcome the idea. See Harold Temperley, *The Foreign Policy of Canning, 1822-1827* (London, 1925), p. 66.

The rebels of Spanish America had thrown open their ports to the outside world, and British and American traders were savoring this new trade, which formerly had been monopolized by Spain. If the autocrats of Europe, led by Alexander I, should next restore the Spanish king to the throne of his ancestors, this purblind Bourbon would no doubt withdraw the recently granted privileges. Neither the United States nor Great Britain—especially the British merchants—found the prospect palatable, and the presumed designs of the Czar were, contrary to his well-reasoned policy, propelling America and Britain into each other's arms.

On a momentous day in 1823 the British Foreign Secretary, George Canning, proposed that the United States join with Britain in a declaration designed to warn the European despots against meddling in the Americas. But Secretary of State John Quincy Adams induced his colleagues in Washington to rebuff this offer and embark upon a lone-wolf course. Entanglement was contrary to our traditional principles, and since in any event the British navy would presumably not permit the European monarchs to come, we could safely issue a defiant declaration under our own auspices.

The twice-told tale of the Monroe Doctrine need not be repeated. But the fact is often overlooked that the Doctrine had two barrels, the first of which was aimed ostensibly at Russia, and the second largely at Russia. With Russian activity on the northwest coast obviously in mind, Monroe warned the powers that there was henceforth a closed season on colonization in the Americas. This applied to England, France, and other nations, no less than to Russia. What they had they might retain, but they must not extend their holdings. The second barrel was aimed at the European despots, who were warned to keep their monarchical systems—and that meant the Holy Alliance and Russian absolutism—out of the New World. If they came, they might threaten our territorial and political security.

Legend again to the contrary, Monroe's memorable manifesto

did not frighten the European monarchs away. They appear not to have had any well-developed plans for intervention, and in any case the stout wooden walls of the British navy stood athwart their course. Alexander I was presumably annoyed by the republican pretensions of the Americans, all the more so because their bombast was so ridiculously disproportionate to their power. The Russian navy, on paper at least, was superior to ours,[7] and had not the British fleet been unwittingly supporting America's policy, the Czar might conceivably have taken vigorous measures.

It is likewise a common error to suppose that Alexander I was so alarmed by Monroe's strong language that the next year he hastened to conclude the treaty by which he withdrew to 54° 40'. The truth is that the policy of contraction had already been agreed upon, and Secretary Adams, who had been vigorously negotiating on the northwest coast problem, was well aware of this fact. The Monroe Doctrine was more in the nature of a general warning to future colonizers, inspired in part by the presumed Russian threat in what is now Alaska, and as such it later proved its worth.

Quarts of ink have been consumed by the subject of who was the principal author of the Monroe Doctrine, President Monroe or Secretary Adams. No one seems to have given Alexander I his due. If he had not made such extravagant claims in his ukase of 1821 and if he had not assumed leadership of the European autocrats in repressing liberal stirrings, the Monroe Doctrine—one of our most useful and enduring foreign policies—probably would not have been issued at the time it was and in the form it was.

---

[7] According to the report of the Secretary of the Navy (*Senate Docs.*, 18 Cong., 1 sess., I, 116) the United States on Nov. 10, 1823, had in active service only one ship of the seventy-four-gun class, as compared with seventy for Russia (*Niles' Weekly Register*, XXVI, 333 [July 27, 1824]). But other American vessels could have been made ready for sea in due time.

7

Alexander I continued his hostility to recognition of the newly born Spanish American republics, and was displeased when the United States formally welcomed them into the family of nations. As late as 1824, the year after the Monroe Doctrine, he was more active than any of his fellow monarchs in encouraging Spain to continue her struggle against the rebels. But by 1825 Russia bowed to the inevitable, and in response to representations from the United States took steps designed to bring about mediation between Spain and her wayward offspring.

Yet the rapidly expanding American republic and the enormous Eurasian absolutism were not always at cross purposes during these troubled years. St. Petersburg did encourage Spain to ratify the treaty of 1819, by which we acquired, among other things, the smiling expanse of Florida. Both Russia and the United States favored independence for the struggling Greeks, although for different reasons. A dispute arose between America and Britain over slaves carried away by evacuating British forces after the War of 1812, and when the issue was referred to the Czar for arbitration under the treaty of 1818, he rendered a decision favorable to us. His findings were presumably based upon a judicial examination of the evidence, but our citizens were disposed to look upon the award as an act of favoritism. And the retreat to 54° 40′ was generally regarded in this country, without too critical an examination of the motives, as a gracious act.

Yet all of these incidents, some of them relatively minor, do not obscure the fact that during much of the time from 1815 to about 1825 American public attitudes toward Russia were unfriendly. As long as the issue of republicanism was uppermost in the two hemispheres, the interests of the greatest despotism and the greatest democracy were bound to clash.

IV

Rifts in the Friendship

"Posterity will read with fainting heart the dreadful tragedy of Poland's fall."—*Buffalo Journal and General Advertiser*, 1832

I

ALEXANDER I died in 1825 of natural causes, unlike many of his predecessors and two of his four successors. With advancing years and hardening of the intellectual arteries, he had forsaken many of his more liberal ideals and *Niles' Weekly Register*, never a devotee of despotism, laid no verbal floral offerings on his tomb. He had been "the soul" of the dreaded Holy Alliance, "the dictator of the continent," always acquiring power "under the semblance of moderation," on the whole perhaps "the most dangerous man of modern times"—not even excepting Napoleon.[1] This portrait was obviously unfair.

A violent though small-scale outburst, known as the Decembrist revolt, attended the accession of Alexander's brother, Nicholas I. Among the rebels were troops who had occupied France and who in some degree had been infected with the virus of revolutionary ideals. The conspiracy was quickly crushed and the ringleaders were brought to trial. It is noteworthy that the defendants alluded repeatedly to the beneficent institutions of the United States and to the inspiring example of that great rebel, George

---

[1] XXIX, 377 (Feb. 11, 1826).

Washington. One of the constitutions drawn up by the conspirators actually provided for a federal system rather closely modeled upon that of the American constitution. All these proofs of the subversive influence of republicanism could hardly have endeared the United States to the absolutist rulers of Russia.

Harsh treatment—the usual lot of defeated rebels—was meted out to the Decembrist ringleaders. Five were hanged and thirty-one condemned to hard labor in Siberia, while the remainder of the one hundred and twenty were exiled to Siberia or sentenced to prison for varying terms. The American public was shocked by the vindictiveness of Nicholas I, who was regarded as the archfoe of liberalism. The death penalty seemed lenient when one thought of the agonized souls who were allegedly chained together and forced to plod hundreds of frostbitten miles into Siberia, there, so the story ran, to be buried alive in the silver mines.[2] When the condemned man entered the shaft, according to one untrustworthy report, funeral services were customarily held at the entrance. But true or not, the tales left an unfortunate impression.

2

The century-long squabbling between Russia and America over tariffs is a significant story, though one almost completely neglected by the chroniclers of our diplomacy. Every major tariff revision by the United States has trampled heavily on the toes of foreign producers, among them the Russians.

The British first enslaved steam in the latter part of the eighteenth century, and won the advantage of a long head start over competitors in inaugurating the Industrial Revolution. Both America and Russia were sprawling agricultural countries, and as a consequence the Industrial Revolution did not come to America until decades after it had changed the face of the British Isles. It did not reach Russia until many years later.

The Jeffersonian embargo of 1807–1809, followed by non-

---

[2] *Niles' Weekly Register*, XXXI, 90 (Oct. 7, 1826).

intercourse and the War of 1812, cut off exports from England to America, with the result that the ingenious Yankees were forced to give birth to their own infant industries. When the shooting stopped, British manufacturers began to dump their surpluses upon the United States, selling them below cost with the intention of smothering the new competitors in the cradle. The wail of these war babies for protection—and they really were "infant" industries in those days—resulted in our first avowedly protective tariff, that of 1816. By 1824, and under the leadership of the magnetic Henry Clay, the protective tariff was being combined with the building of roads and canals for the stimulation of American manufactures, under a bootstrap-lifting scheme known as the "American system."

The Czar and his advisers were no doubt impressed by the success of the American tariff of 1816 in saving and strengthening home industry. They were also learning that the tariff, which had been used by foreigners to harm Russia, could be used by Russia to harm foreigners. Yet during these years the volume of trade between the Empire and the United States was relatively small, and the mutual annoyance caused by tariff schedules was far from serious.

But the notorious tariff law of 1828, known in America as the "Tariff of Abominations," could not be laughed aside, because its unprecedentedly high rates struck a body blow at the Russian iron and hemp industries. (Russian hemp was then highly prized by the United States navy and merchant marine.) Happily the "abominations" were largely pared away from the tariff by reductions in 1832 and 1833, and these concessions caused much satisfaction in Russia.

3

Nicholas I had hardly crushed the Decembrist revolt and established himself on the Romanov throne when he became involved in two wars abroad and a large-scale revolt at home.

The Russian invasion of Persia (1826–1828), resulting from

what the Russians regarded as Persian aggression, was crowned with victory. Two new provinces were acquired, and a new boundary between the two nations was established. The fighting attracted little notice in the United States.

A far more serious conflict between the Russians and the Turks, 1828–1829, erupted after months of rumored hostilities. The American press, unable to secure reliable news from points so far distant, had to devote considerable space to contradicting previously printed tales. A premature report, published in the United States and describing several battles between the Turks and the Russians, proved to be a hoax, possibly designed to manipulate the London stock exchange. With a few changes of names and dates, it was a copy of an official bulletin issued during a former Russo-Turkish War.[3]

The Russian armies started off well, and then, owing in part to overextended supply lines and disease, encountered reverses that somewhat shook the myth of Muscovite invincibility. But regathering their strength, the Czar's warriors captured Adrianople and were soon hammering at the long-coveted gates of Constantinople. The Sultan desperately appealed to the European powers for help. England and Austria, not wishing to have Turkey collapse and leave the Dardanelles in Czarist hands, successfully intervened. By the treaty of Adrianople (1829) the Russians secured a confirmation of their protectorate over the Balkan provinces of Moldavia and Walachia, and made certain gains on the Caucasian coast of the Black Sea.

The impressions that the American public had formed of Russia were not materially changed by these two wars. One journal, apparently not appreciating the significance of the joint-power intervention, praised Nicholas I for the moderation of his terms. But a few newspapers even revealed some pro-Turkish sentiment, partly because our sympathy naturally goes out to the underdog, whether we know the facts of the case or not.[4] And among our

---

[3] *Ibid.*, XXXIV, 348 (July 26, 1828).
[4] *North American Review*, XXI, 400–401 (April, 1830).

more ardent apostles of liberty there was some condemnation of the Russians, who allegedly had betrayed the interests of the revolutionary Greeks by leaving them to the tender mercies of the Turks.

Yet the American press sounded one alarmist note. The Russian Empire, not content with its vast territories, was inexorably getting larger. The gains from Persia and Turkey, while not enormous, testified to an insatiable appetite. When would the Russian giant consent to be caged?

4

The year 1830 was one of revolution throughout Europe, and the bloodiest and most spectacular outburst occurred in Russian Poland. The Poles had long been passionately devoted to national liberty, and although they enjoyed some measure of autonomy under the Russians, they panted for complete freedom. Raising the banner of revolt, they battled not only with firearms but with scythes and pitchforks. The women of Warsaw were reported to have melted down their wedding rings to provide coins for the cause.

The Polish rebels at first enjoyed considerable success, and our citizens, with their deep-seated tradition of liberty, rejoiced over the "glorious tidings" from the "gallant" and "heroic" Poles, while denouncing the "barbaric" Russians. The memory of our own War of Independence was still fresh, and we looked upon the insurrectionists as emulating our worthy example. Nor could we forget such Poles as Pulaski, who had fallen while fighting for American freedom at Savannah, and Kosciuszko, whose engineering contributions had been less spectacular but no less noteworthy.

American enthusiasm for the Poles was expressed in various ways and in numerous places. Books about Poland enjoyed an unusual sale. Orators lashed out against Czarist tyranny, hoping that the northern bear would "skulk back to his marshes and icebergs." Toasts were freely drunk, including one at a Fourth of July picnic: "Poland, be free! or leave the soil to slaves. There is a refuge for your sons in a land of freedom!" [5] We expected that England and France would provide troops for Poland, and were angered when they did not do so. Clinging to our sacred principles of noninvolvement, we would send our blessing and some dollars. A special American committee raised funds, which were sent to Paris, there to be disbursed by an organization under the patronage of the aged General Lafayette. The money arrived too late to be of help in the rebellion, but was used to succor refugees. It is a curious fact that then, as later, the people of the United States assumed that the Poles were fighting to establish a democracy after the American pattern. We did not realize that while some of the revolutionists were ardent democrats, many of the Polish nobles were seeking to set up their own form of home-grown autocracy.

The Russian armies finally gathered momentum and flattened out the opposition. Victory was achieved, so it was reported in America, partly because the Czar's officers had perfidiously broken amnesty terms. At all events a period of cruel repression was begun which, however much exaggerated, was carried on with extreme ruthlessness. The ringleaders were executed, and several thousand families were exiled to the Caucasus. One of the condemned men, while on his way to execution, was said to have gathered a handful of soil and exclaimed, "For this we have fought, and for this we are willing to die!" [6]

Horror tales, many no doubt fabrications, shocked our citizens. A young woman received two hundred lashes for having sent provisions to some unfortunate insurgents dying in the woods. The wife of one ringleader was condemned to receive five hundred lashes for having sheltered a kinsman. She begged that she be executed publicly, so that her fate might inflame the courage of the patriots. Denied this dubious boon, she committed suicide in prison by forcing pins into her bosom.

---

[5] Arthur P. Coleman, *A New England City and the November Uprising* (Chicago, 1939), p. 56.

[6] *Niles' Weekly Register*, XLV, 411 (Feb. 15, 1834).

The Russians not only punished the Polish leaders but embarked upon a program of Russification which continued with varying interludes down to the era of World War I. Former privileges were swept away, and onerous new restrictions were imposed, including attempts to stamp out the Polish language. Late in 1834 *Niles' Weekly Register* reported the following:

> A beautiful Polish girl at a boarding school at Warsaw, aged only 15, who was found playing the national air, "La Pologne n'est pas encore perdue!" [Poland is not yet lost] was seized by the governor, dragged to the guard house, and there whipped and violated by the Cossacks so shockingly, that she died of shame and grief! Many of the Poles, in consequence of their misery have committed suicide.[7]

French, and particularly British sources unfriendly to Russia, gave additional currency to such atrocity stories.

Destitute Polish refugees, the vanguard of a wretched multitude whom Czarist oppression was to cast upon our shores, began to reach New York, and in their personal appearance gave mute evidence of what they had suffered. The New York *American* noted in 1832 that many of them, having sold the few valuables with which they had fled, were being forced to pawn the very coats on their backs. In 1834 a sympathetic Congress passed a bill donating public lands to the impecunious newcomers.

5

Nicholas I was deeply affronted by the anti-Russian outbursts in the American press during and after the Polish revolt. One of the most outspoken critics was the Washington *Globe*, which, because of its intimacy with the Jackson administration, was widely regarded as a semiofficial spokesman. The Russians knew of this connection and naturally took offense. On the basis of their own practices they assumed that since semiofficial journals speak through official inspiration, the Washington government must have planned the attacks. At any rate it could easily stop

[7] XLVII, 135 (Nov. 1, 1834).

them; and because it did not, it was thought to be deliberately unfriendly.

Then, as now, it was difficult to explain the contradictions of our free press to the Russian mind, though Minister Buchanan in St. Petersburg did his best. He found himself under the unpleasant necessity of having to remonstrate to the Foreign Office against the conduct of the Russian minister in Washington, who had imputed insincerity to President Jackson, and who had in effect charged Old Hickory with tacitly encouraging abuse of the Czar while "professing friendship towards the Russian government." [8]

Buchanan suggested to our Secretary of State that, in the interests of international amity, the editor of the *Globe* be urged to refrain from his savage criticism. While upholding the principle of a free press, Buchanan pointed out that there were plenty of other journals of a less official character carrying the burden of attack, and that the cause of freedom would not suffer from the *Globe*'s silence. At all events the unpleasantness blew over, and Nicholas I was soon repeating to Buchanan the ceremonial phrases about Russian-American friendliness.

Buchanan reported in 1833 that the cruelties of the Russian government toward Poland had been much overplayed. It was well known in St. Petersburg that several sons of Polish patriots who had died fighting were receiving their education at the expense of Nicholas I. Because there was no free press in Russia, and because the Czar's newspapers generally chose not to discuss the recent insurrection, the exaggerations of the Poles passed almost without contradiction.

The bitterness engendered in America by the crushing of Polish freedom under Cossack hoofs is usually overlooked by those who describe nineteenth-century Russian-American relations as an era of uninterrupted billing and cooing. This oversight is partly due to the time-honored practice of writing diplomatic

---

[8] J. B. Moore, ed., *The Works of James Buchanan* (Philadelphia, 1908–1911), II, 322.

history solely from official notes and dispatches. The Polish revolt was purely a domestic flareup, like the contemporary nullification movement in South Carolina, and as such was not a proper subject

"BROTHER, BROTHER, WE'RE BOTH IN THE WRONG!"

Queen Victoria admonishes Czar Nicholas I. (From the London *Punch*, 1844.)

for official intercourse. But the absence of a fat diplomatic file does not mean that the American public was not aroused, nor does it mean that during these years the republic was suffused with a warm glow of friendliness for Russia. A writer in the *Democratic*

Review of 1837, striking a curiously modern note, found some solace in the thought that western ideas carried away from Poland by Russian troops would have an undermining effect on Czarist autocracy.[9] Perhaps they did, but the government was well equipped to stamp out dissent.

[9] I, 140 (Oct. 1837).

V

The Calm of Despotism

"My great objection to the country [Russia] is the
extreme jealousy and suspicion of the Government."—
James Buchanan, 1833

I

S T. PETERSBURG (now Leningrad) was not generally
regarded by American politicians as one of the more desirable diplomatic posts. It was reputed to be the most
expensive capital in Europe, and high society spared no expense
in staging brilliant balls. Reciprocity of entertainment was expected, and a failure to hold one's own was regarded as boorish-
ness, despite the fact that then, as now, the salaries paid American
ministers were quite inadequate for their social obligations. Men
like the eccentric Cassius Marcellus Clay were compelled to
mortgage already modest estates.

The atmosphere was strange, with an indefinable mixture of
Byzantium and the Orient; the Russian language was difficult, although French was used in official intercourse; one had to operate
under constant restraint for fear that some careless word would be
picked up by a spy; and one was remote from "God's country."
Communication with Washington was agonizingly slow; one
month for a one-way trip was remarkable speed.

The climate was dangerous to Americans—cold, damp, foggy;
the winters descended early and the Neva River thawed late. The

45

drinking water was vile, the environs were swampy, and the mosquitoes and flies were in proportion, at least John Randolph found them so, to the vastnesses of the country. Francis Dana was sick during much of his unhappy stay. John Quincy Adams kept reasonably well, but he buried his only daughter. George Washington Campbell lost his three oldest children in one week. The half-crazed John Randolph of Roanoke was sent to the gloomy city in the last stages of tuberculosis, and after several weeks was driven to the milder climes of England.[1] Several of our envoys died in the harness; about ten others retired for reasons of ill health, which in some cases was aggravated by the climate; and still others carried back infirmities, usually of a pulmonary or bronchial nature, which contributed to an untimely death. The distinguished South Carolinian, James L. Orr, reached St. Petersburg in 1873. Worn out by the journey he caught a cold, contracted pneumonia, and within a few weeks after his arrival was dead. The wives of the ministers, to say nothing of the subordinate American officials and their families, likewise suffered from the rigors of the climate.

During much of the nineteenth century the tenure of our envoys in St. Petersburg was short, with a few notable exceptions. The caliber on the whole was rather low: men of ability and energy did not take kindly to a living burial near the marshes of St. Petersburg. The Russian post was in addition an ideal place to which the administration could banish political troublemakers, and this accounts in part for the unusual number of bizarre characters who turned up there. Another station which at times served the same purpose was Peking: both were so far away that the diplomatic exile could work little mischief at home. There is much force in the familiar saying that some men are sent abroad because

---

[1] Presented to the Czar, he is alleged to have said breezily, "How are you Emperor? How is madam?" There is reason to believe that the story is apocryphal (William C. Bruce, *John Randolph of Roanoke, 1773–1833* [New York, 1922], I, 638).

they are needed abroad, and others because they are not wanted at home. Still others accepted the St. Petersburg post as a consolation prize when disappointed in higher political ambitions.

Despite such inferior representation, the United States in the nineteenth century managed to rock along. One explanation is that we had relatively little business with Russia, and most of that was of third-rate importance. The Russians moreover were so determined to cultivate our friendship that they could afford to overlook our idiosyncrasies.

2

James Buchanan, who is generally regarded as one of our least successful presidents, proved to be one of our most successful ministers at St. Petersburg (1832–1833). His first impressions, which are recorded fully in his published letters and diary, are unusually illuminating, because they present the Russian scene against the background of his sturdy Americanism.

Buchanan referred repeatedly to "the calm of despotism." The Czar's regime, he observed, was "afraid of the contamination of liberty," as was generally true in Europe during the era of Metternich. There was no free press, no public opinion as we knew it, and little political conversation, and that much guarded. It was impossible for the Russian rulers to understand our government.

The "great objection" of the American envoy was the extreme jealousy and suspicion of the officials. One was forced to hold one's tongue and conciliate the government; spies of the police were everywhere; and one could scarcely hire a servant who was not a secret agent. Severe restrictions were placed on sending children abroad to be educated, or even on traveling in foreign countries, as was later even more true under the Soviets.

Buchanan's mail was so obviously opened that he advised his correspondents to write only comments that were favorable to Russia. The censors did not even bother to reseal the letters carefully, and they used such awkward imitations of the genuine seals

47

"as to excite merriment." "The Post Office American Eagle here is a sorry bird," Buchanan quipped.[2]

The theater was excellent, but the "drudgery of etiquette" in Russian society was wearying. The people were extremely polite, and given to a vast amount of extravagance and show. The upper classes spoke amiably of the United States but were profoundly ignorant of the rising republic. Buchanan met a Russian princess who inquired if the United States still belonged to England. She was astonished to learn that our independence had been recognized by George III a half-century earlier; and she wanted to know if the English language was spoken in the transatlantic democracy.

The bulbous churches and the public buildings of Russia were erected on a grand scale of splendor, yet the worship, Buchanan noted, seemed to consist largely of fetishism, with much obeisance before holy pictures known as ikons. Swindling and other forms of dishonesty were common. The brutally beaten masses were cursed with ignorance, superstition, crudeness, servility, and barbarism; yet they were good-natured rogues who, in spite of their self-crossings, would cheat if they could. Never having known liberty, and never having experienced many of the creature comforts of more advanced nations, they were devoted to their Emperor, whom they affectionately called "the Little Father."

3

The urbane Buchanan was gradually accepted socially, and made friends among the nobility, who invited him to their homes. Yet the conventionally friendly words of the upper stratum did

[2] J. B. Moore, ed., *The Works of James Buchanan* (Philadelphia, 1908–1911), II, 320. George M. Dallas, a successor of Buchanan, recorded a story going the rounds in 1839 that was probably apocryphal. A foreign envoy had complained to the Foreign Office about receiving his dispatches in such a rumpled state as to betray the fact that they had been opened. The Russian official coolly replied, "It must have been done very carelessly: I will give instructions against such negligence in future" (*Diary of George Mifflin Dallas* [Philadelphia, 1892], p. 178).

not conceal a noticeable amount of restraint. The ruling class was well aware that America was a culture bed of republicanism, and the Russian press, which tended to reflect official views, jabbed ill-naturedly from time to time at the youthful democracy, complaining among other things that our inflammatory example was responsible for many of the ills from which Europe was suffering. Buchanan's first impression, which seems to have mellowed somewhat under the spell of upper-class champagne, was that while Nicholas I disliked the United States less than he did either France or England, the ruling group as a whole did not entertain "a very kind feeling for the United States." [3]

The Russians were given an opportunity to show genuine sympathy when, in 1832, South Carolina defiantly nullified the federal tariff and threatened secession. The breakup of the Union, so long heralded and hoped for by European reactionaries, seemed at long last to be coming. Buchanan wrote that the friends of despotism rejoiced and the friends of freedom "sickened at the spectacle." Jackson's vigorous handling of the outburst attracted much attention in the Russian newspapers, and one nobleman told Buchanan it was a pity that such a man was not king of England in place of the spineless William IV. When the crisis in South Carolina was finally weathered without resort to arms, Nicholas I expressed warm satisfaction. He may not have liked democracy, but he disliked Britain and wanted to keep us united as a buffer against her, and he especially disliked rebels. If Jackson had his contumacious Carolinians, Nicholas had his uncompliant Poles.

From the days of Dana the United States had sought a commercial treaty with Russia, under which trade would be regularized, to the advantage of both nations. But the Czar, who insisted that his general economic policy was liberal enough, refused to tie his hands with a specific pact. Buchanan persistently but suavely pointed out to the Foreign Office the advantages, economic and otherwise, that would accrue to Russia from a treaty, and these arguments, combined with the tense European situation after the

---

[3] Buchanan, *Works*, II, 227–228.

Polish rebellion, seem to have convinced the imperial ministers.

Agreement was finally reached in principle, but as was so common in Russia, interminable delays thwarted the drafting of a definitive pact. Buchanan then had a happy inspiration. He suggested that the treaty be signed on the Czar's name day, and the ministers, fully aware of their master's fondness for such niceties, rushed the final stages through with an abnormal burst of speed.

When Buchanan left Russia the next year, Nicholas I departed from precedent by embracing him physically, in the robust Muscovite manner. But the sturdy Pennsylvanian was not swept off his feet by such attentions. Though entertaining a higher regard for the Russians than at first, he rejoiced in his American nationality. He expressed the thought—quite common among his countrymen of that day—that living under foreign despotism had made him a stauncher republican than ever before.

4

Diplomatically speaking, the years from 1832 to 1848, and even to the outbreak of the Crimean War in 1854, are barren in Russo-American relations. American pioneers were pushing west under the propulsion of Manifest Destiny; the Russian people were tending to their own affairs. The secretary of our legation in St. Petersburg wrote home early in 1842 that there was not "an earthly thing to do. . . ." When war threatened between Britain and the United States over the curious McLeod affair in 1841, the Russian Foreign Office, not wishing to see an interruption of commerce and a dissipating of American strength in a useless war, tendered to Washington its friendly offices, which fortunately were not needed.

The only diplomatic problem that caused any considerable exchange of notes between Russia and the United States concerned difficulties on the northwest coast growing out of the expiration of one clause in the treaty of 1824. We still claimed the right to trade with the aborigines in unsettled areas north of 54°40′, but the Russians interpreted the pact otherwise. They ordered out several of our ships, alleging among other things that our traders were ruining the Indians with liquor, which doubtless was in some measure true. These vexations, which continued intermittently for many years, were not ironed out with finality until in 1867 the United States purchased Russia's interests in Alaska.

Additional light is thrown on conditions in the Empire from the American point of view by the subsequently published observations of Minister George M. Dallas (1837–1840), and Secretary of the Legation John L. Motley (1841–1842), who was destined to be the distinguished historian of the Dutch republic. Dallas got along well with the Russian nobility, especially after he had shown his prowess by defeating one of their expert chess players. Motley found the court reserved and complained of "these frigid and rigid Russians." Society was ornate. Dallas was impressed by the handsome dresses of the women but was somewhat shocked by "a most profuse display of the bust." The pomp and ceremony, combined with glittering costumes, reminded Motley of "some prodigiously fine ballet."

Dallas, like Buchanan, was annoyed by the censorship and the omnipresent spies, but he brushed them off with the statement that he had nothing to conceal. Motley observed that conversation was so restrained as to be reduced to banalities about the weather, the heat of the rooms, and a comparison between this year's temperature and that of the same time last year. Secretiveness on the part of the Russians was intense, especially as to the size of military and naval forces, but Dallas shrewdly concluded that the army was not of such strength as to support the view prevalent throughout Europe "of the colossal power of the nation."

The plight of the serfs left a deep impression on both Americans.[4] The moujiks were sheepskin-shirted, greasy, dirty, smelly, long-haired, besotted, and prone to seek in vodka temporary

---

[4] Dallas was struck with the extreme paternalism of the Czar, and in 1837 sent home a copy of a ukase, the second on the subject within six months, prescribing the length, shape, and relation of whiskers, moustaches, and hair (Dallas to Forsyth, Dec. 25, 1837, National Archives [Dispatches]).

escape from their terrestrial hell. Dallas was galloped home one night by a driver who later turned out to be "very drunk." Fortunately, the horse was not.

5

The picture of Russia that appeared in the American publications during the 1830's and 1840's was not so different as one might suppose from that painted by the diplomats in St. Petersburg.

Illiberalism was emphasized by many stories and news reports. Numerous articles described censorship, the expulsion of non-Greek Orthodox priests, and controls over the residence of Russian subjects abroad. Freedom-loving Americans must have been irked by a regulation issued by the imperial legation in Washington which required all Russian nationals and travelers to register. The tale was told of a retired Russian admiral who, after living for some twenty years in Paris, was summarily called home, despite great hardship. When he declined to return, his pension for forty years of service was canceled, and his property in Russia was confiscated.

Barbarity and brutality were the themes of other accounts, some of which related to the further repression of Poland and the jailing of Lithuanian mothers for sheltering their fugitive sons. Several versions appeared of a story to the effect that a Russian duke commanded a trooper to jump a horse repeatedly over an almost impassable barrier of bayonets. When the horse finally collapsed, the rider surrendered his sword to his superior, whereupon he was hustled off to prison. Other tales had to do with difficulties encountered by persons at court because they were not attired in the proper aristocratic dress or because they could not boast aristocratic lineage.

Shocking indeed to the New York *Star* in 1834 was the report that the number of pupils in the schools of Russia totaled only 75,586 out of 56,000,000 inhabitants. The Czar, ever fearful of the leavening influence of liberty, seemingly wanted to keep the people enchained in the bonds of ignorance and servitude. Heavy restrictions were placed upon teachers, both foreign and Russian.

From 1839 to 1845 the American press printed accounts of the Russian war with the Circassian tribes at the eastern end of the Black Sea. The natives put up a stiff resistance, inflicted heavy losses on the invader, and aroused considerable sympathy among our people, who generally applaud the little fellow, especially when he is fighting for his home and hearth. The news of these reverses was coupled with descriptions of the Russian soldier as docile, patient, and cunning, who, on occasion, allegedly had to be flogged into battle.

Many, if not most, of the articles about Russia that were published in America during these years seem to have been rather unfriendly, or to have carried overtones of unfriendliness. One of the favorable reports related how the American minister in St. Petersburg had arranged for an exchange of correspondence between the agricultural societies of the two countries. This envoy had said in a speech that the United States would be glad to send Russia some acorns for oak trees; there was no oak in Europe equal to ours, and no live oak at all. His hope was that the acorns would assist in the development of a more powerful Russian navy, and thereby contribute to maintaining the balance of power and upholding freedom of the seas against Great Britain.

6

During the 1830's and 1840's the Russians, like the Americans, were rapidly extending their frontiers outward. Czarist gains in Tartary and Persia received some notice in our press, and the Baltimore *American* sympathetically thought that the world would be the gainer if Russia, even though Greek Orthodox, took over heathen and backward Turkey.

Less sympathetic was an article in the *American Whig Review* of 1850, entitled "Russian Ambition," which predicted an inevitable war between England and Russia. The Atlantic Ocean was daily becoming less of a barrier, and "the liberty we have winnowed from the chaff of ages" was "too dearly purchased to be abandoned with life." The writer continued on an alarmist note: "When the war shall lie between the Europe of freedom and the Europe of the Vandal and the rehabilitated Hun,—when the Eng-

TURKEY IN DANGER

The Russian bear has predatory designs on his neighbors, including Turkey. (From the London *Punch*, 1853.)

lish people themselves shall gird up their loins for the Holy War, —think you we can turn deafly away, or look on quiescent? [5]

Russian quarantine restrictions at the mouth of the Danube were complained of in 1854 by *De Bow's Review*. They were not only annoying but brutal: women were allegedly forced to strip

[5] VI, 632 (Dec., 1850).

54

before male inspectors. Russia was also reported to have violated treaties in an attempt to fetter the commerce of Hungary, the Danubian principalities, and what is now Bulgaria. The same journal spoke fearfully of the "gigantic encroachments of Russia," pharisaically ignoring the fact that only six years before we had gulped down about one half of Mexico.

In the same year (1854), a writer in the *North American Review* referred pessimistically to Russian Pan-Slavism and its self-appointed task of "regenerating the world." He went on to say:

Supervening upon the fanaticism of race is the enthusiasm of religion, and the humblest boor believes that, either in his generation or after him, the great race of which he is a part will fulfil its magnificent mission of conquering the world and stamping its own nationality on all the inhabitants of the globe, and that the leader in this final crusade is he to whom his political allegiance is due,—the CZAR.[6]

In 1843, in the midst of talk about the Russian peril, *Niles' Weekly Register* published the text of what was alleged to be the will of Peter the Great. It had come from French (anti-Russian) sources, and for this reason the journal expressed doubts as to its authenticity. The document, in parting advice to the Russians, outlined a cynical program of conquest and world domination. The American editor contrasted this statement unfavorably with the exalted and ennobling sentiments of George Washington's political testament—the Farewell Address. The will has since then been proved a forgery by historical scholarship,[7] but it still has some currency, and in the public mind of that day doubtless added something frighteningly concrete to the presumed Muscovite menace.

---

[6] LXXVIII, 534 (April, 1854).

[7] D. V. Lehovich, "The Testament of Peter the Great," *American Slavic and East European Review*, VII, 111–124 (April, 1948).

VI

Ferment in the Fifties

"This [St. Petersburg] is the best school in which to Americanize our countrymen, perhaps that can be found."—Neill S. Brown, 1853

I

THE death agonies of the Polish revolt of 1830 lasted for many years. The American press continued to print lurid tales of Russification and ruthlessness, and in 1839 the Peoria (Illinois) *Register* reported that some two thousand Russian families, fleeing religious persecution, were settling in the Territory of Wisconsin. As late as 1843 the welcome news came that Nicholas I had granted full amnesty to a number of Poles exiled to Siberia and elsewhere for their complicity in the uprising of 1830. But the favorable effect of such tidings was probably more than offset in 1843 by the crushing of a new Polish conspiracy in Warsaw. About two hundred persons were thrust into dungeons, where the most horrible tortures were reportedly used for extorting information.

Yet the American public clung to its faith that the cause of liberty in Poland would one day triumph. These hopes were in some degree kept alive by a spokesman for Poland, a Mr. Tochman, who was referred to as "her national representative in this country," and who foreshadowed the Polish government-in-exile during World War II.[1] The prolonged gasps of Poland for the fresh air of liberty made a host of enemies in America for Russian illiberalism, and further contributed to the incongruity of the avowed friendship between the two nations.

2

The death rattle of Poland was drowned out in 1848 by the spectacular uprising of the Hungarians against Austria under the leadership of the colorful and dynamic Kossuth. The rebels achieved considerable success at the outset, so much so that the Emperor of Austria, acting in the spirit of the defunct Holy Alliance, called in his fellow potentate, Nicholas I of Russia.

The Czar's armies overwhelmed the Hungarians, and the crusher of Poland became the crusher of Hungary. More than that, Nicholas delivered over to the tender mercies of the Austrian Emperor thousands of revolutionists, many of whom were imprisoned, shot, and hanged. The Czar did not himself act as hangman, but in American eyes the blood of another glorious revolution was on his hands.

Senator Hale of New Hampshire proposed an investigation into the wisdom of suspending diplomatic relations with both Russia and Austria.[2] Senator Seward of New York (later the purchaser of Alaska) regarded the conduct of Austria and Russia as stained with an injustice and barbarity which deserved the censure of mankind, and introduced a resolution in Congress designed to grant public lands to refugees from Hungary—a proposal that commanded much popular support.

Senators Hale and Seward were both outspoken antislavery men, and it should be noted that most of the enthusiasm for the Hungarian rebels came from the abolitionist and other antislavery centers of the North. The South, fearing a possible precedent for Northern intervention on behalf of its slaves, was cold toward

---

[1] *Niles' Weekly Register*, LXIV, 235 (June 10, 1843).
[2] Washington *Daily National Intelligencer*, Jan. 8, 1850.

measures designed to promote interference on behalf of oppressed peoples abroad.

The picture was further confused by partisanship. The Democratic party—created by the prorevolutionary, antimonarchical, and antiaristocratic Thomas Jefferson—was then the party of the "outs" and hence more irresponsible. It attempted to make political capital by condemning the incumbent Whigs, the party of aristocracy and conservatism, for not taking more vigorous measures against the "butchers of Hungary."

The refugee Kossuth came to America in 1851, conveyed a part of the way by a United States warship, and made an extensive tour of the country. In the flawless Elizabethan English that he had learned in prison, he publicly urged that the independence of Hungary be recognized by the United States, that the Russian intervention be declared a violation of the law of nations, and that we ally ourselves with Britain to prevent such interference in the future.

The Kossuth craze swept the country like a prairie fire. Resolutions favorable to Hungary were passed by numerous mass meetings and state legislatures, including those of New Jersey, Delaware, and Massachusetts.[3] These pronouncements generally declared that the Hungarian revolution was praiseworthy, that the Russian invasion was an infraction of international law, that a repetition of the intervention ought not to be regarded with indifference by the United States, and that Nicholas I, by giving over the Hungarian patriots to judicial butchery, was guilty of a more infamous act than the Emperor of Austria, who had actually butchered them.

The Kossuth craze gave birth to Kossuth beards, Kossuth hats, Kossuth overcoats, and Kossuth County, Iowa. But the rank and file of our people, though sympathizing ardently with liberty abroad, were not prepared to jeopardize their own freedom by tossing overboard the nonentanglement precepts of the Founding

---

[3] J. B. McMaster, *A History of the People of the United States* (New York, 1893–1913), VIII, 155.

Fathers. Our enthusiasm speedily evaporated, especially when we saw that the fiery Hungarian wanted armed intervention, and Kossuth sailed from America a sadder and perhaps wiser man.

On the diplomatic level, as contrasted with the public opinion level, the Hungarian revolt did not involve Russian-American relations, except in a rather indirect and curious way. In 1853 the Russian Foreign Office remonstrated with Washington against the action of an American naval officer in Turkish waters who had used strong-arm methods to rescue a Hungarian refugee, Martin Koszta by name, from Austrian clutches. Nothing came of this rather gratuitous protest. At all events, the Hungarian rebellion chilled diplomatic and popular relations on both sides of the Atlantic, and caused American alarmists to feel that the Russian monster was a growing threat to all that our Anglo-Saxon civilization held dear.

3

On the eve of the Crimean War the United States minister in St. Petersburg was an able Tennessee lawyer and politician, Neill S. Brown, who served from 1850 to 1853. To a greater extent than any of his predecessors or successors, he included in his official dispatches extended comments on Russian traits, even though much of his information was necessarily based on hearsay.[4] His observations are of unusual value as revealing the reactions of a patriotic American reared in Tennessee during the days of Jacksonian democracy, and also in supporting the truism that there is little new about Russian character. As might be expected in a person of his limited background, he missed completely the

---

[4] This section is based on Brown's official dispatches in the National Archives. Excerpts from a few of them appear at the chapter heads in Walter B. Smith, *My Three Years in Moscow* (Philadelphia, 1950). The story is current in Washington that George F. Kennan, while a secretary of embassy in Moscow during the 1930's, stumbled upon copies of the Brown file, and by selecting certain passages and changing the proper names prepared a dispatch for Washington completely relevant to the current situation.

deeper cultural currents of Russian life, which at that time were noteworthy.

Brown repeated the familiar comments about the vigilance of the secret police, remarking that St. Petersburg seemed to be "in a state of siege." He found the rumor prevalent that even the ministers of the government were spied upon by servants in their households. Brown dared not risk anything in the mails that he was unwilling to have read; those legations that could afford to do so maintained regular couriers and never sent dispatches by post.

Censorship of the press was no less abhorrent to this liberty-loving Tennessean. The annual message of the President of the United States in 1852 was censored where it referred to the desire of certain impulsive Americans to intervene in Europe against despotic oppressors. Foreign books were excluded from Czardom, and there was no Russian publication from which one could derive accurate information regarding revenue, expenditures, the army and navy, or any other matter having a political bearing. Published reports on the current Caucasian war always gave the victory to the Russians, although private advices often told of terrible disasters.

The policy of the imperial government was becoming more antiforeign, and Americans were having increasing difficulty with visitors' visas and customs inspectors. Behind Czarist restrictions lay fear of the subversive impact of liberal ideas on the popular mind. A strong antiforeign group in Russia wished to exclude all outsiders, except for transient commerce. The argument ran that the opening of the door by Peter the Great had brought in enough civilization so that henceforth the Russians could maintain it by themselves. Russian manufacturing, in pursuance of an isolationist philosophy, was being nurtured by a "hot-house system" of protective tariffs.

Secretiveness and mysteriousness were natural accompaniments of the official outlook. The Russian mind seemed "naturally distrustful," especially that of officialdom. The Czar's minister at

Constantinople, so it was rumored, did not trust even his own secretaries with the writing of his dispatches. Government employees would never give out any information worth knowing; one had to rely on stale news or conjecture or on what little one actually saw. Everything was "surrounded with ceremony," and nothing was attainable "but after the most provoking delays." Brown discovered that the Czarist government possessed "in an exquisite degree, the art of worrying a foreign representative, without giving him even the consolation of an insult." [5]

Russian diplomacy, which was "remarkably astute" and "inexhaustible in expedients," perhaps had "no equal." Policy seemed to be guided not by settled principles but by expediency. What might be expedient one day, under a given set of facts, would be inexpedient the next day under the same set of facts.

Graft among officials, especially in the lower echelons, was common, partly because of poor salaries and the multiplicity of bureaus. The recent embezzlement by an officer of more than a million rubles had greatly incensed Nicholas I: if one half of the rumored scandals were true, they were enough to irritate any man to death.

The Russians were "proverbial for their powers of imitation, and equally so for their want of invention," but "they copy well." Everything they had was borrowed, except for their "miserable climate." They fought their battles and constructed their railroads with foreign capital; their best ships were built in England and in the United States. "No nation," observed Brown, "has more need of foreigners, and none is so jealous or ungrateful towards them." [6] Yet on the whole Americans were more highly regarded than others; though republicans, they were not propagandists.

Brown felt that an American minister with an established military reputation would have more weight than a "mere civilian."

---

[5] Brown to Webster, May 27, 1852, National Archives (Dispatches). The other dates listed in the footnotes of this chapter refer to dispatches from the same file.
[6] Nov. 6, 1851.

The Russian government was a military government, and the military was the predominant taste of all, from emperor to peasant. The capital abounded in army officers, with whom valuable contacts could be established. There was much parading of the army and navy. "Display," concluded Brown, "is a passion, as well as a policy with the Russian Government." [7]

Devotion to the army was not entirely pointless. As Brown recorded in this startling passage:

A strange superstition prevails among the Russians, that they are destined to conquer the world, and the prayers of the priests in the church, are mingled with requests, to hasten and consummate this "divine mission," while appeals to the soldiery founded on this idea of fatality, and its glorious rewards, are seldom made in vain. To a feeling of this sort has been attributed that remarkable patience and endurance, which distinguish the Russian soldier in the midst of the greatest privations. [8]

Brown's official dealings were made more difficult by the frenzied applause given in America to Kossuth's fulminations against Russia. The St. Petersburg *Journal* rarely published anything to the advantage of the United States, and printed much that was not. Nicholas I and his court, presumably because of the Kossuth reception, seemed somewhat chilly, but not sufficiently so to justify complaint. The Emperor was the "formidable antagonist of the people"; he was forced to fight free institutions with a hostility and "characteristic cunning" that "admits of no compromise and yields to no relaxation." His government was "consistent"; "it promises no freedom, and gives none."

As time wore on the official atmosphere seemed to warm somewhat toward Brown. He had to concede that he found the Foreign Office at all times courteous toward any requests he had to make, and he had no reason to suppose that it was animated by other than an amicable disposition toward America. He was convinced that Nicholas I "has as kind feelings towards the United States as

[7] April 21, 1853.
[8] Jan. 29, 1852.

he can have towards a country, whose institutions are free." [9]
Such were the impressions that Brown received.

4

The bitterness in America toward the Czar's despotic practices
was in some measure salved by the events of the Crimean War,
1854–1856. This bloody clash, which began as a Russo-Turkish
war in 1853, took on more serious proportions when three other
powers intervened on behalf of the "unspeakable Turk": Britain (fearing for the dismemberment of Turkey), France (ostensibly concerned about the Holy Places of Palestine), and Sardinia
(jockeying for political advantage). To the average American,
with his penchant for the underdog, it looked as though two great
maritime powers—Britain and France—were trying to humiliate
a badly overmatched third. Ironically, while hostilities were confined to Russia and Turkey, some sympathy was expressed
for the less powerful Turk, despite the fact that he was a heathen.

The Washington government was of course neutral, but among
the rank and file of our citizenry there was a surprising amount of
enthusiasm for the Czar's cause. This pro-Russian bias, aside from
underdog preferences and antipathy for Moslem Turkey, was
compounded largely of hatred for Britain, even though France,
our friend of the Lafayette tradition, was fighting at her side.
(The dictatorial Napoleon III was not regarded as representative
of the French people.) A strong undercurrent of Anglophobia
also persisted from the redcoat days of 1776 and 1812, and we
were currently having trouble with the British over fisheries,
filibusterers, Cuba, and Central America. The fear was prevalent
in Washington that if the British and French triumphed over
Nicholas I, they would unite to take a more active role in thwart-
ing the expansion of the United States. The prospect of such intervention, which was strengthened by a public pronouncement

[9] June 25, 1853. Minister Hunt reported to Washington, Jan. 12, 1883, "Nothing would exceed the politeness of these gentlemen but their dilatoriness."

of Lord Clarendon, tended "to Russianize" us, as Secretary of State Marcy put it.[10]

The violently anti-British Irish element in the United States was now politically powerful, thanks to heavy immigration from the Emerald Isle during the potato-famine years of the 1840's. In 1854 a large and enthusiastic public meeting was held in New York to celebrate the return of the prominent Irish agitator, William Smith O'Brien, from the British penal colony in Tasmania. A number of fiery anti-British speeches were delivered, and three rousing cheers were given for the Czar.

In later years Andrew D. White, the distinguished educator and diplomat, testified that pro-Russian sentiment was strongest among the proslavery men of the North, and particularly among the Southern states. There was a general feeling among Southerners that the South and Russia had much in common because both maintained "beneficent" bondage among the lower orders: the Negroes in the South and the serfs in Russia.[11] The Russian legation in Washington actually received a letter purporting to come from three hundred Kentucky riflemen who wanted to try their marksmanship on the Emperor's enemies in the Crimea. But too much significance should not be attached to this appeal. There are always some hotbloods who seek adventure, and it is entirely possible that the British legation received letters from some pro-British Americans who wanted to fight under the Union Jack. In a somewhat different category was the report from Paris that twenty young American medical students had set out to join the Russian medical corps.

At all events a multitude of Americans were hoping that the lordly British would be humbled. Just as Jeffersonian Republicans in 1812 rejoiced over Napoleonic victories and Russian defeats, so many Americans during the Crimean War rejoiced over Russian successes and British reverses. When the rumor proved false that the besieged Czarist stronghold of Sebastopol had not fallen to

---

[10] B. P. Thomas, *Russo-American Relations, 1815–1867* (Baltimore, 1930), p. 116.

[11] *Autobiography of Andrew Dickson White* (New York, 1905), I, 455.

the Allied invader, there was widespread jubilation. A poem in the *United States Review* of 1855 gave praise to the "Defiant, isolated, grand, Sebastopol!" [12] The final surrender of the fortress, late in 1855, dashed American hopes.

5

The first Russian diplomatic envoys in this country were, as already noted, rather poor choices, but the appointment of Alexander A. Bodisco, who served in Washington for nearly twenty years and who ultimately became dean of the diplomatic corps, was conspicuously fortunate. He married an American woman; he gave dinners that were the talk of Washington; and he ingratiated himself by his courtesy, tact, and urbanity. When he died in 1854, a few weeks before the outbreak of the Crimean War, the House of Representatives adjourned for a day so that members might attend the funeral. The Czar much appreciated the unusual honor paid to his envoy.

With the experienced hand of Bodisco withdrawn, control of the legation fell to two young men who were accomplished schemers and who were anxious to exploit the official friendship that St. Petersburg had been assiduously cultivating since 1809. One of them was the chargé d'affaires, Edouard de Stoeckl, who later as minister negotiated the sale of Alaska, and the other was Constantine de Catacazy, who later made himself offensive to President Grant.

The two intriguers, with complete cold-bloodedness, plotted to drag this nation into the war on the side of the Czar. They planned to use the United States as a base for privateers, and they proposed to charter an American merchantman to take a cargo of Russian goods to a Russian port, in an attempt to break the Allied blockade. The British would seize our vessel, and John and Jonathan would again be at each other's throats.

The St. Petersburg Foreign Office was not averse to having the American democracy in the war on the side of autocracy, but it threw cold water on the troublemaking of its representatives. The

---

[12] V, 131 (Aug., 1855).

plots might backfire, in which case Russia would lose the friendship so carefully nurtured—a friendship that might be used to better advantage at a later day. The Czar's government instead courted the United States in various ways, including the lowering of certain tariff schedules.[13]

The cautious policy of St. Petersburg finally paid dividends. The Washington government put an abrupt stop to British recruiting of troops on our soil; it permitted the sale of interned Russian merchantmen; it allowed ships and munitions of war to go to Russia, despite British complaints. It further aided Russian commercial intercourse with the outside world by forcing the blockading British to accept liberal principles regarding neutral ships carrying noncontraband to Russia, or neutral cargoes of noncontraband on board Russian merchantmen. These were time-honored American principles which the British hitherto had resisted and which, under the necessities of the Crimean War, they temporarily conceded to us for the first time. So the United States proved more useful to the Russians as a benevolent feeder-neutral than as an ally blockaded by the British fleet.

On sentimental grounds also Russia and the United States were drawn closer together by a common support of liberal maritime practices, which both had championed since the days of Catherine the Great's Armed Neutrality. Neill S. Brown's successor, when presented to the Czar in 1854, remarked that freedom of the seas was an American doctrine. "And mine too," responded the Emperor, at the same time laying his hand over his heart.[14]

The United States, despite its devotion to democracy, appears to have been the only civilized nation of any importance that was not ashamed openly to avow its sympathy for what was then regarded as a colossus of barbarism and backwardness. Some Americans, who gratefully remembered the mediation of Alexander I in 1812–1813, urged that we repay our debt by similar action during Russia's hour of peril. But nothing resulted from this agitation, partly

---

[13] Thomas, *Russo-American Relations, 1815–1867*, pp. 120–121.
[14] Seymour to Marcy, April 13, 1854.

because the Russians feared that a mediation proposal, coming from a nation regarded as a traditional friend, would be interpreted by their enemies as both collusion and a confession of weakness.

6

The stirring events of the Crimean War unquestionably revived our waning attachment to Russia. The alarmist talk about the Muscovite menace faded rapidly away, for the myth of Russian invincibility lay shattered on the shores of the Crimea. The peasants died bravely, and the Czar's huge man-power reservoir availed little when his inadequate transportation lines broke down. If the Russians could not wage war successfully in their own Crimea, surely they were no threat to the rest of the world. The discerning Andrew D. White, who was with the American legation in St. Petersburg during the conflict, wrote in later years that the Crimean War taught him a great lesson. It was that Russia, "powerful as she seems when viewed from the outside, is anything but strong when viewed from the inside." [15]

British bungling in the Crimea, immortalized by Tennyson's "The Charge of the Light Brigade," was as nothing when compared with that of the Russians. Tales of incompetence and graft, despite Russian censorship, reached the outside world. After the collapse of the Czar's commissariat, Andrew D. White everywhere heard stories of scoundrelism in high places, including money appropriated for army supplies that had been tossed away on the gaming tables of Germany and France.

White no doubt saw Russia under unfavorable war conditions, but he was impressed by the sadness of the people; the squalor of their condition; the brutality, stupidity, and venality of the officials, particularly those who delayed passports unless their palms were appropriately greased; and the rigorous but ineffective attempts of officialdom to censor disagreeable news. When White reached the German city of Breslau on his return, he settled be-

---

[15] White, *Autobiography*, I, 465.

BURSTING OF THE RUSSIAN BUBBLE

Note the many-thonged Cossack whip falling from the hand of
Nicholas I. (From the London *Punch*, 1854.)

fore a cheerful hearth and heard beneath his window, from a
rollicking band of university students, the stirring words of
"Gaudeamus igitur." "I seemed to have arrived in another world,"
he wrote, "a world which held home and friends." [16]

Dismal though the reports were that emerged from Russia,
there can be no doubt that the friendly sentiments of the American people and their government during the war redounded to

[16] *Ibid.,* I, 475.

the benefit of the United States. The Czar, knowing our views on the controversy, did not press us to subscribe to the Declaration of Paris (1856) regarding privateers, and he made it clear that he would observe benevolence toward us in the future should we have to resort to privateering. He also granted certain desirable trade privileges with his possessions in eastern Asia.

But if the Russians appreciated our cordiality, the British definitely did not. After all our loud talk about democracy and freedom, our cousins were shocked to see us morally allied with what they regarded as medieval darkness. British bitterness had not completely vanished when the Civil War broke out five years later, and the lingering animus tended to drive us closer toward the embrace of the Russian bear.

VII

Fires of Civil Conflict

"She [Russia] has our friendship, in every case, in preference to any other European power, simply because she always wishes us well, and leaves us to conduct our affairs as we think best."—Secretary of State William Henry Seward, 1862

I

THE Civil War period marks the high point in the curious chronicle of Russian-American brotherhood. All the powers of the world, including Russia, were technically neutral, but the St. Petersburg government was so conspicuously friendly toward the Northerners that its good will shone out like the ray of a lighthouse. Its benevolent neutrality, moreover, contrasted glaringly with the attitude of certain other governments, notably the French and British, both of which were so unsympathetic as to appear malevolently neutral.

The accusation is often made that Great Britain was hostile to the Union during this critical era. It is true that the landed aristocracy of England had much in common with the planter aristocracy of the South. Yet it is no less true that the disfranchised working classes of the British Isles were sympathetic toward the antislavery North, which was indirectly upholding the cause of free white labor. Caught between these two divergent groups, the London government found it expedient to proclaim an offi-

70

cial neutrality. But it was unable to preserve this neutrality unblemished, partly because Confederate commerce destroyers like the *Alabama* were able to slip out to sea through loopholes in its laws, and partly because the enforcing officials were sometimes pro-Southern in their sympathies.

When the guns began to boom at Fort Sumter in 1861, the British ruling class was prepared to sympathize with the North in its attempt to overthrow the abomination of black slavery. But when Lincoln, with an eye to keeping the pivotal border states in line, had to announce that he was not fighting to free the Negroes but to restore the sundered Union, sentiment in England turned sharply against the North. The British aristocracy had long feared the swelling power of the United States, and if two weak, snarling republics could be made to grow where one strong, united republic had grown before, Her Britannic Majesty's possessions in North America would be more secure. The Northerners, who looked toward the ultimate extinction of slavery, expected warm sympathy from Britain and they consequently regarded cold neutrality as hardly less than veiled hostility.

France, under the slippery Napoleon III, was likewise officially neutral. But while the British government tried earnestly to enforce its inadequate laws, the French government connived openly with Confederate agents. Napoleon was then engaged in his harebrained scheme to prop the Archduke Maximilian on the throne of Mexico, and he rejoiced to see two weaker United Stateses replace the once-powerful Union. If the Southerners and Northerners should unite once more under the Stars and Stripes, they might evict his puppet from the halls of the Montezumas. The Archduke Maximilian was the brother of the Austrian Emperor, and consequently there was much sentiment for the South at the brilliant Viennese court.

The picture was markedly different in Prussia. Among the ruling junker class there was considerable sympathy for the aristocratic slaveowners of the South. But among the masses, who cherished the remnants of a liberal tradition dating from the days of 1848, there was surprising enthusiasm for the North. Hundreds of Germans volunteered for service in the Northern armies, and many others purchased United States bonds. From the standpoint of physical help alone, the friendship of Prussia for the Union was far more substantial than that of Russia, but one does not hear much about it because no tradition of Prussian-American comradeship has sprung up, in fact quite the contrary.

Russia, like the other powers officially neutral, had no desire to plunge into the conflict; yet she was probably the only important nation in Europe whose ruling classes did not openly pray for the breakup of the Union. A handful of Russian officers tried to volunteer at the United States legation in St. Petersburg, and a few Russian officers and men fought in the armies of the North. Colonel John B. Turchin, the "Mad Cossack," was court-martialed after his men had sacked the Southern town of Athens, but he was promoted to a brigadier-generalcy, marched with General Sherman to the sea, and succeeded in personalizing Russian attachment to the Union cause.[1]

2

Why did Russia, the greatest absolutism in Europe, favor the democratic North, while the monarchical and aristocratic classes throughout Europe applauded the gallant Southerners?

The basic answer again presents itself. For more than a half-century, that is since 1809, the fixed policy of the Czar's government had been to encourage the growth of the United States as a potentially strong commercial and naval makeweight against the foes of the Empire. For precisely the opposite reason, the bitterest enemies of Russia, notably Britain and France, hoped that the Union would fall to pieces.

The Russian government and ruling class disliked democracy, but in the interests of the balance of power they favored the Union. Contrary to an erroneous conception, the Russians were

---

[1] Albert Parry, "John B. Turchin: Russian General in the American Civil War," *Russian Review*, I, 44–60 (April, 1942).

not anti-Southern. They merely wanted the North and the South to reunite as speedily as possible; otherwise the two warring sections might kill each other off, and from the standpoint of Russian calculations a completely debilitated Union would be almost as bad as a pair of smaller republics in a partially exhausted state. As was true in 1809 and again in 1812, St. Petersburg was quite frank in making known its realistic concern for the United States.

Another common tie between the autocracy of Russia and the democracy of America was the problem of dealing with insurrection. If President Lincoln had his seceding Southerners, Czar Alexander II had his unrepentant Poles, who in 1863 rose again in open rebellion. With diabolical cleverness the London *Punch* ran a cartoon that had Lincoln say to Alexander II:

> Imperial son of Nicholas the Great,
> We air in the same fix, I calculate,
> You with your Poles, with Southern rebels I,
> Who spurn my rule and my revenge defy.[2]

The American people were torn by conflicting desires in regard to Poland. They deeply appreciated the good will of the Czar, but they were dedicated to the cause of liberty, and since 1830 their sympathies, carefully nurtured by the propaganda of Polish zealots, had gone out to oppressed Poland. The influx of hundreds of thousands of Roman Catholic Irish and Germans since the mid-1840's had intensified interest in the fate of the Roman Catholic Poles. In 1863, after the new Polish revolt had flared up, mass meetings were held throughout the United States at which speeches were made and resolutions were passed. Funds were raised by subscription, and a Polish Aid Committee was set up. In September, 1863, Senator Charles Sumner, chairman of the powerful Senate Committee on Foreign Relations, lent a semi-official air to the agitation by a sensational speech in New York. Breaking a lance for the oppressed Poles and belittling Russian

---

[2] XLV, 169 (Oct. 24, 1863).

friendship, he declared in effect that Switzerland was the only real friend of the United States in Europe.[3]

Yet despite all this agitation the great body of Americans, too deeply preoccupied with their own internal convulsion to show

EXTREMES MEET

The Czar, against a background of massacred Polish rebels, joyously greets Lincoln, against a background of dead Confederate rebels. An example of anti-Russian and anti-United States feeling in the British press. (From the London *Punch*, 1863.)

intense interest in Russia, seem to have been more pro-Russian than pro-Pole. The State Department was torn by no sentimental loyalties or religious prejudices, and hence found it easier to pursue a course dictated purely by self-interest. When France twice asked the United States to join her and Great Britain in a mediation scheme designed to help the Poles, Secretary Seward returned a courteous refusal. We had traditionally pursued a policy of not

[3] *Charles Sumner, His Complete Works* (Boston, 1900), X, 144.

74

intervening in the broils of Europe, alone or jointly. We would appear foolish indeed if we were to assist insurrection in Poland while trying to stamp it out in the South. We were looking forward to the end of the war, when we would be in a position to tell the French to get out of Mexico. When that day came, as it did, our moral position would be much stronger if we could say to the European nations that we had refrained from intervening in European quarrels. By that same token they should refrain from intervening in Mexico.

In brief, the United States did not stay out of the Polish uprising because of any maudlin love for the Czar; every consideration of sound policy prompted our official refusal. But Seward saw to it that the Russian Foreign Office received copies of the correspondence, and St. Petersburg was properly grateful. The London *Times* was less appreciative. "No American can see anything wrong in a Polish war," it sneered, "to which that carried on in Virginia and Tennessee bears so strong a resemblance." [4] To many British aristocrats, Lincoln the oppressor saw eye to eye with Alexander the oppressor, and both were given opportunities to rebuff unwanted joint interventions.

3

Russia and America were further drawn together by the common problem of emancipating servile groups. In 1861 Alexander II issued a manifesto freeing some twenty million white serfs from the overlordship of their masters. This act took considerable courage, because it was bitterly opposed by those, like the slaveowners of the South, who stood to lose a great vested interest. But the emancipation of what one Berlin journal called the Czar's "white niggers" was accomplished without civil war.

Antislavery groups of the North were highly pleased that Alexander II should provide them with so timely a precedent, and the North glowed anew with amity for the Autocrat of all the Russias. Horace Greeley, editor of the influential New York *Tribune*,

[4] Oct. 15, 1863.

applauded the Christianity of the Czar and condemned the attempts of the Confederacy "to make slavery perpetual." The South naturally found such comparisons odious, and the Richmond *Examiner* retorted by making a few itself. Alexander II, it found, was enslaving Poles while emancipating serfs; Lincoln was trying to free black slaves while subjugating white Southerners. Hence the spiritual partnership between the two tyrants was altogether natural. Until this time the Southerners had felt something of a tie with Russia in the common bond of a servile class; now many of them felt as though they had been deserted by an ally.

Lingering memories of the Crimean War likewise influenced relations between the Czarist Empire and the United States. The Russians could not forget the outspoken sympathy of the Americans, and the Americans could not forget the wholehearted appreciation of the Russians for it. Why should the Emperor, rankling from the humiliation and exhaustion of Russia's recent defeat by Britain and France, join in an intervention with his former enemies, against a traditional friend, for the purpose of promoting the interests of those enemies?

The picture was further colored by the fact that Great Britain, hated by Americans and Russians alike, was now a free-trade nation. Both Russia and the United States were trying to build up their industries behind tariff barriers, and the highly protective Morrill tariff of 1861, passed by Congress after enough Southern members had withdrawn, strengthened the community of interest. When Cassius M. Clay, the American minister in St. Petersburg, made a speech in behalf of protection, he was enthusiastically applauded by his audience.[5]

In other respects Alexander II found himself advantageously situated when he sought to ingratiate himself with the United States. In both France and Britain, particularly Britain, there were influential groups that were either pro-Northern or pro-Southern, and they exerted considerable pressure on their governments. In

[5] C. M. Clay, *The Life of Cassius Marcellus Clay* (Cincinnati, 1886), I, 415.

Russia such imperfect knowledge as existed regarding America was to be found largely among the numerically small upper class, so the Czar, unembarrassed by popular opinion, could coolly play a game calculated to serve the best interests of the Empire. As the New York *Nation* later remarked, pro-Northernism was a wise policy for the Russians. If the Union won, it would be grateful; if the South won, it would be so elated that it would quickly forget its grievance against Russia.

4

Early in the war St. Petersburg manifested its benevolence toward the North in various ways. Unlike Napoleon III, it refused to have any traffic with Confederate agents; it took an acquiescent view toward the attempts of the Union to outlaw Confederate privateers; and it used press censorship in such a way as to gloss over Northern defeats and play up victories, while warning readers against news coming over the British Reuter's news agency.

In July, 1861, Prince Gorchakov, the Russian Foreign Minister, sent to the Czar's envoy in Washington an instruction which referred to the North in the friendliest terms and which, when published in American newspapers, gave a lift to drooping morale. The people of the United States were heartened to know that they had one strong friend in an unfriendly world. The *Trent* crisis, later in the year, almost plunged America into war with Britain, and when differences were finally patched up, Gorchakov sent another note expressing his warm satisfaction. Again the impression, both with the Washington government and the public at large, was highly favorable.

Vastly more important than any of these gestures was the attitude of St. Petersburg toward joint-power mediation between the North and the South. In this connection several legends have long persisted. It is commonly believed that Russia, out of her love for the United States, was the chief force in holding back France and Britain from joint intervention—an intervention that would have broken the Northern blockade and ensured independence for the South. Many Northerners agreed with a writer in the *Independent* magazine some years later that we owed "almost as much" to the Russians in 1863 as we did to the French in 1778.[6] What are the facts?

The wily Napoleon III, whose Mexican Maximilian gamble depended largely on the disruption of the Union, was consistently and persistently in favor of mediation. Although possessing the naval power to break the Northern blockade, he lacked the nerve. If Britain would go along with him, all would be well; if not, he would have to mark time. The attitude of Downing Street was crucial, and, popular fancy to the contrary, the most important single force in holding back intervention was not Russia but Britain. This is a fundamental fact that we failed to perceive during the turbulent years of our nineteenth-century Anglophobia and Russophilism.

The St. Petersburg Foreign Office warmly approved of one type of mediation: the kind that without offense to Washington would bring the North and the South together again as speedily as possible. But the Russians would have no part in such a mediation as Napoleon III wanted: the kind that would keep the two sections permanently severed. Although the Czar did not favor such joint-power interference, he nevertheless would not fight to prevent it.

5

The tense autumn of 1862 was the most dangerous period of all from the standpoint of foreign intervention in the United States. The North had suffered a series of costly beatings on the battlefield, and increasing numbers of critics in England believed that in the interests of humanity the fratricidal fighting should be brought to an end. The London cabinet had under serious advisement a scheme to join with the French in mediation. The British expected that St. Petersburg would decline to go along, but they

[6] LVI, 649 (March 24, 1904).

felt that at least as a gesture of courtesy the Czar should be invited —an attitude which strongly indicates that Alexander II's position was not crucially important.[7] There was actually a tendency in British thinking to write off Russia as a major military influence, following her exhaustion in the Crimean War and the subsequent dislocation of her social structure resulting from the emancipation of the serfs.

The British cabinet officials, learning of General Robert E. Lee's proposed invasion of Maryland, decided to suspend their decision on intervention pending news from the American front. The Southern invader was halted on the hard-fought field of Antietam in what was virtually a drawn battle. President Lincoln took heart from this dubious success to launch his preliminary emancipation proclamation, which added immeasurably to the moral strength of the North by committing it belatedly to the freeing of the slave as well as the preserving of the Union. The cause of the North did not seem so shaky as before, and cooler heads in the British cabinet recoiled from the prospect of a head-on clash with the Yankees.

In November, 1862, Downing Street flatly refused to join Napoleon III in his mediation scheme, and among other reasons listed the unwillingness of the Russian government to co-operate. This savors of an excuse rather than the real reason. If the British had chosen to intervene, with or without the company of France, they had ample power to break the Union blockade, without having to call upon Alexander II's navy, which happened to be scandalously worm-eaten and weak.

Several conclusions may be hazarded. The Czar was opposed to intervention, but passively rather than aggressively so. There can be no doubt that his unwillingness to go along with the other powers was a factor that entered into their calculations, but it seems to have been a minor rather than a major factor. If Antietam had resulted in a crushing Confederate victory, the British and

---

[7] E. D. Adams, Great Britain and the American Civil War (London, 1925), II, 40.

the French would probably have intervened, with or without the blessing of Alexander II. The decisive event was the indecisive battle of Antietam; and, to repeat, the major brake on intervention was Britain, not Russia.

Intangibles are often more important than tangibles, and myths are often more important than facts. The well-known opposition of the Russian Emperor to intervention gave rise in the North to the ill-founded feeling that he was holding back the unfriendly powers and would continue to do so. The Union triumphed in 1865 largely because, after suffering a disheartening series of reverses, it was able to overcome a spirit of defeatism. A realization that the United States had one firm friend in Europe who was restraining its enemies bolstered faltering Northern morale, and—although this can never be proved—may have spelled the difference between quitting and continuing on to victory. The tangible contributions of Alexander II during the conflict have been much overrated, but the seemingly intangible contributions, based though they may have been in part on fiction, were of substantial value.

The Russian Fleet Myth

"The movement of those [Russian] fleets spoke a
language which was well understood by the nations of
Europe, and that language was 'hands off!'"—Representative G. S. Orth, 1868

I

ONE of the few specific incidents that the people of the
United States remember in connection with Russian-
American relations in the last century, if they remember anything at all, is that during the darkest hour of the Civil
War, when England and France were presumably threatening
armed intervention, two "splendid" Russian fleets "swept" into
the ports of New York and San Francisco. The Czar thus served
notice on the interventionist powers, so the legend runs, that if
they came to our waters they would have to reckon with Russian
guns shooting the same language as that of the Americans. The
British and French forthwith took the hint, and the Union was
saved.

About all that is true in this version is that during the autumn
of 1863 two Russian fleets did drop anchor in the two American
harbors. Historical scholarship has shorn away the added mythol-
ogy, but the legendary tale lives merrily on, especially in the
world of journalism, which hates to see a pretty tale stabbed
through the heart by a researcher's pen.

The bare facts may be outlined. On September 24, 1863, two Russian warships appeared off New York City, joining the one already there and heralding the arrival of a fleet of some six vessels, which gradually gathered over a period of several weeks under the command of Admiral Lessovsky. Their arrival caused much excitement, especially in New York, partly because Russian ships were a strange sight in the harbor, partly because there were four French and three British warships there with crews of some 5,000 men, partly because Anglo-French intervention seemed possible, and partly because the visit had not been preceded by the slightest warning. The close-mouthed Russians had guarded their secret well.

This unexpected visitation was naturally interpreted by a host of Americans as a concrete expression of Russian friendliness, as indeed in some measure it was. Many Northerners also assumed that Alexander II, not content with refusing to acquiesce in the mediation proposals of his fellow sovereigns, had sent his squadrons to America so as to interpose physical force should the British and French fleets attempt to interfere.[1] It was widely believed that Admiral Lessovsky had sailed under "sealed orders," which would be opened only in the event of a showdown with the European powers.

The American people, it should be added, were not so gullible as they appear to have been. For some weeks prior to the appearance of the fleet the rumor had been widespread, both in America and Europe, that Russia and the United States were about to conclude an offensive-defensive alliance, under the terms of which the Czar would unite with Lincoln in repelling Anglo-French intervention. The coming of the warships seemed to be ocular proof that the alliance had been signed, or was about to be, and that the Russian fleet was here to carry out its provisions.[2]

This interpretation took on even greater reality when, on

---

[1] See Philadelphia *Daily News*, Oct. 1, 1863; Windsor *Vermont Journal*, Oct. 10, 1863.

[2] New York *Herald*, Sept. 15, 25, 1863; Richmond *Whig*, Aug. 29, 1863.

October 12, 1863, nearly three weeks after the initial surprise in New York, a Russian fleet of some six warships began to gather in San Francisco Bay, under the command of Rear Admiral Popov. His coming, though dramatic, did not create so great a sensation as that in New York. The initial surprise had worn off; the force was smaller; San Francisco was far removed from the main theater; and Popov, who had visited San Francisco before, was a familiar figure.

The Czar's government, with characteristic taciturnity, offered no explanations. The Russian minister in Washington was instructed to say, if asked why the vessels had arrived, that they had come for "no unfriendly purpose." This was true, so far as it went. The visitors toasted the time-honored friendship; they kept gravely quiet regarding the object of their visit; and their enigmatic silence seemed to give assent to such naïve interpretations as the Americans cared to put on their presence. When the Russians were told that they had come because they loved the United States, and that it was the Emperor's intention to defend the Union, they could not very well interrupt with vehement denials. If the Americans wanted to read into the visit a more friendly objective than existed, the Russians would do well to hold their tongues and drink another glass of champagne. The more indebted Alexander II could make the Americans feel to his Empire, the more he might count upon them to support his policies in the future.

The Russians have been condemned for numerous sins, but this myth, like that of the cordial Catherine II and the amiable Alexander I, was made in America, not in St. Petersburg.

2

The arrival of the fleets could hardly have been better timed from the standpoint of their psychological impact. The tide of civil conflict had swirled in favor of the North at Gettysburg and Vicksburg, nearly three months earlier, but that was less apparent then than now. Much stern fighting loomed ahead; Northern operations in Tennessee were encountering setbacks; and there was still a strong chance that a wave of Copperhead defeatism would extinguish the fires of unionism. The high point of Anglo-French intervention had been reached a year before, but this fact is clearer in retrospect than it was at the time. There were still persistent rumors of French interference, and the construction of two powerful ironclad rams was being pushed by the Confederates in British yards, ostensibly for the purpose of breaking the Union blockade. Two days before Admiral Lessovsky's two ships reached New York, the American press reported word from London that the rams had been ordered detained pending an adequate explanation of their destination,[3] but this was not the final detention that came later.

The North seemed to be urgently in need of friends, and the unexpected visit of the Russians dramatically highlighted the fact that Alexander II was not only our one true friend but that he seemingly was prepared to fight on our side. "God bless the Russians!" exclaimed Secretary of the Navy Welles, and this sentiment was echoed throughout the country.[4]

The spontaneous outburst of enthusiasm for the visitors, especially in New York, was as heartfelt as it was effusive. The inhabitants of the metropolis welcomed the opportunity to express in a tangible way their appreciation of a country—the *only* great power in Europe—that had seemingly stood by us during the early years of the war, and presumably would continue to do so in the future. Deputations from various states arrived in New York to pay their respects, and the New York Central Railroad arranged to take a party of Russian officers to Niagara Falls. The fleet visited Washington and Boston, and everywhere the guests were plied with expensive liquors and gorged with rich foods. Elaborate balls were held, with generous libations to Lincoln the Emancipator and Alexander the Liberator, and the bearded Rus-

---

[3] New York *Times*, Sept. 22, 24, 1863.
[4] *Diary of Gideon Welles* (Boston, 1911), I, 443.

sians whirled their fair partners across the ballroom floor with Slavic abandon.

At the various banquets the Russian spokesmen tactfully stressed the ancient amity, and as tactfully avoided reference to the Polish rebellion or the European crisis. American after-dinner orators, speaking more prophetically than they realized, toasted the time when Russia would dominate the Old World and the United States the New World. "Providence has decreed," declared General Hiram Wallbridge in New York, "that there shall be two great hemispheres, one the Eastern and the other the Western. The one shall be represented by Russia, and the other by the United States." [5]

Talk of an offensive and defensive military alliance was redoubled, despite the then hoary admonition of George Washington against foreign entrapments. *Harper's Weekly*, noting that both America and Russia were nations of the future, urged a compact with Alexander the Liberator as a brake on the ambitions of Britain and France. No such formal entanglement was effected, but then and for many years later Americans commonly referred to Russia as our "ally." The very fact that such an alliance could be seriously discussed in 1863 is eloquent testimony to our regard for the Russians and to our need for foreign support.

The welcome to the visitors in San Francisco was warm, though perhaps less overwhelming. During a disastrous fire some two hundred Russian volunteers helped man the water buckets, and the grateful citizens raised funds and provided gold medals for those who were injured. A great ball was attended by the Russian officers and the socially elite, at which portraits of Lincoln and Alexander II adorned the walls. Supper was served at eleven o'clock in the evening, the last strains of the dance orchestra died away at five in the morning, and a few guests were still present at six. Rumor had it that two Confederate commerce destroyers might sail into the harbor and begin to bombard the city, and

---

[5] London *Times*, Oct. 15, 1863.

Admiral Popov, under the spell of his enthusiastic reception, was so carried away as to issue orders for his men to repel the Confederates if the need arose. Apprised of this unauthorized zeal, St. Petersburg flatly countermanded Popov's orders. The Russian fleets had not come to America to fight the South.

3

The mystery was not definitely solved in this country until 1915, when Dr. Frank A. Golder, drawing upon the official Russian records, published an article in the *American Historical Review*.[6]

The Russo-Polish crisis came to a head in 1863, with a strong possibility of interference by the British and the French. If intervention should occur, an armed clash would follow, and the Russian fleet would be bottled up in the Baltic by the British, as it had been during the Crimean War. The Russian Siberian squadron would be set upon jointly by the British and French, who had better telegraphic facilities and who consequently would get word of hostilities first.

The objective of the Russian high command was to get its fleets away from these vulnerable mousetraps, base them on neutral ports, and utilize them as individual commerce destroyers, in the manner of the *Alabama*, to prey on the rich and vulnerable merchant marine of the enemy, especially Great Britain. For such purposes the United States was ideal. San Francisco and New York were well situated for access to shipping lanes; and the Russians, after carefully nurturing American good will all these years, could count upon a hospitable reception. The presence in the United States of these potential raiders would presumably exert pressure on the French, and particularly on the British, to go slowly in the Polish crisis. At all events, when the storm had blown over and the fleets had served their purpose, the commanders were ordered home in 1864, but not until they had further ingratiated themselves with the "best people," official and

---

[6] XX, 801–812 (July, 1915).

otherwise, by reciprocating American hospitality with brilliant banquets.

The Yankees are proverbially sharp traders, and at first glance it seems strange that they were so largely taken into camp or—more accurately—took themselves into camp. But the rumors of an imminent alliance explain a great deal. One should also note that the Northerners were so wrought up after years of tension and bloodshed that they were more than ordinarily ready to believe what they wanted to believe.

But a good many of our better-informed citizens, though evidently only a minority, perceived that there was more to the Russian naval demonstration than met the eye. The unsavory Congressman Benjamin F. Butler, who was perhaps judging Russian motives by his own, somewhat later expressed the view that there was a selfish purpose involved. Senator Charles Sumner also guessed the essential truth, as did a considerable number of our more discerning newspaper editors.[7]

Yet these surprisingly accurate speculations evidently made no more than a slight dent on the public mind. They emanated from only a minority of the newspapers, and often appeared inconspicuously in small type. They ran counter to what we wished to be the truth regarding Russia's friendliness and unselfishness. They were admittedly guesses, and we are inclined to accept editorial guesses with a grain of salt, especially when placed against such concrete facts as the presence of the Russian fleets and the unconcealed friendliness of the officers and men.

One final point must be made. There was nothing essentially incompatible between the theory that the Russians had come because of friendship and a possible alliance against common enemies, on the one hand, and the theory that they had escaped to sea so as to be able to ravage the commerce of prospective foes,

---

[7] The present writer has analyzed the reactions of seventy-four contemporary American newspapers, and his findings will be published in an article entitled, "The Russian Fleet Myth Re-examined," in a forthcoming issue of the *Mississippi Valley Historical Review.*

on the other.[8] Even granting that the Czar had dispatched his ships primarily to confound his enemies, this did not mean that they had not been sent secondarily to assist us. If Russia had become involved in war with France and Britain, and if we had been drawn in as well, the Russian commerce raiders, using American ports, could have subserved our interests as well as those of Russia by attacking the joint enemy.

Yet the important thing is not what the historian unearthed in 1915, but what the mass of our people thought in 1863–1864. We believed—increasingly so with the passage of time—that the Russians had come to succor us, morally if not physically, and highly important attitudes and decisions were grounded on this interpretation.

4

A number of smaller legends sprouted from the main legend, and they remain to be dissected.

The two fleets did not "sweep" magnificently into the harbors of their destination, for if they had left their home ports as units they would have excited the suspicions of potential foes. In New York the ships straggled in over a period of some three weeks; in San Francisco they entered days apart. The presumed significance of their coming was consequently somewhat slow to be recognized.

Neither fleet was powerful nor in good condition. The Russian navy has traditionally been stronger on paper than on water. Two of the major ships that were to have come to New York had to be left behind as unseaworthy. They were all wooden, and although the larger vessels had engines, the principal propellant was wind. During the voyage it was discovered that the sails did not fit properly; the sea pounded in through the port holes; the sailors were inexperienced; the food was poor; and scurvy broke out before the crews sighted Manhattan. The San Francisco squadron was in similarly wretched shape; one of the vessels was wrecked

---

[8] Chicago *Tribune*, Sept. 26, 1863; New York *Herald*, Sept. 25, 26, 1863.

off Point Reyes, some thirty miles from its destination.[9]

The assumption that these few antiquated and poorly manned ships could have repelled a combined Anglo-French fleet is foolish, and the Russian Admiralty presumably knew it. Britain was still Mistress of the Seas, and both she and France had powerful, ironclad vessels in their navies, any one of which could have disposed of the entire Russian fleet with ridiculous ease, much as the clumsy Confederate *Merrimac* had crushed the wooden Union ships at Hampton Roads a year earlier. The real threat of the Russian fleets was not in a slam-bang naval engagement, but in the possibility that each one of them would put to sea as a raider against poorly defended merchantmen.

The contemporary belief in America that the Russian fleets prevented Anglo-French intervention in the Civil War will not hold water. As already pointed out, the real threat of such intervention had passed a year before, in the fall of 1862, when the British had drawn back for entirely different reasons.

The Russian fleet coup did create something of a sensation in Europe, and on the whole it was about as displeasing to the British and French as it was pleasing to the Americans.[10] The threat to British commerce may have been important in causing Downing Street to consent to an amicable settlement of the Polish crisis, but proof of this contention has yet to be forthcoming. The published writings of contemporary British statesmen, who were preoccupied with more pressing problems, are singularly lacking in references to the Russian squadrons. The English press, likewise preoccupied, paid relatively little attention to the surprise visit, as was true of the continental newspapers. The pontifical London *Times*, which had a semiofficial connection with Downing Street, regarded the New York maneuver as a routine cruise and sneered at the Americans for making such a fuss over it. This

---

[9] San Francisco *Daily Bulletin*, Sept. 28, 1863.

[10] A remarkable booklet published in France at the time guessed accurately the purposes of the fleet visit and sneered at the perfectly natural moral alliance between the brutal and oppressive Yankees and the no less brutal and oppressive Tartars (Félix Aucaigne, *L'alliance russo-américaine* [2e éd., Paris, 1863]).

JOHN BULL AND LOUIS NAPOLEON DESCRY UPON THE HO-
RIZON A CLOUD ABOUT THE SIZE (AND SHAPE) OF TWO BIG
MEN'S HANDS, AND ARE FRIGHTENED NEARLY OUT OF THEIR
BOOTS BY THE PHENOMENON

The supposed consternation caused in Europe by the appearance of the
Russian fleet and the fraternizing of Russians and Americans. (From *Harper's
Weekly*, 1863.)

great journal, at least initially, expressed no alarm over commerce
raiding, but it did betray fear as to the expansionist ambitions of
the American and Russian giants.[11]

Certain British observers, as well as some Americans, regarded
the Russian demonstration as a warning to Napoleon III in

[11] London *Times*, Oct. 15, 1863.

Mexico, for commerce destroyers could have done serious damage to his line of communications with Maximilian. But proof that such a possibility influenced French or British policy likewise has not yet been uncovered.

Countless variants of the Russian fleet myth may be found in American newspapers and magazines since 1863. To mention them all would merely add to the confusion. But one persistent version must be scotched, for it has been given additional currency by the published letters of Franklin K. Lane, Woodrow Wilson's Secretary of the Interior. The tale is that Secretary Seward in 1863, seeking a demonstration against the British and French, arranged for the visit of the Russian fleets with the understanding that the United States would pay the expenses. This was later done in a secretive way at the time of the purchase of Alaska for $7,200,000. Of this sum $1,400,000 was for the territory, and $5,800,000 for the expenses of the fleet.[12] The whole story is nothing but a fairy tale from the Washington whispering gallery.

5

The episode of the fleets, in itself of no great importance, had astonishingly wide repercussions.

The morale of the United States received a definite boost at a time when it needed stimulants, and Secretary Seward was no doubt encouraged to pursue his policy of dealing boldly with prospective enemies. The American public was in no mood to look a gift fleet in the hatch, and this explains why the rotten wooden ships seemed "splendid."

The United States may have served as an unwitting instrument to restrain the British and French, and to help bring about an amicable settlement of the Polish affair. If the dispute had flared forth into a general war, it might easily have involved the North.

It is possible—though not yet proved—that both Paris and London thereafter decided to treat the United States more deferentially. Otherwise they might drive Washington into the

---

[12] *The Letters of Franklin K. Lane* (Boston, 1922), pp. 260–261.

much-talked-about alliance with Russia, which in turn would be inimical to their schemes.

The presence in America of the Russian officers and men aroused our interest in faraway Russia. Eugene Schuyler, a distinguished scholar-diplomat, and Jeremiah Curtin, a truly great linguist, were inspired by their contacts with the visitors to perfect their knowledge of the Russian language, and they went on to serve their country most usefully in the legation at St. Petersburg. They also, through translations and original writings, further acquainted the American public with Russia.[13]

The Russian officers who had been so hospitably received were favorably impressed with the United States, and when they returned to Kronstadt, they entertained the American minister on board their flagship, while a Russian military band, utilizing musical notes rather than diplomatic notes, alternated in playing "Yankee Doodle" and the Russian national anthem.

Careless commentators, in speaking of the warm gratitude of the American people for Russia and her fleets, overlook the fact that this enthusiasm was not shared by the South.[14] The Southerners could not applaud the anti-interventionist stand of Alexander II, inasmuch as Anglo-French intervention would have ensured Confederate independence. To them it seemed perfectly natural that the dictatorial and South-repressing Yankee should be allying himself with the dictatorial and Poland-repressing Cossack.

Yet Northern gratitude was undoubtedly deep and tenacious. When Alexander II was murdered by an assassin's bomb in 1881, Secretary of State Blaine dispatched an effusive note for the eyes of his successor. Blaine referred to Alexander II's refusal to join

---

[13] Schuyler did much to introduce Russian literature to the American public when he published a translation of Turgenev's *Fathers and Sons* (1867) and Leo Tolstoy's *The Cossacks* (1878). He also completed a book on Turkistan (1876), which was critical of Russian administration. Curtin published important English translations of Russian authors, notably Alexis Tolstoy, and wrote books on Russian myths and folk tales.

[14] See Richmond *Enquirer*, Sept. 29, Oct. 6, 1863; Richmond *Dispatch*, Oct. 7, 1863.

in mediation, as well as to his open declaration in favor of the North. Fearful that the unfriendly nations of Europe might intervene, continued the American Secretary, the Emperor dispatched "a large and powerful [?] fleet of war vessels as a proclamation to the world of his sympathy in our struggle and of his readiness to strike a blow on the side of the Union if any foreign power should strike a blow in aid of the insurrection." The United States, Blaine concluded, deeply appreciated the Czar's act of favoritism to the Union, "even at the risk [?] of plunging his own empire into war." [15]

If the Secretary of State of the United States should thus in official form tell the Russians why they had sent their fleets to America, why should they be so boorish as to point out to him his various errors? They no doubt were happy that, in serving their own realistic ends, they had incidentally reaped such a rich harvest of good feeling. Gratitude is a species of international currency which may be deposited for use on that day when one needs friends.

6

The fleet myth has outlived all others in Russo-American relations, primarily because of its opportune timing, its emotional impact, and its picturesque quality. It kindled a fire in the hearts of our citizens which caused the disputes of the past to melt away and the amenities of recent times to stand out in sharper relief. It unquestionably rendered the Union cause substantial moral assistance, but the American people were artless in assuming that because the results were good the purposes must also have been unselfish. Our citizens simple-mindedly concluded that Russia not only loved us but had always loved us, and they began to remember more vividly the legend of the kindly Catherine II and the devoted Alexander I and all that these monarchs had presumably done for us, while losing sight of Polish repressions,

---

[15] *Papers Relating to the Foreign Relations of the United States, 1881* (Washington, 1882), p. 1014.

Hungarian stabs in the back, Slavic menaces, and autocratic repressions.

The fleet myth also projected a mighty beam into the dark uncertainties that lay ahead in Russo-American relations. We could forgive much in a nation that had stood by us so valiantly and gallantly in our most critical years. Long after much bitterness had been generated between the two nations near the end of the century, long after the historic friendship had ceased to be much more than an empty phrase, countless Americans still remembered the Russian fleets and refused to face up to the reality that a new era had dawned.

If a legend is believed long enough and earnestly enough by enough people, it almost becomes a fact. On occasion, as in 1863, it is more important than a fact.

The Purchase of Alaska

"There is little doubt that a like offer [of Alaska] from any other European government would have been rejected."—James G. Blaine, 1884

I

THE heavy fogs of St. Petersburg were doubtless disagreeable during Civil War days, but the diplomatic atmosphere was far more agreeable for our envoys than that of some other European capitals, notably London and Paris. The American minister had little to do but to keep the Russians friendly, and this was not a difficult task because they were determined, in their own interests, to remain friendly.

Cassius Marcellus Clay represented the United States during the early years of the war. Although a Kentuckian, he was an abolitionist who had campaigned for Lincoln in 1860, and as a reward had been led to expect the secretaryship of war. When this proved impossible, he was awarded the St. Petersburg post as a consolation prize. The administration must have been relieved to get him out of the country, because he was a singularly ill-balanced, violent, and vindictive character. During his long and hectic career in America he became involved in numerous canings, duels, bowie-knife stabbings, and shootings.

Despite his ungovernable temper and disregard of etiquette, Clay formed a warm attachment for the Russians and conceived of his task as the easy one of cultivating their good will. He entertained on such a lavish scale that, according to his own unreliable account, his invitations were much sought after. He found the Russian upper crust genial and hospitable, and the women very beautiful. On his final return home he brought with him a Russian boy, whom he named Launey Clay and whose parentage he refused to divulge.

Clay was recalled in 1862 to provide a sanctuary for Secretary of War Simon Cameron, about whose head a storm of financial scandal was breaking in connection with War Department contracts. Fortunately Cameron had little to do. He reported that he was "spared the necessity of advocating our cause," for he found a "constant desire to interpret everything to our advantage." His secretary of the legation was the poet Bayard Taylor, who complained that the social treadmill was wearisome and who noted that the guests spoke "French nothings with great elegance." [1]

Cameron returned to America in 1863, when the stench in the War Department had subsided, and was succeeded by his predecessor Clay. The fiery Kentuckian took to himself much undeserved credit for having kept Russia in line during the Civil War and for having paved the way for the Alaska purchase. The fact that Russian-American cordiality could have survived the tempestuous ministrations of this crude character is further evidence of an almost unbreakable community of interest during these anxious years.

2

In April, 1866, Alexander II narrowly escaped death when a newly emancipated serf, with great presence of mind, struck the arm of the assassin, and the pistol discharged harmlessly into the air. News of the providential deliverance moved the American

---

[1] Henry Bergh was secretary of legation, 1863–1864. Scandalized by brutality to horses in St. Petersburg, he returned to the United States and founded the American Society for the Prevention of Cruelty to Animals (*Scribner's Monthly*, XVII, 878–879 [April, 1879]).

people deeply. They had lost their own great emancipator a year earlier, and their hearts went out to the other great emancipator who in the recent war had been their good "ally."

Congress promptly passed a joint resolution, which was most unusual, expressing deep satisfaction over the Emperor's good fortune. Such a pronouncement would normally have been presented through ordinary diplomatic channels, but our gratitude to Russia was so great that ordinary methods would not suffice. We would send the resolution by a special naval mission, led by a clumsy Civil War monitor.

The enterprise was headed by the corpulent but engaging Gustavus Vasa Fox, who had served capably as Assistant Secretary of the Navy during the late war. The Russians outdid themselves in reciprocating the hospitality shown their officers in America, and Admirals Lessovsky and Popov were among the hosts. Busts of the Czar and portraits of Washington, Lincoln, and President Johnson were in evidence, and the American President, nearing impeachment, was treated with far more respect than was being shown him at home. There were immense menus and innumerable toasts "To the Great Empire of the East and the Great Republic of the West." Flowery speeches paid tribute to the ancient friendship, reaching back to Catherine II and sealed by the events of the recent conflict. There was also much playing of national songs, and some kissing of the Americans and tossing them into the air, in the exuberant Muscovite fashion for which the visitors were not fully prepared.

At a gala dinner in St. Petersburg, Fox read a poem written especially for the occasion by Oliver Wendell Holmes, which began:

> Though watery deserts hold apart
>   The worlds of East and West,
> Still beats the selfsame human heart
>   In each proud Nation's breast.

The eighth stanza referred to the recent conflict:

When darkness hid the starry skies
        In war's long winter night,
One ray still cheered our straining eyes,
        The far-off Northern light! [2]

Fox read in English, and when a Russian interpreter translated the poem, shouts of "encore" forced a second reading, after which the translator was enthusiastically tossed into the air.

Surprising tributes from all over the Empire indicated that the tradition of friendship had penetrated to the very mudsills of society. Flowers and telegrams were showered upon the visitors. Fox and his entourage traveled widely, and in one place the peasants, in a tribute ordinarily reserved for members of the imperial family, laid their garments in the road for the visitors to walk upon. The mission at length departed, stuffed with good food and good liquor and good will, and bearing appropriate gifts from Alexander II, including a diamond-studded snuff box.

News of the Fox mission, surprisingly enough, received hardly more than routine coverage in the American press. The excitement was too far away; insistent problems were close at hand (including reconstruction in the South and Napoleon III in Mexico); and Russian friendship, especially after the fleet visits, was no novelty. The Czar's benevolence could be taken so completely for granted that it was not particularly newsworthy. The New York *Herald* even begrudged the unnecessary expense to the taxpayer of "Mr. Fox's Pleasure Trip," pointing out that by the time he reached St. Petersburg the resolution he was bearing would long since have been published in the Russian newspapers.[3]

But the Fox love feast undoubtedly did much to publicize and cement the now traditional cordiality. In both countries abundant opportunity was given to review the friendly acts of the recent and remote past, while unpleasant incidents were avoided. The Russians were delighted to have a chance to greet their democratic brothers from beyond the sea, and the American people were

---

[2] *The Poetical Works of Oliver Wendell Holmes* (Boston, 1887), p. 255.
[3] New York *Herald*, May 18, 1866.

gratified to learn that their Russian "allies" had received the visitors so enthusiastically. A speech by the distinguished Russian statesman, Prince Gorchakov, was so effusive as to revive considerable comment, both in Europe and in America, as to the imminence of a full-dress Russian-American alliance.

One final contribution merits mention. The Russian people were afforded an unusual opportunity to learn something about the United States and to discard some of their false impressions. Jeremiah Curtin, who was attached to the St. Petersburg legation, tells of the little Russian girl who was surprised to find that the Americans were not red-skinned.[4]

3

In 1867 Russia unexpectedly sold Alaska to the United States for the bargain price of $7,200,000, and this strange transaction contributed powerfully to the myth of a sentimental Russian-American friendship. Gradually the impression took root that the Czar transferred his huge American possession to the United States for a pittance because he liked us and wanted to do us a favor, and as a result we ought to feel everlastingly grateful.

The Alaska purchase legend, like the fleet legend, has a concrete basis in fact, because there can be no denying that the sale did take place for $7,200,000. But why did Russia sell, and specifically why did she sell to us?

The naked truth is that Russian America (as Alaska was called in the prepurchase era) had become a burdensome economic liability. The Russian-American Company, under whose monopoly the territory was being systematically ravaged, had mismanaged its affairs badly, and its accumulated woes were about to be tossed into the lap of the Czar's government, which did not want to be bothered with them.

Alaska moreover was strategically indefensible by weak-navy Russia against a strong naval power, like Great Britain. In the recent Crimean War, London had consented to the neutraliza-

---

[4] *Memoirs of Jeremiah Curtin* (Madison, Wis., 1940), p. 113.

tion of Russian America, presumably because an attack might stimulate a quick sale to the Yankees, with unpleasant complications. But the Russians could not count on being so lucky in the future. In short, Alaska was an uneasy hostage to Great Britain.

Another Russian fear grew out of the proven rapacity of the westward-moving Americans. The spirit of Manifest Destiny had not completely died; and the rumor that a colony of polygamously prolific Mormons was going into Alaska had caused a momentary scare in St. Petersburg. If a gold rush should start, as one had recently into British Columbia, the Yankees would probably swarm in and take over, as they had in West Florida and Texas. It was obviously sound strategy to sell out for even $7,200,000, rather than wait and lose everything, including face, and perhaps be defeated on the battlefield in the bargain. The misconception is that the stupid Russians sold without any knowledge whatever of the gold and other natural resources of the vast area. The fact is that they knew of some gold deposits in Alaska, and they sold because they knew of them, not because they were ignorant of them.[5]

The decision to dispose of Alaska was prompted by still other considerations. The Russian Empire had overextended itself into North America, half a world away from its capital, and European colonialism in the western hemisphere during the nineteenth century had generally proved unprofitable. Certain advisers in St. Petersburg were urging that Alexander II make Siberia his easternmost outpost, because it was contiguous and easily defensible.[6] The Russians also wanted a freer hand in Europe and the Far East: they were still eyeing the Dardanelles covetously, and they were on the march across Asia, with Britain attempting

---

[5] See A. G. Mazour, "The Prelude to Russia's Departure from America," *Pacific Historical Review*, X 311-319 (Sept., 1941).

[6] Hunter Miller, "Russian Opinion on the Cession of Alaska," *American Historical Review*, XLVIII, 530 (April, 1943).

to thwart their progress. High on the list of those who might buy Alaska were the unsophisticated Americans, whose gratitude had been brought to a high pitch during the recent Civil War, and whose continuing cordiality was looked upon as a strong asset in the current diplomatic war with Great Britain. There was still some friction with Washington over the Northwest Treaty of 1824; and the Russian-American Company, by its arbitrary tactics, was a constant irritant to Yankee traders. Why take a chance on ruining a priceless friendship while scrambling for a few kopecks of trade on the Alaska coast?

But rubles could not have been a vital consideration with the Russians, even though the Czar's government was in financial difficulties during much of the nineteenth century. The sum involved was relatively small. Yet it was not to be laughed aside, particularly when the alternative seemed to be the loss of Alaska, plus the loss of a valuable friend, plus the loss of what millions of dollars Washington was willing to pay.

4

There was never any real doubt in St. Petersburg during these months as to the logical prospective purchaser of Alaska. The one nation that could use it most effectively to thwart the ambitions of Russia's hereditary foe, Great Britain, was clearly the United States.

Alaska, though a liability to the Russians, would strengthen the maritime power of the Americans and add to their natural resources. The transfer would apply the pincers to British Columbia, which would then be squeezed between American territory on both the north and south. Friction would develop between the United States and Great Britain, in line with the Russian policy of divide and conquer. (Serious trouble did arise later between the Americans and the Canadians over such problems as seals and boundaries.) After the Yankees had pinched off British Columbia and had caused that rich apple to fall into the basket of Manifest

Destiny, they would next apply the squeeze to the rest of Canada. When it was annexed, the American republic would be further strengthened and the British Empire would be correspondingly weakened.

The Russians had some misgivings about the United States as a neighbor—a United States that had already demonstrated its power and rapacity—and considerable uneasiness was expressed as to the wisdom of having the Americans only fifty-six miles away from Siberia, across the Bering Strait.[7] But such doubts were completely overbalanced by other and more immediate dangers.

The legend must therefore be discarded that the Russians sold Alaska primarily because they liked the United States. Alexander II and his advisers logically and cold-bloodedly decided to unload their frozen asset in such a way as to secure the maximum benefits to the Russian Empire. They found that the United States best fitted into their schemes, and in pushing the sale they naturally sought to capitalize on the warm friendship that we had developed for them during the recent war. The Czar was doubtless pleased that self-interest so neatly dovetailed with doing a good turn to a republic that had shown such enthusiastic appreciation of his conduct. But if he had concluded that some other nation would better subserve the interests of the Empire, he no doubt would have attempted to dispose of the territory elsewhere.

5

The Russian minister in Washington, Edouard de Stoeckl, cleverly dropped a hint that the Emperor might be persuaded to sell Alaska, and Secretary Seward, who happened to be an expansionist of undiscriminating voracity, rose avidly to the bait. Not only was Seward a Manifest Destinarian with trans-Pacific and polar visions, but he presumably hoped to stage a spectacular success that would improve the position of President Johnson, who was then facing impeachment. Seward was much too eager a purchaser to be a good bargainer, and he settled for $7,200,000,

---

[7] *Ibid.*, p. 525.

"THE BIG THING"

OLD MOTHER SEWARD. "I'll rub some of this on his sore spot: it may soothe him a little."

The Alaska purchase is here interpreted as a maneuver by Secretary Seward to help out President Johnson. Note the sneering references to walruses, polar bears, Eskimos, and icy peaks. (From *Harper's Weekly*, 1867.)

although we now know that Alexander II would have sold for $5,000,000.[8]

The land-surfeited Americans, who had scarcely heard of Alaska and who wanted no part of it while staggering under the burdens of reconstruction, were shocked to learn that Seward had consented to pay out so much of the taxpayers' money for a mass of fog-girt and walrus-covered icebergs, peopled by a few Siberian convicts.[9] Derision was heaped upon "Walrussia," "Seward's Polar Bear Garden," the "land of short rations and long twilights." But Secretary Seward, fearing that the sale would be hooted out of court, discreetly launched a campaign of education, designed to inform the press of the varied natural resources of Alaska. He also wined and dined influential Senators, and succeeded in enlisting the support of Charles Sumner, the oratorical big gun of the Senate.

Seward's campaign of education gradually began to bear fruit. As the debates in both Senate and House reveal, our people were influenced by the potential economic resources of Alaska, by the commercial value of the area in our Pacific development, by the improvement of our strategic position, by the giant stride in the direction of our Manifest Destiny, and by the banishment of one more monarchical flag from the Americas, even though it was that of our great and good friend the Czar. Finally, the purchase dealt a popular blow to Britain by snatching the choice Alaskan morsel from her grasp and then enveloping British Columbia.

If the heated discussions in the American press and in Congress are an accurate guide, the most forceful argument for accepting the bargain was economic. We were actively interested in the resources of Alaska and in an improved commercial position in the

---

[8] F. A. Golder, "The Purchase of Alaska," *American Historical Review*, XXV, 419–420 (April, 1920).

[9] Some little attention had been focused on Alaska, and further notice had been taken of Russian friendliness, when in 1863 the American telegraph promoter, P. McD. Collins, secured a right of way from the St. Petersburg government for a line across Siberia and Russian America (*Senate Misc. Docs.*, 38 Cong., 1 sess., No. 126). The construction abruptly ceased in 1866, when Cyrus Field successfully spanned the Atlantic.

Pacific. The only other argument that seems to have been of comparable importance—and at that it ranked considerably below the economic argument—was Russian friendship.

Russia, it was repeatedly pointed out, had been our only real supporter during the recent conflict. We had solicited the territory from her (thanks to Seward's eagerness), and the Czar, out of the depths of his regard for us, had consented to sell us Alaska for a song. We could not in these circumstances throw it back into his face; that would be a shabby way to treat him for his loyalty. Besides, we might need his good will at some time in the future.

With almost unanimous voice the members of the House of Representatives agreed that Russia had been our true friend, as proved by her sending the fleets, but some doubts were expressed as to whether genuine friendship called for such a sacrifice as taking over "Seward's Icebox" and paying millions of dollars for it. Representative Benjamin F. ("Beast Ben") Butler argued that if it was necessary to pay out $7,200,000 to retain her amity, then pay it out and refuse to take over the territory.[10]

The Alaska purchase treaty slid through the Senate with little difficulty, thanks to the subtle lobbying of Seward, but strong opposition developed in the House against the necessary appropriation. Certain of the members, who were scandalously involved in a personal way, insisted that the money be held up until the Russian government consented to pay the enormously inflated Perkins claim, growing out of an alleged contract by an American to provide military supplies during the Crimean War. The House at one time seemed to be so hopelessly deadlocked that Minister Stoeckl suggested to his superiors in St. Petersburg that the Emperor give the territory to the Americans outright, and thus shame them into paying. Alexander II promptly vetoed the suggestion; the grasping Yankees might prove utterly shameless. Stoeckl was forced to resort to high-priced lobbyists and publicists, as well as to some

---

[10] The present writer has analyzed the debate in Congress and the press in "Why the United States Purchased Alaska," *Pacific Historical Review*, III, 39–40 (March, 1934).

bribery among Congressmen, before the appropriation was finally passed. He then asked to be permitted to go somewhere else where he might breathe a less fetid atmosphere, perhaps not realizing how liberally he had contributed to the existing odor.[11]

6

The American masses accepted the transfer of Alaska with considerable reluctance, and with the hope rather than the confident expectation that it would pan out with gold, fish, and furs—as it fortunately did. As time wore on and as the riches of Alaska became increasingly apparent, we began to feel genuinely grateful to the Russians for having conferred so substantial a favor upon us. Thus we fell into the common but misleading habit of reading back into the past the mood of the moment. But at the time of the sale there actually was some complaint that the Russians had taken unfair advantage of our friendship to dump Alaska on us.

The aftertaste for the Russians was likewise not altogether pleasant. They particularly resented the injection of the dubious Perkins claim into the discussion. Minister Cassius M. Clay, writing many years after the event, reported that Prince Gorchakov was so aroused by the Perkins affair that, with veins on forehead bulging, he exclaimed, "I will go to war before I will pay a single copeck." [12] Clay is not a trustworthy witness, but there is no denying the fact that the Russians were deeply annoyed.

The Russian government, like that of other expansionist nations, has developed a tradition of hanging on to its already disproportionately huge possessions. It has never permanently surrendered, in peace or war, any other area comparable in size to Alaska. In 1867 this tradition, combined with an ingrained hostility to foreigners, aroused some opposition in Russia against letting the territory go. Yet Minister Clay—again the unreliable witness—found the transaction generally acceptable, partly because of the cordial feeling for the United States. "Well," Clay reported one

[11] Golder, "The Purchase of Alaska," pp. 423-424.
[12] *The Life of Cassius Marcellus Clay* (Cincinnati, 1886), I, 406.

Russian as saying, "we have sold to you too cheaply, but it's all in the family." [13]

The reasons of the Russians for selling Alaska seemed sound, at least at the time. One miscalculation was the assumption that the United States would continue to be the traditional friend of Russia and the hereditary enemy of Britain. Events have turned out otherwise, and Alaska has become a vital strategic area which the Russians could well wish they had never sold. The territory of the United States now extends to the Bering Strait and beyond, and Americans today are somewhat less nervous than they would be if Soviet bombers were perched on the line of 54° 40'—the one-time southern boundary of Russian America.

---

[13] Clay to Seward, May 10, 1867, National Archives (Dispatches).

X

Cracks in the Ancient Friendship

"Welcome, thrice welcome! but not as a stranger,
Come to the nation that calls thee its friend!"
  —Oliver Wendell Holmes, "Welcome to the Grand
  Duke Alexis," 1871

I

THERE is a homely adage to the effect that when the mush gets too thick it burns. The mush of Russo-American cordiality became almost unmanageably thick during the Civil War, and then thickened to the burning point about the time of the Fox mission. The beginning of the scorching process dates from approximately the time of the Alaska purchase, which left slightly bitter feelings on both sides of the Atlantic.

The good-will tour of the Grand Duke Alexis, the third living son of Alexander II, helped to postpone for a time any serious friction, but even it generated considerable embarrassment. The visiting dignitary reached New York in November, 1871, there to receive a royal welcome, which included a huge band trained to play Russian airs. This was but the beginning of a seemingly unending round of parades, balls, and receptions. From New York to Washington the young nobleman was cheered by curious crowds, but in the nation's capital, which was accustomed to celebrities, his reception was lukewarm, and his formal presentation to President Grant at the White House passed off without incident. Alexis returned to New York, pushed north to Boston, then to Canada, and then to Chicago, whose burned-out ruins he viewed and for whose relief he contributed generously. At Milwaukee,

THE GRAND DUKE'S RECEPTION

COLUMBIA. "My long-lost ALEXIS! I am so glad you have come!"

The gifted cartoonist Thomas Nast pokes fun at the exuberance of America's welcome. (From *Harper's Weekly*, 1871.)

which boasted a considerable Russian population, the enthusiastic multitude had to be held back by bayonets. At St. Louis, Alexis was snowballed by mischievous boys whom he regarded good-naturedly, and he presented a diamond bracelet to the blond burlesque queen, Lydia Thompson, in appreciation of her performance. Traveling west to Omaha, he went on a "buffalo shoot" with "Buffalo Bill" Cody and a party of Sioux Indians, and upon killing his first victim telegraphed the glad tidings to his imperial father. The rigors of "roughing it" were assuaged by taking along sandwiches and champagne.

Returning through Kansas, the Grand Duke was greeted by an original ode of welcome, patterned after the "Battle Hymn of the Republic," the chorus of which ran:

> Ho! for Russia and the Union!
> Ho! for Russia and the Union!
> Ho! for Russia and the Union!
> The Czar and Grant are friends! [1]

Moving on into the South, Alexis encountered small crowds and restrained enthusiasm, particularly at Memphis. Evidently the states lately in rebellion did not entertain grateful thoughts toward the nation that had stood by the Union so steadfastly. After visiting New Orleans, the imperial party sailed from Pensacola, Florida.

Alexis was described as a handsome six-footer, and it is not surprising that the women turned out in conspicuously large numbers to greet him. Nor is it surprising that "Alexis garniture" and "Russian green" quickly became favorites with the ladies. The size of the welcoming crowds was no doubt also due in large measure to curiosity. "If it had been a Crim Tartar," opined *Harper's Weekly*, "or a king of the Cannibal Islands, or a white elephant, the excitement would have been precisely the same." [2] There was, moreover, a suspicion that the visit had provided an opportunity for the high society of the Gilded Age to outdo itself with competitive displays of extravagance.

Alexis had inspected the schools of Boston, and it was generally assumed that he would carry back enlightenment to Russia. His coming also served to divert popular attention from the more nauseous aspects of the Catacazy affair, which will be discussed shortly. But despite the sneering of *Harper's Weekly*, there can

---

[1] New York *Herald*, Jan. 23, 1872.
[2] XV, 1146 (Dec. 9, 1871).

be no doubt that the visit did much to underscore our gratitude to Russia by reviving recent memories and enabling us to embroider upon them. Probably the most enduring result of the visit was poetical. Oliver Wendell Holmes again broke into verse, this time in his memorable "Welcome to the Grand Duke Alexis," which was sung to the Russian national air by the children of the public schools:

> Bleak are our shores with the blasts of December,
> Fettered and chill is the rivulet's flow;
> Throbbing and warm are the hearts that remember
> Who was our friend when the world was our foe.[3]

Holmes sent this poem and another inspired by the occasion to his historian friend, John Lothrop Motley, then stationed at The Hague. Motley, who had seen something of Czardom at first hand, wrote that he did not appreciate too highly the affection which was "supposed" to exist between Russia and America, and which at any rate was "a very platonic attachment." He added cynically, "Being founded, however, on entire incompatibility of character, absence of sympathy, and a plentiful lack of any common interest, it may prove a very enduring passion." [4] At all events, Holmes's poetical offerings were major props in the perpetuation of the Russian-love myth.

2

Constantine de Catacazy was another of the poorly balanced diplomats whom it has been the ill fortune of both Russia and America to send to each other's shores. A clever and engaging person of undoubted shrewdness and unscrupulousness, he had already had a scandalous career. While a young secretary of legation in Rio de Janeiro, he had run away with the wife of the aged Neapolitan minister. He managed to live down this incident, and after commending himself through his cleverness to the Foreign

---

[3] *The Poetical Works of Oliver Wendell Holmes* (Boston, 1887), p. 256.
[4] G. W. Curtis, ed., *The Correspondence of John Lothrop Motley* (New York, 1889), II, 336.

Office, finally reached Washington, this time properly married.

St. Petersburg instructed Catacazy to oppose the offensive Perkins claim, no doubt thinking that he would do so temperately. But the envoy was so deeply angered by evidences of graft and improper pressures that he betrayed an excess of zeal. He traduced President Grant and Secretary of State Fish in private conversations, which was most indiscreet, and broke into the press in an abusive campaign against President Grant, which was highly irregular. Infinitely inventive, he turned out to be a liar, intriguer, and forger; among other things he fabricated notes from St. Petersburg approving his conduct which he showed around Washington.

Catacazy's sins would have been intolerable even if he had confined himself to the relevant Perkins claim, but he did not. The Anglo-American Joint High Commission was then laboring in Washington over American grievances against Britain—grievances that were so serious as to threaten war. Although the Russian press generally supported the American cause, Catacazy apparently assumed that the Czar's interests would be promoted if the British were enmeshed in controversy with the United States. He therefore buttonholed the representatives of both nations and did what he could to disrupt the negotiations by exciting their prejudices. Once the treaty was signed, in spite of his persistent efforts at sabotage, he schemed to prevent its execution.[5]

Secretary Fish made it clear to the Russian Foreign Office that Catacazy was personally offensive and that his replacement by a more tactful successor was desired. In normal circumstances this request would have been promptly granted, but Catacazy could not be immediately recalled without grave difficulties. The Grand Duke Alexis was about to depart on his good-will tour, and protocol demanded that he be shepherded about by an envoy of ministerial rank. A substitute could not be sent overnight, and if the United States insisted upon Catacazy's immediate dismissal, the tour of Alexis would have to be canceled. Preparations for the

---

[5] Fish to Curtin, Nov. 16, 1871, National Archives (Instructions).

Grand Duke's visit had been preceded in Russia with much fanfare, and a sudden cancellation would be interpreted in Europe as having serious international implications, with much loss of face for Russia. The Foreign Office moreover appears to have believed that unsavory political forces were behind the Perkins claim, and it was naturally disposed to accept the reports of its own envoy. Besides, the peremptory recall of a minister was regarded as a serious step, not to be undertaken without deliberate investigation.[6]

A compromise agreement was finally worked out. President Grant, who was deeply angered, would not formally receive Catacazy except when the minister was with Alexis, and under no circumstances would Grant engage in conversation with his traducer. The Russian Foreign Office promised to recall the meddlesome envoy as soon as the imperial visit ended, provided he was tolerated in the meantime. The already disagreeable situation was made more difficult when the Czar and his henchmen developed the suspicion that we did not trust the Russian government to carry out its promises, and that we were preparing to bundle Catacazy out of the country ourselves.

3

When the Grand Duke Alexis reached Washington and took up his abode at the house of the Russian minister, President Grant, although receiving him as a caller, could not invite the noble sightseer to dinner at the White House without having Catacazy come along. Hence no invitation was tendered. This ostracism made a most painful impression in Russia, where social slights were taken more seriously than in the Land of the Free. Alexander II was especially distressed by the affront which had been shown to the Grand Duke and indirectly to the Crown itself.

---

[6] The Russian Foreign Office pointed out that the American minister, Cassius Marcellus Clay, had engaged in dubious speculations and in a violent "fistication" in the rear of the entry to the imperial opera box during a gala performance, but no request was made for his recall (Curtin to Fish, July 9/21, 1871, *ibid.* [Dispatches]).

As agreed in advance, Catacazy was recalled after the Grand Duke left Washington, but there was some little delay in the choice of his successor, perhaps partly as a mark of displeasure. Gradually the Russian court began to perceive that the objectionable envoy was not a trustworthy public servant. It was revealed that he had pocketed $3,000 in a deal involving the purchase of a lot in New York City for a Greek Orthodox Church. He was also so ill advised as to publish a pamphlet in Paris defending himself, in disobedience of the express orders of the Emperor, as a result of which he was dismissed from the imperial payroll and his pension stopped.

This unfortunate imbroglio, which was widely aired in the press of two continents, marked a downward lurch on the path of amicable relations. The New York *Tribune* held that the affair ended the honeymoon period, while the New York *Nation* believed that Catacazy had ruptured the "entente cordiale" of Civil War days. This magazine shrewdly re-examined the bases of the "love," and concluded that the two nations had nothing in common "but size."

The Russian press spoke in favorable terms of the popular welcome accorded Alexis, as did the Czar and Czarina at social affairs attended by the American minister. But a chilly undercurrent in official and royal circles could not be concealed. Alexander II was pleased by the cordial reception given Catacazy's successor, and in June, 1872, he remarked to the American envoy with evident feeling that he accepted this as evidence that the United States wished to "*revive* the friendship and kind relations" which had never previously been interrupted.[7] Later in the year our minister in St. Petersburg reported that the re-election of Grant had occurred without any official expressions of satisfaction, quite in contrast to the many congratulations received from other members of the diplomatic corps.

With the passage of time, and with Catacazy's continuing acts of folly, the Czar showed more friendliness toward America. Late

---

[7] Curtin to Fish, June 2, 1872, *ibid*. Italics inserted.

in 1873 he met our minister and remarked that Alexis had returned full of praise for "the gallantry and hospitality of our men and of the beauty of our women." The American replied that the Grand Duke "was so handsome and dignified" that "our young ladies all fell in love with him." Alexander II laughed and remarked, "Yes, and he with them." [8]

The Catacazy affair, in itself of no fundamental importance, elicited more official correspondence than almost any other subject from 1809 to 1917. Among other things it illustrates how thin-skinned the traditional brotherhood really was.

4

From the year of the Fox mission in 1866 to the assassination of Alexander II in 1881, developments in Russia on the whole continued to cast a lengthening shadow over the ancient attachment.

Liberty-loving Poland was almost continuously in the American public eye. Once the uprising of 1863 had been stamped out, the Emperor embarked upon a savage program of Russification. The Polish language suffered further restrictions, the remnants of Polish nationality were obliterated, and the Roman Catholic clergy were so severely handled as to bring about a rupture in 1866 between St. Petersburg and the Vatican. All of these oppressive measures were odious to red-corpuscled Americans, and especially to Roman Catholic Americans.

The non-Russian Baltic peoples, after a similarly protracted experience with Russification, were more firmly incorporated into the Empire. Forward-looking Americans were distressed by the thought that both in Poland and in the Baltic provinces the crude Cossack was pulling a superior civilization down to his own inferior level. The New York *Nation* lamented in 1872 that what was going on in Poland and the Baltic area "probably surpasses in cruelty and brutality anything the modern world has ever seen. . . ." [9]

---

[8] Jewell to Fish, Dec. 10, 1873, *ibid.*
[9] XIV, 37 (Jan. 18, 1872).

The decade of the 1870's also witnessed on an increasing scale the violent outbursts of Russian revolutionaries, who deliberately resorted to terrorism as a means of bringing about desperately needed reform. In the 1870's and 1880's there was not a single year when the news dispatches from Russia did not contain reports of the trials or executions of prominent agitators. While decent Americans could not applaud the employment of the bomb as an instrument of reform, the impression deepened that only an intolerably tyrannical government could evoke such excesses. Terrorism was a constant and frightful reminder of the iron hand of autocracy.

5

During the same years, 1866 to 1881, American public sentiment on the whole was less offended by the conduct of Russia in the international theater. These were the decades when Russian armies were on the march across Asia. Countless skirmishes and battles were fought with the natives east of the Caspian and north of Persia and Afghanistan. The British were alarmed, because Persia controlled the lifeline to India, and because Afghanistan dominated the gateway to India. But while the American people rather indirectly shared this concern through British journals and other media, their fear was markedly less. The theater of conflict was too far away, and we were too busy building railroads, wiping out Indians and buffalo, and otherwise extending our own frontier.

Events in the European international arena, as contrasted with those in Asia, were generally of more interest to Americans because closer to home. Alexander II took advantage of the Franco-German War (1870–1871) to regain the right, lost in the Crimean conflict, to refortify Sebastopol and maintain a Russian fleet on the Black Sea. American opinion seems to have been favorable to Russian demands, and our minister in St. Petersburg was forced to deny the ridiculous rumor that President Grant had offered the Czar an American fleet to assist in forcing the Dardanelles.[10]

---

[10] Curtin to Fish, Dec. 19, 1870, National Archives (Dispatches).

Alexander II looked upon himself as the special protector of the Christian Slavs in the Balkans, where he sought to establish Russian ascendancy among the satellite states then under the Sultan's overlordship. When the Turks began to butcher the infidel Christians on an appalling scale, especially in Bulgaria, the Russians, stirred in some degree by a Pan-Slav impulse, went to war with Turkey (1877–1878). After early setbacks, the Czar's warriors captured Adrianople and drove toward Constantinople. The panicky Turks sued for peace, yielding concessions that left Russia much more powerful in the Balkans than Great Britain and Austria-Hungary desired. A war crisis speedily developed. After a protracted period of dangerous uncertainty, the Russians were forced into an international congress in Berlin, as a consequence of which they relinquished dominance over the Balkans, although regaining a part of Bessarabia and retaining the recently won Armenian districts at the eastern extremity of the Black Sea.

Popular sympathy in America seems to have been on the side of Alexander II in his war with Turkey, for the anti-Christian butcheries of the Sultan's soldiery had placed the Turk outside the pale.[11] The Slavic crusade to free the Balkan Christians was in some ways reminiscent of our own recent crusade to free the slaves. The Congress of Berlin was admittedly a stinging diplomatic defeat for the Czar, but even so the Russians had recaptured some of the military prestige lost in the Crimean War. They had also made substantial territorial gains, and had given proof of their power to surge eastward across Asia. Fears of the so-called Muscovite menace were again revived.

6

The Turkish crisis unfortunately reopened the old sores of the Catacazy affair. In the winter of 1876–1877 a Russian fleet, with

---

[11] Anomalously, this was but one of the numerous occasions in the nineteenth century when liberal, democratic, and Christian Great Britain, seeking to strengthen her Empire, supported Moslem and despotic Turkey, while autocratic and absolutist Russia championed Christian and popular movements in the Ottoman Empire.

the Grand Duke Alexis as one of its officers, came to the United States. The Emperor's minister in Washington, unlike his predecessor in Civil War days, volunteered an explanation. The Russian warships, threatened by superior Turkish units in the Mediterranean and unable to secure reinforcements from the icebound Baltic, were ordered to winter in friendly American ports. Secretary Fish assumed that the Russians were also interested in cutting off munitions shipments for Turkey, and in pinning down British naval units at Halifax and Bermuda.[12]

Alexis was actually under imperial instructions to repair the damage growing out of President Grant's social slights during the previous visit. The plan was that he should call on the President, but when the rumor gained strength in St. Petersburg that Grant had announced his determination not to return the contemplated visit, the Russian court did not want to expose itself to another affront. It therefore sought advance assurances from the President that the call would be returned. The American minister reported from St. Petersburg that a sudden frostiness had sprung up, and that it would be a pity if the two nations should drift back into "the cold and restrained position" following the Catacazy episode. "These people," he added, "will love us if we will only let them do it." [13]

President Grant and his successor, President Hayes, both agreed that courtesy would require a return of the ducal call, but they both insisted that the dignity of their high office forbade specific social bargains. A cordial invitation was issued to Alexis, who, after consulting his father, returned a "very peculiar" refusal. The Emperor simply would not permit the visit without advance assurances of a return, so none was made. The Grand Duke, who arrived at Charleston, by-passed Washington on his journey north, and although the imperial family seemed pleased by the warmth of his second public reception, no ground was gained in patching up old diplomatic troubles. Secretary Fish believed that the Russian

---

[12] Fish to Boker, March 7, 1877, National Archives (Instructions).
[13] Boker to Evarts, March 19, 1877, *ibid.* (Dispatches).

government was trying to extort from the Grant administration some kind of statement that could be construed as an apology.[14]

Another naval movement of perhaps greater significance occurred a year later, when the Russo-Turkish crisis deepened and war between Russia and Britain seemed imminent. In April, 1878, the Russian steamer *Cimbria* aroused excitement in the United States and abroad when it sailed from a Baltic port with some sixty officers and six hundred seamen, presumably to man four armed steamers acquired in America for the ostensible (and actual) purpose of raiding British commerce in the event of war. The *Cimbria* arrived at a Maine port in due season, but fortunately Anglo-Russian differences were composed without resort to arms.[15] England-haters in the United States, who vividly remembered that our merchant marine had been ravaged in the Civil War by the British-built *Alabama*, would have rejoiced to give their cousins a dose of their own medicine, while those same cousins expressed alarm and resentment over American connivance with the "barbaric" Slavs.

The employment by the Russians of hospitable ports in the United States on these two occasions further demonstrated the value of the American connection to them. These incidents should have convinced some of our citizens, and possibly did, that the fleets had come to the United States in 1863 for similarly realistic purposes.

7

In 1881 Alexander II was torn to pieces by an assassin's bomb, after a half-dozen or so attempts on his life had failed, some of them by a miraculously narrow margin. By one of the tragic ironies of history, he had signed on that very day a decree authorizing steps toward certain needed reforms, but his nerve-shattered successor promptly suppressed the imperial edict.

---

[14] Fish to Boker, March 7, 1877, *ibid.* (Instructions).
[15] See L. I. Strakhovsky, "Russia's Privateering Projects of 1878," *Journal of Modern History*, VII, 22-40 (March, 1935).

The rank-and-file American, while deploring murder, has normally looked upon the removal of monarchs, by violent means or otherwise, as an incident in progress. A painful impression was created in Russia by Socialist meetings in New York and Chicago which applauded the assassination. But such views in America were those of an inconsequential minority. The grief of our citizenry was widespread, and the official expressions of condolence were more than ordinarily sincere. The memory of the assassination of Lincoln was still fresh, and we shared with the Russian masses a common sorrow. Alexander II was regarded as our only true friend during the Civil War, as evidenced by his opposing multipower intervention and by sending his fleets, and he had also sold us Alaska, which by 1881 was clearly turning out to be a bargain.

By an unhappy coincidence, only four months after the murder of the Czar, and while the Russian legation in Washington was still using black-bordered stationery, President Garfield was fatally shot by an assassin. The Russian government reciprocated our earlier condolences, and the two peoples were in some degree drawn together temporarily by a common sorrow.

With the passing of Alexander II a personal tie in Russian-American relations was severed. It would have been broken even if his successor, Alexander III, had been a zealous liberal, which he definitely was not. Just as the death of Franklin D. Roosevelt, who was much admired by the Russians, marked the end of an era, so the death of Alexander II, who was much admired by the Americans, spelled the end of the golden age in Russian-American relations.

XI

Pogroms and Prisons

"Every country has its own constitution; ours is absolutism moderated by assassination."—Remark attributed to an anonymous Russian in the nineteenth century

I

WHEN Catherine the Great seized her share of Poland late in the eighteenth century, she got more than territory. She managed to pick up one of the largest concentrations of Jews in the world, although to be sure there was a considerable sprinkling of them elsewhere in her empire. Medieval Europe had long looked upon the Jew as an infidel who had crucified Jesus, and after the Russians took over Poland, they imposed certain restrictions on residence, movement, and occupation. At least as early as 1820 references appeared in the American press to Russian ill-treatment of the Jewish unbelievers.

The Jews are a sober, enterprising, and acquisitive people, which the lethargic Russian peasant certainly was not, and in spite of adverse conditions growing out of industrialization, some of them prospered, at least comparatively, in the midst of poverty. They were the traditional moneylenders and middlemen, in which capacity they were naturally unpopular. They were also vodka sellers, and by capitalizing on the national weakness for alcohol, contributed to the debauchery of the masses. As is so often the case in such circumstances, the envy, prejudice, and bigotry of the peasant in Russia were aroused against the Jews, who allegedly trampled and spat upon the sacred Greek Orthodox ikons. The hoary and horrendous tale would not down that the Jews practiced "ritual murders"—that is, the secret sacrifice of Christian children to obtain blood for their passover cakes.

The Jews as a group—particularly the young and well-educated—resented the restrictions under which they labored, and there was a tendency among them to join the ranks of the revolutionists, thus bringing down upon themselves the wrath of the Czar and his bureaucrats. These officials further objected to the Jews on the ground that they were a veritable nation within a nation—a clannish element that was resourceful in escaping military service and otherwise unwilling to support the state. Jewish sympathizers outside the Empire replied that it was unfair to segregate these unfortunates and then condemn them for being exclusive.

Even before the murder of Alexander II in 1881, the persecution of the Jews had been somewhat accelerated. In 1879 Representative Samuel S. Cox of New York City, where many Jews had found a haven, pressed in Congress a joint resolution which sought to amend the treaty of 1832 so that Russian Jews who had become naturalized American citizens would not be discriminated against when they returned to their native hearths. This move was inspired by the case of Herman Rosenstraus, who had purchased property in Russia for a sewing machine company, but who could not take title because of his Judaic faith.[1] The resolution passed the House, but not the Senate, and in succeeding months Cox was indefatigable in seeking information from the President regarding the status of American Jews in Russia. The next year, 1880, the Secretary of State, responding to a petition from the Union of American Hebrew Congregations, directed the United States minister in St. Petersburg to make such representations as would best subserve the interests of religious freedom.

The lid blew off in 1881, following the assassination of the

---

[1] *Cong. Record*, 46 Cong., 1 sess., p. 1891 (June 10, 1879).

Czar by revolutionists, with whom the Jews were in some degree identified, at least in the peasants' minds. In Warsaw the mob ran amok for three days; in Kiev, so the report ran, not a single Jewish house escaped damage. Christians chalked crosses on their houses, or exhibited holy images illuminated by lamps, to fend off the fury of the mob. The outrages were not confined to Russian Poland but occurred generally wherever there were concentrations of Jews. Representative Cox, in demanding action, made an impressive speech to Congress in which he listed 167 places where in 1882 there had been riots, burnings, pillagings, rapings, and murders.[2] Estimates in the American press placed the property damage at $80,000,000 and the number of families reduced to beggary at 100,000.

The failure of the Russian authorities to bring a speedy end to these orgies testified to the bitterness of feeling among the peasants, as well as to the impotence of the St. Petersburg government or its willingness to let the masses run riot against the Jews rather than brood over their own hard lot. More than one critic, in Russia and abroad, accused the officials of conniving at these holocausts.

2

Tens of thousands of terrified Jews fled from their burning homes to neighboring countries, and additional tens of thousands sought sanctuary in the American Canaan. The first large stream of these destitute and bewildered people began to flow into New York in 1882. Significantly, this year marks the beginning in our history of the New Immigration—the influx on a considerable scale from southern and eastern Europe—and Russian Jews constituted a substantial part of it.

Before 1882 most of the Jews in America were German Jews, of a relatively prosperous class, and they were not numerous, totaling about 230,000 for the entire United States. When the flight from Czarist Egypt began, Russia had approximately half

[2] *Cong. Record*, 47 Cong., 1 sess. (Appendix), pp. 651–658 (July 31, 1882).

of the Jews in the world. Now the United States has nearly half of them.[3] The exiles of the 1880's unfortunately arrived in such a shattered state—mentally, physically, financially—that they did not constitute as good stuff for citizenship as they would have had the exodus taken place under normal circumstances.

American newspaper readers were shocked to learn of these pogroms, and their sensibilities were even more deeply rasped when with their own eyes they saw the ragged and terror-stricken hordes crowd into our eastern cities. Decent citizens the country over burst forth in a spontaneous outcry against this latest exhibition of man's inhumanity to man, and similar responses were forthcoming from the British and other civilized peoples. The American protest was significantly nation-wide, and not confined to Jewish centers or to Jewish pressure groups. A large indignation meeting was held in New York in February, 1882, and another in Philadelphia in March, 1882, from which a memorial was sent to Congress urging appropriate representations at St. Petersburg.

Representative Cox continued his demands for action and condemned the apathy of his colleagues in Congress. To the argument that we should not jeopardize the ancient amity, he replied that we "want no friendship with a rule so entirely tyrannous." The officials in the State Department were definitely embarrassed. Technically, it was no business of ours if Russian subjects murdered other Russian subjects of a different faith, any more than it was the business of Russians if American citizens lynched other American citizens of a different hue. But if hordes of impoverished Negroes had descended upon Russia as a result of such persecutions, St. Petersburg no doubt would have protested. In these circumstances and in response to public pressure, the State Department tactfully voiced its displeasure.

The position of the United States was not so strong morally as

---

[3] By an ironical twist the Soviet regime now accuses the Americans of anti-Semitism and prides itself on the absence of it.

we could have wished, for we had done a thorough job of exterminating certain Indian tribes, and during the 1880's and 1890's our lynching rate was higher than it has ever been since then. We had also been murdering dozens of pig-tailed Chinese in San Francisco and elsewhere; and the year 1882, when the Russian-Polish Jews began to arrive in formidable numbers, was also the year that we officially excluded Chinese coolies. Apologists for the Russians were aware of these skeletons in our closet, and had an unpleasant habit of rattling them in our faces.

3

Vicious persecutions of the Jews continued in Russia throughout the 1880's, despite our vigorous disapprobation. Pro-Jewish petitions poured in on Congress from numerous groups, and various resolutions were introduced requesting information, expressing sympathy, or demanding protest and protection. In 1890 Representative Cummings of New York sponsored a resolution in which he deplored the persecution of the Jews, all the more so because Russia was our "firm friend" and had gained imperishable glory by emancipating the serfs and protecting Christians against the Turks. Two large groups of Missourians endorsed the position of Cummings, as did the legislature of Idaho.

Embarrassing questions were also being raised in Congress and elsewhere as to the treatment of naturalized American Jews in Russia, and Representative Dungan of Ohio in 1892 introduced a joint resolution directing severance of diplomatic relations with Russia.[4] This extreme proposal naturally received no serious support. The national platforms of both Democratic and Republican parties in 1892 contained popular planks expressing sympathy for the persecuted Jews. Disquietingly large numbers of Russian-Jewish expellees were becoming labor agitators in the United States, and this development was regarded as a further black mark against the Czarist regime. Nor did the American people relish

---

[4] *Cong. Record*, 52 Cong., 1 sess., p. 5228 (June 10, 1892).

having their fair land used as a kind of dumping ground for Jewish malcontents and other unfortunate by-products of Russian cruelty.

Anti-Jewish attacks began to taper off markedly about 1891. Outside Russia it was assumed, although not proved, that the improvement was in response to an outraged world opinion. It was also assumed that influential Jewish banking houses, notably the Rothschilds, were acting as a brake by putting difficulties in the way of the Czar's borrowing operations, which were then huge and not as successful as St. Petersburg had hoped.

The Jewish problem was more or less acutely in the American public eye during the thirty years from 1881 to 1911. It probably did more than any other single grievance to sour the somewhat synthetic good will that had been built up over the years between Russia and the United States. Even by itself it would have aroused much antagonism, but our resentment over the butchery of Jews was deepened by a concurrent exposé of Siberian prisons and other Czarist cruelties.

4

No one critic did more to rip away the veil of fancy from Russian despotism, and expose it to the American public in all its nakedness, than George Kennan.[5] No one person did more to cause the people of the United States to turn against their presumed benefactor of yesteryear. Yet the unique contributions of this remarkable man have been largely overlooked by historians, perhaps because he wrote for the reading public and not for the diplomatic files.

The ordinary American in the 1880's knew vaguely of Siberia as "God's frozen country," to which undesirable characters were banished by Czarist edict. Occasional tales of hardship and terror drifted out of these silent solitudes, but on the whole the vast half-

---

[5] A distant relative (not an uncle, as commonly stated) of another expert on Russian affairs, George Frost Kennan, whose distinguished career as a foreign service officer began in 1927 (Kennan to author, Feb. 10, 1949).

continent was a no man's land to our people until George Kennan wrote about it.

In 1865, when only twenty years of age, Kennan was selected by the Western Union Telegraph Company to be a member of its expedition to Siberia for surveying a possible telegraph route across Russia, Siberia, the Bering Strait, and Alaska. Young Kennan lived in Siberia for two years, enduring temperatures that dropped to 60 degrees below zero. The surveying enterprise came to an abrupt end when news arrived that Cyrus Field in 1866 had successfully laid his cable across the Atlantic, and Kennan returned home after a perilous journey by dogsled. His adventures were published in a book entitled *Tent Life in Siberia* (1870), and attracted wide attention. In the same year Kennan traveled to the Russian Caucasus to study conditions there. After engaging in various occupations, he became best known, both in England and America, as a fascinating and authoritative lecturer on Siberia.

In 1885 Kennan was commissioned by the *Century Magazine* to return to Siberia, accompanied by the gifted artist George A. Frost, and to prepare a series of articles on the alleged horrors of the Siberian prisons. Conservative by nature, Kennan embarked on his mission thinking that the unfavorable reports had been much overcolored, and rather sympathizing with the Russian rulers in their efforts to get rid of fanatical revolutionists.[6] His known predisposition in favor of the government was probably responsible for his being allowed to study conditions at first hand without molestation, except for one brief arrest in Siberia after he had accidentally walked past a prison three times.

Kennan, who was able to speak Russian fluently, actually found conditions horrible beyond belief, and his exposé is a classic of thoroughness and dramatic force. His findings were published (1888–1890) by the *Century Magazine* in a long series of articles, beautifully illustrated by Frost's sketches, and subsequently they appeared in two volumes, *Siberia and the Exile System* (1891).

---

[6] George Kennan, *Siberia and the Exile System* (New York, 1891), I, iv.

The articles had a tremendous impact, both at home and abroad. They were not only widely circulated but, what was more important, they were read by editors, lawyers, preachers, and others who were in a position to give wide currency to the author's discoveries. The series stirred up a heated controversy in the press, and Kennan was tireless in defending himself and his methods against critics. He also supplemented and implemented the printed word by several hundred highly popular and somewhat sensational public lectures.[7]

Kennan's agitation was largely responsible for the establishment of the English Society of the Friends of Russian Freedom in 1890. This group was organized to spread propaganda about Russian despotism in the hope of achieving reform. The idea quickly took hold in America, chiefly in Boston, where the American Society was formed with similar objectives. Among the members were Julia Ward Howe (author of "The Battle Hymn of the Republic"), James Russell Lowell, Phillips Brooks, Edward Everett Hale, and Samuel L. Clemens. An American edition of the magazine *Free Russia* was issued regularly and further aroused our people against Czarist practices.

5

What did Kennan find that so shocked the sensibilities of his readers and auditors?

The condemned man or woman often received no trial; habeas corpus, an Anglo-Saxon concept, was unheard of. The victim was banished, with or without stated reason, for a definite or indefinite term, by what was called "administrative order," all of which was time-honored Russian practice but repugnant to our American ideals of justice. University students were suddenly imprisoned on false charges for years on end, not because they had

---

[7] William W. Ellsworth, *A Golden Age of Authors* (Boston, 1919), pp. 258–277. Dr. George H. Blakeslee told the present writer in 1948 that Kennan spoke to the student body of Connecticut Wesleyan University. During the intermission the speaker retired behind the stage and reappeared in Siberian prison garb with chains attached to his feet.

committed a crime, but because they might turn out to be revolutionists. The prisons were overcrowded to as much as four times their capacity, and there was a vast amount of suffering from hunger, cold, sickness, and bereavement. Frost's sketches showed delicate men and women, chained together in gangs, plodding off hopelessly into desolate wastes of ice and snow.

The police were brutal; many of the arrests were arbitrary; and solitary confinement without cause was common. The torture of loneliness was partially relieved by communication through the knock or tapping alphabet, by which the inmates were able to spell out messages to one another through thick stone walls.[8]

Lashings and knoutings were common, and the prison authorities were guilty of numerous other abuses and barbarities. Yet the Russian masses were not shocked by all this inhumanity. In generations past they had learned to accept misery and degradation with composure, as if they were the normal incidents of life. Suicides were not infrequent. Kennan told of a woman medical school student who cut her throat with a piece of broken glass after two years of solitary confinement in a fortress.

The callousness of the prison officials was beyond belief. Wives and mothers were used as live bait. The prisoner would be promised an interview with them; he would be allowed to glimpse them anxiously waiting to see him; and then he would be dragged away in the hope of extorting a confession. One prisoner, a young girl who died of brain fever in prison, was buried quietly at night without the knowledge of her relatives. When the mother, who had been led to believe that the funeral would occur later, appeared at the prison the next day, she was informed that the burial had already taken place. Upon asking the chief of police where her daughter had been interred, she was told, "That is our business." Kennan's summation of the incident is moving:

Imagine that your only daughter, a schoolgirl, still in her teens, had been arrested upon a vague charge of disloyalty; that she had been

---

[8] The same type of thing, as later used by prisoners of the Communists, is vividly described in Arthur Koestler, *Darkness at Noon* (New York, 1941).

thrown into prison and kept there a year in solitary confinement without a trial; that she had died at last of brain fever brought on by grief, anxiety, apprehension, and solitude; that you had not been permitted to stand by her death-bed; that you had been deceived as to the time of her funeral; and that finally, when you went humbly and respectfully to the Chief of Police and asked where your murdered child had been buried, that you might at least wet the fresh earth of her grave with your tears, you had received the contemptuous answer, "That is our business," what would you have done? [9]

After interviewing numerous unfortunates, including half-starved and heartbroken women, many of them of good families and delicate frame, some of whose babies had starved or frozen to death, Kennan could neither sleep nor sit still. He suffered a breakdown of health and strength in the trans-Baikal region.

6

Kennan's name is so imperishably associated with Siberian prisons as to obscure the fact that he wrote with equal force about conditions elsewhere in the Russian Empire.

Tyranny was everywhere in evidence, and Kennan was unsparing in exposing its ugliness. Penniless people were flogged by the thousands for nonpayment of taxes. The secret police were sleeplessly vigilant. Foreigners had to receive permission to get into Czarland, permission to get out, permission to stay longer than six months, and they had to notify the police every time they changed their boarding place. "In short," concluded Kennan, "you cannot live, move, or have your being in the Russian Empire without permission." [10]

Censorship was rigidly enforced and stupidly exercised. Law and justice were maladministered. The servants of the law were not always highly intelligent. Photographs of the terrorist Degaiev were sent out showing him in six different poses: with and without cap, with and without beard, and with and without mustache. A

---

[9] *Century Magazine*, XXXV, 297 (Dec., 1887).
[10] *Ibid.*, XXXVII, 891 (April, 1889).

tipsy police officer jailed four suspects, and went around saying that he had found four of the accursed Degaievs, and that he was going to hold them until he could find the other two.

Bribery and graft of various kinds were commonplace. One corrupt police official found a corpse and dragged it around to the houses of several wealthy persons for temporary deposit, and these householders, rather than become involved in the clutches of the law, paid him handsomely to take it elsewhere.

Kennan further criticized paternalistic control of the peasant:

From the time when he leaves his cradle and begins the struggle of life down to the time when his weary gray head is finally laid under the sod, he must be guided, directed, instructed, restrained, repressed, regulated, fenced in, fenced out, braced up, kept down, and made to do generally what somebody else thinks is best for him.[11]

7

Kennan did not disapprove of everything he observed. He actually found a number of honest and intelligent officials, caught in the toils of the system, who were anxious to lay bare its defects in the hope that some reform might be accomplished. He drew a sharp distinction—and one that was increasingly being made in American minds—between the Russian bureaucracy and the Russian peasants. "As for me," he concluded, "my sympathies are with the Russia of the people, not the Russia of the Czars; with the Russia of the provincial assemblies, not the Russia of the secret police; with the Russia of the future, not the Russia of the past." [12]

Nor was Kennan the only writer to expose the brutalities of the Czarist system. His findings supplemented and confirmed the tales of Russian exiles like Kropotkin and Stepniak, some of whose reports were being published directly in the American press or republished from British journals. But Kennan's accounts carried

---

[11] *Ibid.,* p. 890.
[12] *Ibid.,* XLVI, 472 (July, 1893).

more weight because he spoke as an American citizen and not as an embittered expatriate.

Russophiles in this country, as well as Russian spokesmen abroad, condemned Kennan for stressing the exception rather than the rule, which he no doubt did on occasion to make his point. Apologists for Czardom wrote books proving that conditions in the Russian prisons were on the whole good and that, if capital punishment prevailed in the Empire to the same extent as in certain western countries, many of the exiles about whom Kennan was shedding tears would long since have been hanged for murder or attempted murder. Siberia was a penal colony, said these apologists, and Australia, when it had been used as such, presented many shocking scenes to the civilized world. Finally, Kennan's accusers charged that he had unethically abused the hospitality of his hosts, after accepting all the favors shown him, by writing his savagely unfair indictment.

Kennan not only vigorously defended himself against his critics but took the offensive by challenging the bases of the ancient friendship. Pointing out that any "disinterested alliance" should be based on a "nobler feeling than hostility to Great Britain," he went on to demonstrate that Russian regard for the United States during the Civil War had been dictated "by self-interest rather than by friendship." [13] Even if it had been otherwise, the American people owed nothing to the existing regime of Alexander III, beside which that of his father, Alexander II, had seemed comparatively liberal. Journals like the Cincinnati *Gazette* agreed that the events of the Civil War should not blind us to current wickedness.

The activities of Kennan, whether at the writing desk or on the lecture platform, helped rivet the horrified attention of our people on Siberia. At the close of a Kennan lecture in Philadelphia in 1889, an association was formed which drew up a petition beseeching Alexander III to reform the terrible prison system, and citing the Civil War friendship on which his father had set the seal of

---

[13] *Ibid.*

his approval by sending the fleet to New York. The *Century Magazine* reported that from 1,200 to 1,800 signatures a day were being affixed to the appeal.[14]

The New York *Evening Post* in 1890 remarked that not even the time-honored cordiality was proof against the inhumanities which Kennan had exposed, and suggested that the Russian Empire be made to feel that no decent government wanted anything to do with it. The Philadelphia *Ledger* in the same year went further and urged that the civilized nations refuse to have any traffic with Russia until she had abandoned her atrocious practices, just as they refused to have official dealings with cannibals.

8

Czarist censors were not unaware of the incendiary influence of Kennan's articles, for they liberally scissored or blacked out pages of the *Century Magazine* that reached Russia. The journal itself published a facsimile of an obliterated page that had been returned from a subscriber. Kennan announced that the blacked-out articles had been hectographed, and although at least one young Russian was jailed for having them in his possession, they were circulated from hand to hand even to political exiles in remotest Siberia. The author is credited by his admirers with having written the *Uncle Tom's Cabin* of the Russian revolution—that is, with having had a large hand in inflaming the Russian masses against their masters, and thus inciting them to revolt against the Romanov's in 1917.

George Kennan was a private citizen, and the Russian Foreign Office could not properly lodge an official protest against his activities. But the *Century Magazine* for February, 1893, published a statement by Pierre Botkine, secretary of the Russian legation in Washington. It was doubtless written under instructions from St. Petersburg, or at least with the approval of the Foreign Office. The editor of the magazine stated that insofar as he knew this kind of communication was without precedent.

---

[14] XL, 636–637 (Aug. 1890).

Botkine flatly challenged the lurid version of Siberian prisons presented by Kennan, and pointed out that credible witnesses had told an entirely different story. He explained away the Russification of minorities, the persecution of Jews, and the intolerance of the Greek Orthodox Church. Russia, he argued, was not a complete despotism, and there was some liberty. In any event, autocracy was "as natural and satisfactory" to Russians as was the republican form of government to Americans, and the people cheerfully submitted to it and prospered under it. As for persecuting revolutionists and anarchists, the United States had itself executed anarchists implicated in the infamous Haymarket Riot of 1886 in Chicago.

Botkine's references to the ancient friendship fairly oozed sweetness and good will. Although the two governmental systems were so divergent, he said, the two nations were "natural and disinterested allies, who have never fallen out, and are drawn to each other by bonds of sympathy." Then Botkine played his trump:

Which was the first of the nations to extend to you a brotherly hand, and to bring to you moral support from abroad, in the hour of trial during your civil war? I need not remind you that it was Russia; for though years have passed since then, the story of the arrival of our fleet at the port of New York in that period is yet fresh in the memory of the appreciative American people.[15]

The appeal of Botkine elicited speedy responses from both Russophobes and Russophiles. Some newspapers, like the New York *Sun*, asked for a suspension of judgment and appealed to the presumed debt owed to Catherine II, Alexander I, and Alexander II. Others scorned the historic attachment as largely selfish, a view vigorously espoused by Kennan, who was pleased to note that the power of world opinion had evidently forced the Russian government to emerge from behind its "wall of silence and indifference" and defend itself.

Kennan continued intermittently to write about Russia—

---

[15] XLV, 612 (Feb., 1893).

Romanov, revolutionary, Bolshevik—until his death in 1924. With considerable boldness he returned to St. Petersburg in 1901, and after a stay of three weeks was politely ordered to leave.[16] The incident aroused little interest in the United States. As far as exposing the wretchedness of Russia and erasing glamour from the Czarist regime, Kennan had already done his great work. Through him his countrymen had been led to examine realistically the unnatural friendship between the Republic of the West and the Despotism of the East.

[16] *Foreign Relations, 1901* (Washington, 1902), pp. 451-452.

XII

Despotism at Home
and Dominance Abroad

"The twentieth century belongs to us."
—St. Petersburg *Novoye Vremya*, 1895

I

IN THE era before the American Civil War the influence of Russian literature in the United States was virtually nil. Not until 1867—coincidentally the year of the Alaska purchase—was the first translation of a Russian novel published in America. It was Eugene Schuyler's translation of Turgenev's *Fathers and Sons*, which depicted the conflict between the old and new forces of Russian society in such a way as to arouse the reactionaries and divide literate Russia into two camps. The government seized on Turgenev's term "nihilist" as one with which to besmirch reformist tendencies.

The novels of Turgenev continued to increase in popularity with American readers, and in the 1870's and early 1880's a dozen or so new titles by this talented writer were translated. By the middle 1880's a veritable flood of translations from the Russian began to pour from our press, with Leo Tolstoy now the most popular author.[1] Among these translations were four in 1886 by

---

[1] Thirty-four titles by Tolstoy alone were available by 1890. See Royal A. Gettmann, *Turgenev in England and America* (Urbana, Ill., 1941), p. 111. The Library of Congress catalog shows one Tolstoy translation in 1885, six in 1886

the gifted Isabel F. Hapgood, whose role in introducing Russian literature to the American public has never been properly appreciated. Noteworthy among the four was Gogol's *Dead Souls,* a satirical treatment of graft in the days of serfdom.

Why American readers should have developed a strong taste for Russian novels in the 1880's and 1890's is difficult to determine. Among possible factors were the recurrent Anglo-Russian crises, labor disturbances in the United States reflecting Russian anarchism, and the activities of George Kennan in focusing the spotlight on Czarist practices.

At all events, the popularity of Tolstoy continued to mount, and his influence was felt in the field of morals as well as literature. By espousing pacifistic and nonresistant principles (which were repugnant to Czarism), he commanded a strong following among American idealists, a number of whom, including William Jennings Bryan, made pilgrimages to his home. In 1889 a Tolstoy Club was organized in Boston, and ten years later it had over one hundred members.

Russian novels excel in stark realism. American readers received an indelible impression of the blighting hand of despotism and bureaucracy (Gogol's *Dead Souls*); of coarseness, stupidity, and ignorance; of general resignation and apathy; of sadness, gloom, dreariness, pessimism, melancholy, despair, and suicide; of poverty and drunkenness; of squalor, misery, debauchery, and sordidness (as in Dostoevsky's *The Brothers Karamazov*); of oppression, suffering, and cruelty; of morbidity, abnormality, and gruesomeness (as in Dostoevsky's *The Idiot*, the author of which was himself an epileptic); and of murder and butchery (as in Gogol's *Taras Bulba*).

To what extent such descriptions were accepted by a large American reading public as fact or fiction, one will never know.[2]

(including *Anna Karenina* and *War and Peace*), nine in 1887, eight in 1888, and five in 1890.

[2] The impressions left by the novelists were supplemented by popular lyceum lecturers in the United States like Bayard Taylor and Andrew D. White (Harvey

But probably tens of thousands of our citizens were further repelled by a government that permitted such terrible conditions to persist.

2

The thirst for Russian novels in the 1880's and 1890's was paralleled by a similar thirst—possibly whetted by the same factors—for newspaper and magazine articles about Mother Russia. From such sources, which were abundantly available, what picture did the American reader receive of the Czarist Empire?

Russification of both religion and nationality was continuing apace under the slogan, "One language, one church, and one government." In particular, the persecution of the Roman Catholics in Poland and of the Mennonites and Dukhobors in Russia aroused much sympathy in the United States—a nation dedicated to freedom of worship.

The church was represented as sterile, superstitious, and idolatrous, with much prostration before religious pictures (ikons). The priests were portrayed as degenerate, immoral, grasping, and ignorant. The chief procurator of the Holy Synod, Constantine Pobyedonostsev, who assumed that high office in 1880 and who extended his influence over civil affairs as well, was regarded abroad for about a quarter of a century as the prototype of reaction, illiberalism, anti-Occidentalism, and religious persecution. The excommunication of the kindly and world-famous Tolstoy by the Orthodox Church in 1901 was an event that shocked the United States and other civilized nations.

The bureaucracy clogged the gears of progress with inefficiency, extravagance, procrastination, red tape, and graft. The departments were overstaffed and underpaid, and the bureaucrats were under strong compulsion to seek additional income by devious means. In the armed forces from 1894 to 1902 there were more than a half-dozen notorious cases of corruption or selling

---

Wish, "Getting Along with the Romanovs," *South Atlantic Quarterly*, XLVIII, 351 [July, 1949]).

secrets to foreign powers. (Some of these affairs foreshadow the Soviet purge trials of the 1930's.) Numerous other cases of forgery, pilfering, or plundering became public scandals. Andrew D. White learned that in the war with Turkey the Russian army had suffered from a shortage of shoes, and when he asked where they were he was told by an officer, "In the pockets of the Grand Duke Nicholas."

The bureaucrats, as described in our press, were not only corrupt but excessively suspicious and sometimes stupid. In 1892 Poultney Bigelow was commissioned by the United States government to cruise along the shores of the Baltic in a special canoe, for the purpose of observing what had been done to preserve the beaches against wind and wave. Accompanying him was the distinguished artist, Frederic Remington, who was to prepare sketches. According to Bigelow's angry but untrustworthy tale, they were spied on, their mail was opened, and they ran into a veritable net of police obstruction. The hatch of their canoe had purposely been left unlocked so that it might be easily examined, but during an inspection tour a bureaucrat smashed through the mahogany deck with a hatchet. After both men had abandoned their plans in disgust following a seemingly interminable wait, they were told that permission had been granted. Bigelow's one-sided and unfair account of his experience, published by *Harper's Magazine* in 1893, lost nothing in the telling.[3]

A favorite theme of the American press was Russian censorship. Such well-known works as Carlyle's *French Revolution* and Lecky's *History of European Morals* were placed on the prohibited lists. Russian newspapers were under restraint to print nothing discreditable to the government, such as the accidental sinking

---

[3] LXXXVI, 294–306 (Jan., 1893). The unpublished official reports sent home by the American diplomatic representative in St. Petersburg, whose views may have been warped by an understandable animus, reveal Bigelow as an importunate, unbalanced, and lying exhibitionist. The Russians courteously granted him the desired permission without unusual delay, presumably as a concession to the traditional friendship. They did not care to have artists in canoes snooping around fortified places, and a like request from the Germans or the British would no doubt have been flatly denied.

of a naval vessel. Censorship of foreign newspapers was conducted with vigor if not discernment. Pages or paragraphs were cut out, inked out (with a special inked roller), or pumiced out. Curious Russians would come around to the foreign embassies in St. Petersburg, including the American, to read the unmutilated London *Times* and other journals. They would also have their friends abroad clip the objectionable articles and send them in by registered mail. The censors were guilty of incredible stupidities; they would blot out harmless paragraphs and take no notice of serious attacks on the government. In 1892 the American *Review of Reviews* noted that its character sketch of the Czar, which it had regarded as eulogistic, had been cut out bodily.[4]

3

The plight of the Russian masses, only recently "liberated" from serfdom, elicited much sympathy in the United States. They were pictured as hungry, indolent, improvident, fatalistic, degraded, shaggy, ragged, unkempt, uncouth, and reeking in Oriental filth. One traveler described Russia in 1892 as "the land of the flea and the home of the slave." The poor peasant was bewildered and illiterate; he was the victim of vodka as well as usury, which was often the by-product of vodka. Excessive drinking was a national disgrace and, besides returning a revenue to the government, kept the people in a stupor. Alcohol was the opiate of the masses.

A glaring deficiency in Russian society was the almost complete absence of a middle class. The chosen few lived in magnificent mansions; the inert masses existed in wretched hovels. Emancipation had proved to be an immense illusion. The people seemed to be less well off than in the days of serfdom; then they could obtain the necessities of life; now, particularly in the industrialized areas, they were half-starved wage slaves. Andrew D. White returned to Russia as United States minister in 1892—a Russia that he had known in the 1850's. He found little visible betterment in the lot of the masses. As his train drew into St.

---

[4] V, 150 (March, 1892).

Petersburg, so he recorded, the peasants "with their sheepskin caftans, cropped hair, and stupid faces, brought back the old impressions so vividly that I seemed not to have been absent a week." [5]

Yet numerous observers agreed that the peasant was blessed with good humor, native intelligence, and a deep loyalty to the Emperor, who was not regarded as the author of all these misfortunes nearly so much as the bureaucrats. It was further agreed that if the heavy hand of paternalism could be removed from the backs of the people, they would show some signs of initiative.

Despotism was everywhere entrenched; the state was everything, the individual nothing. Mild suggestions of reform invited reprisals. Seizure was swift; disappearance mysterious; punishment summary and often barbarous, supplemented by liberal applications of the knout and many-thonged Cossack whip. The Czar lived in daily dread of death, and his army of secret police, fantastically estimated at 50,000 in St. Petersburg alone, was everywhere. Not even the mail of the imperial family was believed to be above surreptitious scrutiny, and those upper-class families who could speak English did so lest their servants relay their lightest word to the authorities. The Emperor demanded blind obedience, and he shared the unenviable distinction with the Sultan of Turkey of being the only ruler in the civilized western world to deny his people a constitution. Thus was Czarism delineated for the American newspaper and magazine reader.

4

The assassination of Alexander II in 1881 touched off a redoubled persecution of revolutionists, but little was accomplished. In the absence of free speech or the ballot box, violence seemed to be the only possible means of expressing discontent and hastening reform. Pitiless repression led to more violence, and more violence led to more repression, in an upward-spiraling vicious circle.

---

[5] *Autobiography of Andrew Dickson White* (New York, 1905), II, 7.

Tales of terrorist outbursts were commonplace in the American press during the 1880's and 1890's. From 1882 to 1904 hardly a year passed in Russia without some major assassination or attempted assassination. About a half-dozen plots were uncovered which had as their object the murder of the Czar or Czarevitch. Numerous attempts, some of them successful, were made upon the lives of high public functionaries, as a result of which scores of agitators were arrested, tried in huge mass trials, convicted, and banished or imprisoned.

The universities were hotbeds of revolutionary ideas. Hundreds of students were trained for white-collar positions, but in the absence of a substantial middle class there was no adequate employment for them. The Czar, it was believed, recognized the dangers of educating people so that they could perceive and protest against his tyranny. Violent demonstrations among students, a considerable number of them women, resulted in wholesale arrests and the closing of universities. These protests occurred periodically in the 1880's and 1890's, and from 1900 to 1903 were extremely serious. Mounted Cossacks were employed to disperse or trample down the demonstrators; a state of siege at one time was proclaimed in Moscow; and the government dismissed hundreds of youths from the universities and conscripted them for military service in the Far East. These demonstrations, coinciding with violent labor disorders, brought Russia to the verge of civil war on the eve of the great conflict with Japan in 1904.

The manhandling of students, added to all other evidences of illiberalism, excited the indignation of sympathetic Americans. Revolution was freely predicted, and in 1891 the Philadelphia *Record* prophetically remarked: "With so many elements of combustion in Russia it would not be surprising if at an early day its despotic government should be swept away by a revolution more terrible than that which destroyed the French monarchy in 1789." [6]

Patriotic Americans were increasingly disturbed by the flotsam

---

[6] *Public Opinion*, X, 347 (Jan. 17, 1891).

of anarchists and other agitators which Russian oppression was tossing upon our shores. The terrible Haymarket Riot of 1886 in Chicago resulted in the conviction of eight anarchists. Although predominantly German, their incendiary tactics could not be disassociated from those spawned in the ideological pesthouse of Russia. Chicago newspapers referred to groups of strikers as composed of "foreign scum, beer-smelling Germans, ignorant Bohemians, uncouth Poles, wild-eyed Russians." [7] In 1892 Henry Clay Frick, a millionaire industrialist, was shot and stabbed in his office, though not fatally, by a Russian-Jewish anarchist, Alexander Berkman. The assassin was allegedly incited to the deed by his anarchist mate, the gifted agitator, Emma Goldman, who was also of Russian-Jewish birth. In 1901 President McKinley was shot and killed by another anarchist, Leon F. Czolgosz, the American-born son of parents who had emigrated from Russian Poland. He likewise had been influenced by Emma Goldman.

5

While the Russian government was driving its malcontents westward to the haven of America, its armed forces were pushing eastward across Asia with inexorable force. Russia of the 1880's and 1890's put forth a burst of expansionist activity that finds few parallels in modern history. In 1884 a Russian army defeated the native tribes and captured Merv, near the frontiers of Persia and Afghanistan. The British were shocked by this latest coup, which threatened India. Succumbing to a fit of "Mervousness," they pointed excitedly to alleged violations of Russian promises and voiced loud complaints about the untrustworthy Muscovites. The American press was much less alarmed; in fact there was considerable rejoicing among Britain haters that our old "ally" Russia had stolen a march on our hereditary enemy, the "land grabbing" Great Britain, by doing some land-grabbing of her own. In 1885–1886, following much anxious talk about the Russian menace to

---

[7] See Harry Barnard, "*Eagle Forgotten*": *The Life of John Peter Altgeld* (Indianapolis, 1938), p. 83.

Persia, London worked out a settlement of the Afghan boundary problem with St. Petersburg.[8]

Four years later, in 1889, a party of about 150 Russians made a curious missionary-commercial foray into Ethiopia, involving themselves in trouble with France; and in subsequent years, largely because of religious affinity, Russia indicated a continuing interest in the African kingdom. In 1891—a turning point in modern European history—the Russian despotism of the east clasped hands in entente with the French republic of the west.

This ill-matched marriage of convenience was conceived in pure selfishness, as are all unions of a similar nature. The French republic had about as much in common with absolutist Russia as had the United States, but a common hatred—this time of Germany—drew them together. France, with her dwindling birth rate, feared another Teutonic invasion, and Russia, though less apprehensive, distrusted the theatrical Kaiser Wilhelm II. Besides, the financially decrepit Russian government needed large French loans, which were ultimately forthcoming, to promote an ambitious program of railway construction and other projects. Thus in the words of John Hay the cultured French Marianne became the "harlot" of the uncouth Russian moujik, to the accompaniment of reciprocal fleet visits. At the port of Kronstadt, in Russia, Alexander III stood bareheaded while the hitherto banned "Marseillaise," revolutionary battle hymn of the "infidel Republic," blared forth from a Russian band.

The newspapers of the United States, forgetting that our own republican alliance with monarchical France in 1778 had been no less strange, were sharply critical of our hereditary French friends. Yet there was some feeling of sympathy for France that the seriousness of her peril should have forced her into such an unnatural union. Comments seemed to suggest that our ancient

---

[8] In 1885, as a result of Russian hospitality to the survivors of the *Jeannette* polar expedition, a United States naval officer was sent to Siberia with presents of gold watches and other testimonials to about thirty Russians. This was the most conspicuous of several similar cases that aroused American gratitude (*Foreign Relations, 1885* [Washington, 1886], pp. 665–669).

attachment to France was still of higher sentimental value to us than our more recent tie with Russia. The Boston *Transcript* believed that the Czar was "always a risky, shifty sort of an ally," and that when his interests demanded he would back "out of an alliance." The St. Louis *Republic*, under the heading "A

"NO YOU DON'T!"

The Russian bear, trespassing in Afghanistan, droolingly views the riches of India. A cartoon expressive of British fears. (From the London *Punch*, 1885.)

Possible Crime," blamed France for having taken a step that would "lengthen Siberian chains and widen the sweep of the knout. . . ." [9]

6

With her western borders bolstered by the French entente and with French gold available for her treasury, Russia was freer than before to push eastward. She again threatened the British in India

[9] *Public Opinion*, XI, 429 (Aug. 8, 1891); XI, 578–579 (Sept. 19, 1891).

by reaching the Pamir Ridge (the "roof of the world"), and after a period of crisis adjusted the dispute amicably in 1895. In the same year she played a leading role in the coalition of powers which forced the Japanese to disgorge their hard-won gains of the Sino-Japanese War. Three years later she secured for herself the richest of those gains as a leasehold from China—the coveted ice-free Port Arthur. From 1898 to 1904, when the Russo-Japanese War broke out, she became involved in friction with Britain over Turkey, Persia, and Tibet. In the Far East she betrayed a strong interest in Korea, and more than a strong interest in Manchuria, which she occupied in 1900 during the Boxer difficulties and which she showed a strong reluctance to evacuate, despite firm commitments to do so.

The Russians not only spread rapidly and contiguously, but they clung to what they had acquired with Anglo-Saxon tenacity. Like a huge mass of quicksilver, when blocked in an area like Afghanistan, they would flow elsewhere into a place of less resistance, like Manchuria. In these ventures, like their Soviet descendants, they showed infinite patience. Their magnificent sweep across Asia, which had been going on for more than a century and which perhaps only Americans could really appreciate, made a deep impression in the United States and invited comparisons with our own concurrent exploitation of the Great West. A few journals even expressed satisfaction that the frostbitten bear, after having been caged so long, had finally been able to bathe his paws in the relatively warm waters of the Yellow Sea.

The American press on the whole viewed the Russian advance along the Persian and Afghan borders with considerable indifference, though mildly condemning the use of deception and force. These places were too far away; we had no vital interests there; and besides, the Russians, for all their backwardness, were carrying a superior culture to less advanced peoples.

But the press of Great Britain was filled with almost hysterical apprehension, overlooking the fact that Britain herself had acquired much territory by questionable methods. The British were worried about the energy, youth, and expansiveness of Russia; about her "inexhaustible" man power, her huge army, and her navy, which was rapidly being augmented with specially designed commerce destroyers obviously aimed at England. Alleged Russian duplicity and mendacity were constantly harped upon by British writings, conspicuous among which was Kipling's immortal appeal in 1898, "Make ye no truce with Adam-zad—the Bear that walks like a Man!" British merchants in Liverpool, Manchester, and Birmingham feared that the Bear would claw shut the markets of Manchuria and deprive British manufacturers of a lucrative business.

After the friction between Russia and Britain came to a head over Persia and India, the British press and propagandists began to speak more frequently of the "inevitable war." "We believe," declared a writer in the British *Blackwood's Magazine* (1896), "that to our race will fall the ultimate supremacy of the world; Russia believes exactly the same of herself. Sooner or later the two ambitions must collide, and we had better be making ready for that great day at once. To allow Russia to absorb all possible strength before the conflict is to put a premium on defeat and ruin." [10]

7

If American opinion was relatively indifferent to Russian penetration eastward, the same could not be said of Russian penetration westward, especially into the Balkans. An aroused Baltimore *American* asserted in 1886:

Russia's ambition is sleepless and insatiable. It goes ahead, step by step, through intrigue, through treachery, through diplomatic mendacity, through anything that helps it onward. Her policy is to get more territory, and what difference does it make if her material interests suffer, if her debt piles up, and if her people remain poor? It makes a great difference, however, with other nations. The powers of Europe are becoming very tired of Russia's trickery. The peace that

[10] CLX, 147 (July, 1896).

now exists is a mere strip of red tape around Pandora's box. Once it is broken, the effect will be terrible for a time, and many lives will be lost, but the final result will be a gain for the world and a big advance in the civilization of Eastern Europe.[11]

American observers were especially concerned about Russia's ill-concealed determination to dominate Bulgaria. We were apostles of popular sovereignty and self-determination; and in Bulgaria the Russians were apparently seeking to impose their ways upon a weaker people. A number of the Bulgarian leaders had been introduced to American principles of freedom and democracy at Robert College in Constantinople, which received financial support from contributors in the United States. The president of this institution wrote for an American journal in 1886 that the policy of the Russians was incomprehensible unless they sought to reduce Bulgaria to "a state of anarchy, and then to occupy it." The New Orleans *States* resented the threats of the "Muscovite bully," while the Memphis *Appeal* branded the Czar a "common robber." [12]

The huge armies massed under the banner of Imperial Russia aroused further fears. American critics were frank to say that the Czar's militarism was a primary factor in the increasingly onerous burden of armaments throughout Europe. "Marse Henry" Watterson's Louisville *Courier-Journal* in 1890 viewed the Northern "Colossus" with grave concern, for the Russian had "proven his ability to fight like the European, and to deceive like the Asiatic." In the Far East, continued this journal, the Muscovite was pursuing "devious diplomacy," and he pressed forward both "by arms and by chicanery," whichever best suited his purposes. He had tricked "half the tribes of central Asia" out of their territory, and now menaced the Celestial Empire of China.[13]

Similarly apprehensive statements, most of them less extreme, can readily be found in the American press during the 1890's.

---

[11] *Public Opinion*, I, 502 (Oct. 9, 1886).
[12] *Ibid.*, I, 502, 503 (Oct. 9, 1886).
[13] *Ibid.*, X, 56 (Oct. 25, 1890).

Alarmists generally agreed in referring to the Russian "Colossus of the North" as a grasping and greedy monster whose thirst for conquest was insatiable. Czarism was threatening the peace of Europe and of the world, and was menacing the very foundations of western civilization. The prescient if pessimistic Henry Adams, writing privately in 1899 after a trip to Russia, noted the vast passive energy of the Empire. He believed that the two future centers of power were Russia and America. "Some day," he concluded, "perhaps a century hence, Russia may swallow even her [America]; but for my life-time I think I'm safe." [14]

The year 1895, when the Sino-Japanese war ended, marks a turning point in American attitudes toward Russian imperialism in eastern Asia. We began to show increasing suspicion of Czarist machinations in North China and Korea, where American merchants and missionaries were developing an important stake. These areas were geographically far away, but economically and spiritually fairly close to home. American and Russian interests seemed destined to clash in a significant way for the first time in three quarters of a century. The future looked dark indeed for the historic friendship.

---

[14] W. C. Ford, ed., *Letters of Henry Adams, 1892–1918* (Boston, 1938), p. 213.

XIII

Malnutrition
and Extradition

"Can we have friendship between tyranny and liberty; between Asiatic despotism and modern civilization; between the inertia of barbarism and the spirit of progress?"—Representative John O. Pendleton, 1892

I

THE gathering gloom in Russian-American relations near the turn of the century was temporarily dispelled by one pleasant interlude—the generous response of our people to the great famine of 1891–1892.

More than a half-dozen serious famines had cursed Russia from 1801 to 1891, and others were to follow, more or less periodically. In a country of such vast extent and such inadequate means of transportation, it was difficult to shift surpluses of grain to districts where there were shortages. The crop failures of 1891, which followed a searing drought, proved to be the most disastrous thus far in Russia's disaster-ridden history, and brought death to the doors of some 36,000,000 sufferers. Close upon the heels of the third horseman, famine, galloped the first horseman, pestilence. Epidemics of typhus and cholera claimed thousands of victims, including the famous composer, Peter Ilich Tschaikovsky, who had made a triumphal visit to America in 1891, two years before his death.

The simple call of humanity elicited a warm response from American hearts, even though we were repelled by anti-Jewish barbarities and other evidences of despotism. Our own harvests had been bountiful in 1891, following the terrible drought of 1890 in the Middle West, and as a kind of thank offering we were prompted to share our good fortune with our starving friends. The millers of Minneapolis donated flour; Iowa set up the Russian Famine Relief Commission; and the Nebraska farmers contributed some 1,500,000 pounds of corn meal.[1] One train of twelve cars loaded with corn left Nebraska for the east coast— an original Friendship Train. Altogether five ships bore gifts of grain to Russian ports, and a number of Americans went along to distribute supplies and nurse the sick.

Aside from pure humanitarianism, we regarded this succor as a partial repayment for the help that we felt Russia had given us during the Civil War and earlier, and the ancient debt was again discussed and rediscussed. One may safely assume that the outpouring would not have been nearly so sizable or so spontaneous if the famine had been in China or India. All of the grain came from private donations, as did much of the transportation. Contributions of money, some of them pathetically small, poured in from all over the country. Secretary of State Blaine forwarded to our minister in St. Petersburg a contribution of $11.51 from the public schools of Florence, South Carolina. By contrast the British, who felt no obligation to repay a debt, gathered a relief sum which in American eyes was regarded as indecently small.

2

Speed was of the essence, so a resolution was introduced in Congress authorizing the Secretary of the Navy to transport the grain in United States naval vessels and to charter merchant ships at a cost not to exceed $100,000. After slight opposition the proposal slipped through the Senate by a vote of 40 to 9. But the House was not to be stampeded, and it debated the measure with

[1] See W. C. Edgar, *The Russian Famine of 1891 and 1892* (Minneapolis, 1893).

a warmth that revealed a changing state of mind regarding the Russians.

Advocates of the scheme stressed the dictates of humanity and our age-old debt to Russia. They also pointed out that the Navy had been used to transport supplies to the starving Irish in 1847 and 1880. (But there were vastly more Irish than Russian voters in the United States.)

Opponents of the measure alleged that reports of the famine were grossly exaggerated; that the current Congress had been elected on an economy pledge; that the Treasury was badly depleted; and that the Czar had a huge gold reserve, which he was spending on unnecessary armaments. He had himself allegedly brought on much of the existing distress through his bungling or that of his red-taped bureaucrats. If he was so solicitous for his people, so the argument ran, let him use some of his gold surplus to charter empty ships in American ports.

Other critics of Czarism charged that a nation which would persecute the Jews so viciously had no claims on our sympathy. The reply was that the Russian people, not the nobles, were starving, and that the peasants had been incited against the Jews by their own rulers. An attempt to stipulate that Jews should not be debarred from American food shipments was shunted aside as insulting to the Czar. A few outspoken Representatives were so bold as to challenge the validity of the traditional cordiality. Conspicuous among these was Representative Pendleton of West Virginia, who declared that Russia was "a menace to modern civilization" and "a threat to the peace of the world. . . ." He insisted that there could be no true friendship between two nations so antipathetic in their basic institutions; real friendship could come only when Poland was free and a halt had been called to the persecution of opinion and religion.[2]

The decisive argument against the resolution was the hoary cry of states rights. During the recent drought in the Middle West, various Congressmen had sought to appropriate money for the

---

[2] *Cong. Record*, 52 Cong., 1 sess., pp. 163–164 (Jan. 6, 1892).

relief of their constituents, but they had been thwarted by the constitutional argument that the national government is not a charitable agency and that federal funds could not legally be disbursed to the states. The eloquent young Representative William Jennings Bryan, observing that his adopted state of Nebraska had recovered from the drought and was now giving grain to Russia from her surpluses, reaffirmed the states rights view. Besides, he argued, where was the United States to stop? Famines and floods occurred all over the earth every year, and to discriminate in favor of Russia would make for bad feeling. In the absence of full investigation, Bryan declared, it would be folly to vote the proposed appropriation "to one of the most despotic of nations." [3]

The House, by a count of 165 to 72, finally struck out the grant of $100,000, which meant that the Navy was to carry the grain in the only ship it had available for cargo purposes, the old sailing frigate *Constellation*. This weather-beaten craft, built in 1798, was entirely inadequate, so the whole question of federal aid was postponed indefinitely by a close vote of 93 to 87. Humanitarians and Russophiles throughout the country were outraged, and demands poured in on Congress for reconsideration. Several such efforts were made but they all bogged down, and the relief program had to be handled entirely by private philanthropy.

While Congressmen were criticizing Russia in increasingly outspoken terms, the press was not silent. Much was said about the callousness of the Czar's government, about its failure to take ordinary precautions, about its botching relief work and hampering foreign missions, about its remorseless collection of taxes from starving peasants, and about the continued grafting by the bureaucrats and nobles in the midst of catastrophe.

Yet the spontaneous outpouring of the American people, despite Jewish pogroms and Siberian prisons, was a powerful tribute to the strength and tenacity of the ancient friendship. The Russian government, though to some degree humiliated by having to accept charity from foreigners, bestowed gifts on the bearers

---

[3] *Ibid.*, pp. 160–161 (Jan. 6, 1892).

and expressed warm appreciation. As tokens of gratitude one peasant at Easter time sent to the Americans three colored eggs, together with a touching letter. A Russian poet, referring to three of the five ships that had brought alms, wrote:

> From Behring strait to Louisiana
> Our heart is on thy welfare set:
> "Missouri," "Conemaugh," "Indiana,"
> A Russian never shall forget.[4]

3

The year after the famine relief program was carried through, distinct unpleasantness developed between Washington and St. Petersburg over the fur seals of the North Pacific. This is hardly what one would have expected, because both nations had seal herds, and it was assumed that Russia would see eye to eye with the United States in protecting them against foreign poachers, chiefly Canadians.

The seals, who knew nothing about the sanctuary of territorial waters, ranged far out to sea, where they were indiscriminately slaughtered. In the early 1890's Russian and American patrols, aroused by this butchery, illegally seized Canadian poachers outside the three-mile limit. (Ironically, in doing so the United States was in some degree associating itself with the pretensions of the Czar in 1821 to jurisdiction over the high seas.) The Canadians and British protested energetically against the highhanded conduct of the American authorities, and the resulting dispute was finally referred to an arbitral tribunal in Paris.

The Russian Foreign Minister, aware of a common interest in the seals, assured the American envoy that he would do what he could to support the case of the United States in Paris. Specifically, he promised that Russia would stand firm in claiming ownership

---

[4] *Review of Reviews*, V, 700 (July, 1892). Much criticism was voiced abroad when the first four relief ships were greeted with gallons of champagne and fine feasts in town halls. Russians, whether Czarist or Communist, have characteristically set much store by keeping up appearances.

of seals on the high seas if it owned the breeding grounds; refrain from any agreement with Britain regarding its own seizures that would embarrass the United States; and instruct the Russian ambassador in Paris to give the American case moral support.[5]

The Russian promises unfortunately were not kept. While the Paris tribunal was still sitting, St. Petersburg secretly came to an understanding with the British regarding earlier cases. The Foreign Office agreed to pay pecuniary damages to London for the seizure of two British ships outside the three-mile limit, but refused indemnity for four taken inside Russian territorial waters. This was a tacit admission that the Americans had an unsupportable case, and shortly thereafter, whether influenced by the Russian action or not, the tribunal handed down a decision adverse to the United States.

Andrew D. White, then our minister to Russia, was angered by the apparent "treachery" of St. Petersburg. The Russian seal herd was much smaller than ours; and this fact, combined with what seems to have been a desire on the part of the Czar to cultivate better relations with Britain, apparently accounted for what we regarded as bad faith. White also assumed that the social lobby of the British had been highly effective with the Russians, for the British envoy in St. Petersburg was something of a snake charmer.[6] In his chagrin White thought that the Russians were overrated as statesmen.

This episode again underscores the fact that Russian-American relations at that time operated on two levels: the one of private diplomatic negotiation and the other of public opinion. The Russian "betrayal" attracted little popular attention, but it was deeply disturbing to the Department of State. Jewish pogroms and Siberian prisons were of scant concern to the diplomats, but they were deeply disturbing to our people.

The problem of the three-mile limit also affected Russian-American relations in a more direct way. Intermittently during

---

[5] White to Foster, Nov. 16, 1892, National Archives (Dispatches).

[6] *Autobiography of Andrew Dickson White* (New York, 1905), II, 20.

the post-Civil War years, Russian cruisers would seize or otherwise molest American fishermen or whalers approaching the coast of Siberia. Ordinarily these incidents attracted little public notice and were adjusted with a minimum of friction. The most notorious cases involved the confiscation of four American vessels in the early 1890's. After protracted negotiations the dispute was referred to a Dutch arbiter, who in 1902 ruled that the craft had all been taken outside the three-mile limit, in some cases with unnecessarily harsh treatment, and assessed the Russian government damages totaling nearly $100,000, with 6 per cent interest.[7] But even this case, which affected only a few people in a remote area, received relatively little space in the American newspapers.

4

A curiously neglected episode in 1893 testifies to the increasing distaste of American citizens for Russian tyranny.

Until the 1870's a treaty providing for the mutual extradition of escaped lawbreakers was not particularly wanted by either the United States or Russia. No American felon in his right mind would seek asylum in police-ridden Russia, and relatively few persons, criminal or otherwise, were then coming to the United States from the Czar's domain. But the need for an extradition treaty became more pressing with the rise of terrorist groups and the flight to America of anarchists and other agitators sought by the Russian police.

After protracted negotiations an extradition treaty was signed in 1887, but it languished in the Senate. In 1893 it was revived, debated in secret session (as was the rule in the nineteenth century), and finally approved. The action of the Senate was greeted by an astonishing roar of public protest.

The American ideal had traditionally been to permit extradition of common malefactors but not persons accused of political offenses. The assassination of the head of a state, particularly where no other means of effective protest existed, had long been viewed

---

[7] *Foreign Relations, 1902* (Washington, 1903), Appendix I.

by us as a political crime and not a common crime. But the new extradition treaty with Russia stipulated that any person attempting to assassinate the head of either state, or a member of his family, would be regarded as a nonpolitical criminal and hence extraditable.

Protest meetings multiplied throughout the United States, and an avalanche of resolutions descended upon the Senate, both before and after the approval of the treaty. Refugee Russian revolutionaries, fearing for their own skins, joined the chorus of denunciation. Jewish immigrants, many of whom had seen Russian injustice at first hand, protested vehemently. Countless Americans who had been influenced by the Kennan articles and other exposés were aroused, and Kennan himself threw his formidable pen into the fray.[8]

5

The principal objections to the treaty may be listed briefly. To regard political assassination as a criminal offense was a departure from hallowed tradition. Pulaski, it was recalled, had been under accusation for an attempt on the life of the King of Poland when he fell fighting for American independence. The treaty was onesided: Russia would retrieve escapees from America but we would not seek American refugees fleeing to Russia. Czarist justice was not founded on Anglo-Saxon principles, and extradition should be confined to nations whose juridical systems were similar to ours, which would exclude China, Turkey, and Russia. In large areas of the Czar's domain, as Kennan pointed out, there was no trial by jury. Refugees who fled to our shores almost invariably escaped from Russia by forging passports, and since forgery was an extraditable crime under the treaty, when the culprit was retrieved on this pretext, the Czar could accuse him of some political wrongdoing, whether trumped up or true, and then banish him to Siberia by mere administrative decree.

Other objections were hardly less forceful. The treaty had been

[8] See *Forum*, XV, 283 (May, 1893).

secretly debated and hastily rushed through, without giving sovereign American opinion a chance to be properly heard. This was a denial of the democratic process quite in keeping with Czarist practices. To make a treaty with the Russians would dignify their archaic and illiberal judicial system with the seal of our approval, and hence erect a barrier against future reform. Finally, the American people were in effect asked to make slave catchers of themselves for the Russian secret police, in a manner disagreeably reminiscent of the fugitive slave law of 1850.

The defenders of the treaty, conspicuous among whom were administration supporters, argued that Britain had an extradition treaty with Russia which went even further; that the United States had a similar assassination clause in treaties with Belgium and Luxemburg; and that to argue that St. Petersburg would recover a criminal on the grounds of forgery and punish him for something else was to accuse Russia of bad faith. (George Kennan forthwith spoke up and said that there was ample evidence of bad faith.) A few voices protested that Russia was our old "ally," that she had saved us during the Civil War, and that not to surrender a murderer of the Czar, our great and good friend, was "barbarous." [9]

The uproar against the treaty apparently intensified after its approval by the Senate, and a formidable agitation developed for abrogation. The earlier remonstrances, especially those of 1890, had poured in on Congress primarily from laboring groups, such as barbers, bricklayers, and cigar makers, and notably from concentrations of German immigrants. But the outcry of 1894 was much more widespread. Petitions demanding abrogation inundated Congress from large groups of citizens in Colorado, Connecticut, the District of Columbia, Illinois, Iowa, Kansas, Louisiana, Michigan, Mississippi, New York, Ohio, Pennsylvania, South Carolina, and Wisconsin. Resolutions were passed by the senate of the state of Ohio, by the assembly of New York, and by the legislature of Illinois. Among the petitioners was the aged but vigilant Julia Ward Howe. A Society for the Abrogation of

[9] *Public Opinion*, XV, 264 (June 17, 1893).

the Russian Extradition Treaty was formed, and it dispatched appropriate representations to Washington.[10]

In response to this tremendous outpouring a half-dozen or so resolutions were introduced into Congress demanding an abrogation of the treaty, but they all fizzled out. The Senate, which at times is notoriously unresponsive to public pressure, was not to be stampeded, and gradually popular interest shifted to other subjects. But the amazing thing is that so much spontaneous protest could have arisen over an issue that did not affect either the pockets or lives of the workaday American. We were undoubtedly more sensitive about freedom then, possibly because we were closer to the day when we had not enjoyed it. And as between our fundamental liberties and Russian friendship, especially after the pogroms and other barbarities, Russian friendship would have to take a back seat.

6

The years between the extradition treaty of 1893 and the Spanish-American War of 1898 were enlivened by a few incidents which indicate that the ancient attachment still had a few sparks of vitality.

Occasionally minor friction arose over Greek Orthodox opposition to American missionaries and other proselyters, but all this was ironed out amicably. More disturbing were the restrictions that St. Petersburg imposed on foreign life insurance companies, which were diverting business from local Russian enterprise. Vigorous pressure was brought to bear by American companies on the State Department, but little progress was made, despite extensive diplomatic representations. Under the existing regime, so Minister White reported, the trend was toward isolation and antiforeignism, even at the expense of more rapid economic progress.

In 1893 the native Hawaiian dynasty was toppled, with improper assistance from American troops, and an annexation treaty signed by the white oligarchy was rushed to the United States

[10] *Cong. Record,* 53 Cong., 2 sess., pp. 5499, 5666.

Senate, from which it was soon withdrawn by the scrupulous President Cleveland. Minister White in St. Petersburg reported that both official and public opinion was entirely favorable to the annexation desires of the United States.[11] The Russians, who had no great fondness for either the British or the Japanese, could hardly have preferred them as occupants of the Pacific paradise.

The panic of 1893, which caused a critical shortage of gold in the United States Treasury, prompted a friendly though unpublicized gesture by St. Petersburg. In April, 1893, Minister White cabled that Russia, after refusing other foreign powers, was prepared to lend us a large amount of her gold surplus for one or two years. White later explained that the Russian offer of $60,000,000 probably grew in part out of a hatred of western European financiers, some of whom were Jews, and out of a desire to keep them from making money from America's financial plight. Washington delayed more than four months before replying. Finally under White's prodding Secretary of State Gresham thanked the Russian government for its generous offer, and explained that we were relieved of the necessity of accepting it.[12]

The United States, being a democracy, could not so readily reciprocate this courtesy. In August, 1895, the Russian legation in Washington inquired in a "very confidential" note if Russia could purchase fifteen million ounces of silver at the market price. The State Department replied that this could not be done without act of Congress, so the request was not pressed.[13] Congressional action would have involved both delay and undesirable publicity.

These two overlooked incidents illustrate the fact that official relations were still being maintained on a formally friendly plane, even though our people, with mounting stridency, were referring to Russia in less than friendly terms.

---

[11] White to Foster, Feb. 20, 1893, National Archives (Dispatches).

[12] White to Gresham, April 26, 30, 1893; Gresham to White, Sept. 2, 1893 (received), *ibid.*

[13] Somow to Adee, Aug. 11/30 [*sic*], 1895, *ibid.* (Notes). The stamped date indicates that the note was received on Aug. 12, 1895.

The Sunset of the Century

"There is no danger that the Czar of Russia will disarm. If he ever does his own subjects will get him."—Chicago *News*, 1902

I

A DIPLOMATIC revolution in the closing years of the nineteenth century kicked the last major prop from under the historic Russian-American amity. Great Britain, faced with the rising might of Germany and other perils, now found her vaunted isolation dangerous rather than "splendid," and cast about for friends if not allies. Finding her transatlantic offspring bulging with power, she began an era of "patting the eagle's head." The flattered Yankees, who had hitherto made great sport of "twisting the lion's tail," responded with increasing cordiality, despite a heavy residue of Anglophobia.

The British were conspicuously friendly toward the United States during the Spanish-American War, and their naval officer at Manila Bay, Captain Chichester, lent moral support to Admiral Dewey when the latter was at loggerheads with the Germans, even though such aid has been grossly exaggerated by legend.[1] Misery loves company; and when in 1899 we lightheartedly shouldered the liabilities of imperialism while listening to the siren

---

[1] T. A. Bailey, "Dewey and the Germans at Manila Bay," *American Historical Review*, XLV, 59–81 (Oct., 1939).

call of Kipling's "White Man's Burden," we unwittingly created another common tie with the Mother Country.

Hatred of England had long been one of the mainsprings of American regard for Russia, and now that the transatlantic kinfolk were burying the blood-stained hatchet, the republic of William McKinley and the despotism of Nicholas II were bound to drift farther apart. The movement was temporarily slowed when a rebellion of the Boers in South Africa against the British crown placed something of a strain on the new Anglo-American friendship. A vast amount of sympathy was expressed in the United States for the overmatched Dutch rebels, much of it in a rich Irish brogue. Formidable numbers of our citizens saw eye to eye with the Russians in upholding freedom of the seas against the British blockade of South Africa, and in hoping for the discomfiture of Queen Victoria's Empire.

The Spanish-American War of 1898 had been under way about a month when Count Cassini, the first envoy of ambassadorial rank from Russia, presented his credentials in Washington. Fresh from diplomatic triumphs in China, he was notorious for his denial of the Cassini convention, which he had negotiated while in Peking; and the belief was current that his lying went above and beyond the call of diplomatic duty. Cassini's appointment was presumably dictated by his knowledge of China, regarding which the American public was taking a more active interest as a result of Russian encroachments; and the suspicion was prevalent that he had been sent to lull and gull the stupid Yankees.

On the day of his official presentation to President McKinley, Cassini referred tactfully but untruthfully to the "unalterable friendship," "without the least cloud having ever arisen to disturb relations." [2] During ensuing months he continued the somewhat unconventional practice, begun by Botkine in 1893, of giving out statements to the press. He sneered at the newly born British love for the United States as a "ruse." He alleged that during the Civil War the Czar "out of pure friendship" had offered gold (?) and

---

[2] New York *Herald*, June 24, 1898.

ships, and had given orders to Admiral Lessovsky to place his fleet at the disposal of the Union and make war on France and England should they recognize the Confederacy. A knowledge of Alexander II's intentions, according to this garbled version, held the hostile powers in check. At the same time that Cassini was falsifying history and radiating good will, he was operating under instructions which read: "While remaining in the aura of Russian-American friendship you must make every endeavor to create conflicts between the Federal Government and England and Japan." [3] The slippery diplomat labored zealously to carry out both the letter and spirit of these instructions.

2

The attitude of Russia during the Spanish-American hostilities of 1898 in some measure reflected the changing diplomatic atmosphere. As during the Civil War, although with less warmth, St. Petersburg was officially noninterventionist and correctly neutral. Actually, there was considerable sympathy in official circles for Spain, but the decision was reached that a hands-off policy would best subserve the ends of the Empire. In 1897 the Russian government rejected a Spanish-inspired proposal, presented by the Czar's French ally, that Russia and France extend their good offices to the United States and Spain. A handful of Russians did attempt to volunteer for service in the American armed forces, but they may have been fugitives from boredom or absolutism. Significantly, the Russian press, while referring pleasantly on occasion to the time-honored tie, was not above criticizing American methods and pretensions.

The ruling class of Russia naturally could not generate great enthusiasm for the American cause. Spain was a monarchy, and so was Russia, only more absolute. Spain was the underdog, or quickly proved to be. France, for various reasons, was friendly to

---

[3] E. H. Zabriskie, *American-Russian Rivalry in the Far East, 1895-1914* (Philadelphia, 1946), p. 202. In later years the Bolsheviks published Cassini's instructions in an effort to discredit the Czarist regime by exposing its hypocrisy.

Spain, a fellow Latin country, and ever since the entente of 1891 France and Russia had drawn closer together. Russia had some skeletons in her closet, notably the persecutions of Jews and other minorities, and being opposed to intervention in her own affairs, she could not afford to applaud American interference in Cuba on the ground of Spain's mistreatment of the *insurrectos*.

The feud between the bear and the lion still persisted, and since the British were notoriously sympathetic toward the United States, the Russians were repelled from entering the same camp with them. As for the Far East, Nicholas II could not welcome with open arms a meddlesome new power which, based on the Philippines, might interfere with his monopolistic designs on Manchuria and North China.

The semiofficial St. Petersburg *Novoye Vremya* was annoyed by the holier-than-thou prating of the Americans about intervening in Cuba for humanity; the Russians had repeatedly fought against the inhumanity of the Turks. The St. Petersburg *Novosti* openly urged that the "senseless and criminal" Spanish-American War be ended. If, declared this sheet, the European powers insisted jointly on a cessation of the conflict, America would have to give in, "as her position with two long and exposed coast lines, is not such as could withstand the combined fleets of two or three European powers." [4] Anglophiles and Russophobes in the United States eagerly seized on this statement as reflecting official Russian views, but the *Novosti* was actually an obscure and unofficial journal.

The Czar's government on the whole did not regard the fate of the Philippines as a critical issue. From the point of view of Russia the islands could better have remained in the hands of senile Spain, but the United States, the traditional friend, was a more agreeable tenant than either Britain or Germany, who were potential foes. When a St. Petersburg newspaper condemned American annexation in an editorial that received wide publicity, the

---

[4] Cited in J. K. Eyre, Jr., "Russia and the American Acquisition of the Philippines," *Mississippi Valley Historical Review*, XXVIII, 553 (March, 1942).

Foreign Office ordered a rebuttal, which was published in one of its own semiofficial mouthpieces. This reply, a copy of which was sent to the American Embassy for proper credit, reaffirmed neutrality and good will toward the United States.[5]

3

As back-seat riders the Russians did figure in an unsuccessful attempt to head off the Spanish-American War by joint mediation. Germany, France, and Austria-Hungary were the most active proponents of the scheme. The Russian government later explained that it went along with the six-power representations only after the other nations had adhered, and only after it had made sure that the mediation was in the interests of humanity.[6]

Anglophiles in the United States seized upon this incident to play up the recently born friendship of Britain, and to pooh-pooh the insincere friendship of Russia during the Civil War. The numerous foes of England in America were forced to magnify Russian assistance, and the shopworn tale of the fleets was once more dusted off and pressed into service.

But the British continued to keep a vigilant eye on American friendship. In 1902, four years after the Spanish war, they alleged that one of the powers (presumably Austria-Hungary) had been put forward by the others to lead intervention. But London had succeeded in quashing any effective interference. This revelation caused a flurry of excitement in the European capitals, and Britain was accused of deliberately stirring up trouble. As in 1861–1865, the truth seems to be that England was the most important single power in blocking intervention. But die-hard American Russophiles and Anglophobes were not easily silenced, and numerous allusions were again made to Alexander II's assistance during the Civil War.

Regardless of who had been the friend of whom in 1861 and 1898, it was evident that the United States, having recently

---

[5] Peirce to Hay, Nov. 19, 1898, National Archives (Dispatches).
[6] Tower to Hay, Feb. 26, 1902, *ibid.*

emerged as a formidable power, was worthy of courtship. The Chicago *Tribune* published a pointed jingle entitled "Who?":

"Who befriended Uncle Sam?"
"I," said John Bull,
"I used my pull.
I befriended Uncle Sam."

"Who helped him lick Spain?"
"I," said the Kaiser,
"I stood right by, sir.
I helped him lick Spain."

"Who stood off the Powers?"
"I," said the Czar,
"I was right thar.
I stood off the Powers."

"Who's his friend now?"
"I," said they all,
With unanimous bawl.
"I'm his real friend now!" [7]

4

The Spanish-American War had not yet officially ended when, in August, 1898, Nicholas II startled the civilized world by proposing, through his foreign minister, an international conference for the limitation of armaments.

The call came at a most unexpected time from a most unexpected source. If such an appeal had gone forth from the Queen of Holland or the President of Argentina, it would not have been looked upon with excessive suspicion. But the reactionary Nicholas, who officially espoused the scheme, had shown little devotion to idealism, and he certainly had not revealed a conspicuously pacific disposition. Russia's army was the largest in the world; she had whipped up recurrent war scares; and she was bending her frontiers outward, particularly in Manchuria. Less than six months

---

[7] *Literary Digest*, XXIV, 250 (Feb. 22, 1902).

earlier she had wrenched Port Arthur from the senile grasp of China.

American newspapers on the whole applauded the imperial invitation and hoped for a successful conference. If Nicholas II should accomplish his purposes, his name would be universally

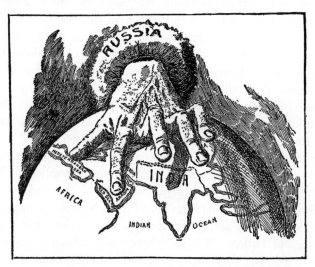

PADEREWSKI'S SPAN NOT IN IT WITH ALEX'S

Even at the time of the call for the Hague Conference much uneasiness existed in America regarding Russian imperialism. Paderewski was the famous Polish piano player, and the Czar (Nicholas II) is mistakenly referred to as Alex. (From the Denver *Republican*, 1898.)

blessed. Some religious journals were ecstatic in heralding the dawn of an era when swords would be beaten into ploughshares. The generally favorable reaction to the Czar's leadership was no doubt partly prompted by a persistent but weakening feeling of indebtedness reaching back through Civil War days to the era of Catherine the Great.

But the thunder of applause by no means drowned out the muttering undertone of criticism. The dream of universal disarmament was attacked as futile and impractical. Nicholas II, as the Boston *Transcript* noted, had the Romanov "queer streak"; he was too visionary and too lacking in force to accomplish anything.[8] And even if he had the will, would the strong military faction in St. Petersburg permit him to carry through his plans?

The American chargé in St. Petersburg reported that Russian opinion was none too favorable. Ever since the days of Peter the Great the idea had been hammered home that the army was not only the glory and blessing but the very safety of the country. Also, the humanitarian aspects of the Czar's program did not appeal to Slavic fatalism and semi-Oriental traditions, all of which, combined with other factors, had bred a callous disregard for human life. The Russian diplomatic corps, reared in the military tradition, branded the scheme Utopian, although quite a few of the Russian intelligentsia thought it commendable.[9]

In the United States and elsewhere abroad the most gnawing question was: Where was the Ethiopian in the cordwood? Was the financially shaky Russian behemoth unable to stand the continued strain of an enormous army? Was Nicholas II hoping to use his budgetary savings for intrigue and corruption in China, Persia, and Turkey? Perhaps his spectacular invitation was just a ruse to gain time for military preparations. The dominant note of the critics was fear of Russian motives. The Memphis *Commercial-Appeal* argued that Russian sincerity was "always subject to a discount," that if the Czar ever felt "really strong" he would not hesitate to violate his promises, and that if Russia really craved peace she was "absolutely unprepared for war." [10]

The loudly heralded conference finally met at The Hague during May and June of 1899. Nothing of consequence was accomplished in the direction of disarmament. The Germans, who relied on the speedy mobilization of their army, were unwilling to shackle their terrific striking power. The Russians moreover had failed to make adequate preparations for the conclave. The dele-

---

[8] *Public Opinion*, XXV, 300 (Sept. 8, 1898).
[9] Peirce to Hay, Nov. 9, 1898, National Archives (Dispatches).
[10] *Public Opinion*, XXV, 428 (Oct. 6, 1898).

gates, though mouthing pat phrases about Nicholas II's idealism, were distrustful of Russia. Andrew D. White, who was one of the American representatives, remarked that probably at no time since the world began had "so large a body come together in a spirit of more hopeless skepticism as to any good result." [11]

Disappointment over the failure to secure a reduction of arms blinded many critics to the fact that ground had been gained in the codification of international law and in the setting up of the Permanent Court of Arbitration. But as far as Russia was concerned, the harvest of suspicion and disillusionment tended to weaken the prestige of Nicholas II.

5

Russification of minorities meanwhile had been going forward inexorably, notably in the Baltic provinces and in Poland. Andrew D. White concluded that the Russians were jealous of those possessing a superior civilization, and sought to drag other peoples down to their own level. The plight of the Poles was in some measure personalized by the brilliant piano playing of Ignace Jan Paderewski, who first toured the United States in 1891, and by the novels of Henryk Sienkiewicz, best known for *Quo Vadis?* (1895). Less well known but nevertheless important in arousing admiration in America for his people was his trilogy of novels, published from 1890–1893, which immortalized the heroic struggle of the Poles in the seventeenth century against Cossacks, Turks, and Swedes.

In 1890 reports began to reach America of the faint beginnings of Finnish Russification, but not until 1899 did the campaign shift into high gear. The Grand Duchy of Finland had been taken over in 1809 by Russia following the defeat of Sweden, and Alexander I had sworn a solemn oath, binding himself and his successors, to respect the Finnish constitution and the rights and privileges that the Finns had enjoyed under Swedish rule. Finland had prospered, despite niggardly natural resources, and had attained the highest

---

[11] *Autobiography of Andrew Dickson White* (New York, 1905), II, 256.

degree of civilization in the Russian Empire. The Finns were intelligent, literate, industrious, thrifty, sober, and moral; their traditions were hardly less liberal than those of contemporary Britain; their economic and political institutions were stable; and their loyalty to the Empire, quite in contrast to the Poles, was beyond question.

The Czar's officials could of course make out a case for Russification. Why should a semi-independent state exist within the Empire, especially one that controlled the strategic approaches to St. Petersburg? Why should the Finns possess rights and privileges which the Russians themselves did not enjoy? Would not the Finnish way of life, which comported so ill with autocracy, prove dangerously contagious? And from the administrative viewpoint, the Russification of Finland would bring greater unity to the Empire for fiscal and military purposes. But the only way to achieve this goal was to violate the pledge given to Finland by Alexander I and repeated by his successors in the coronation oath. Nicholas II, persuaded by reactionary bureaucrats, proceeded to do precisely this.

The "Finnish Reign of Terror," which dated from 1899 to 1905, and which attracted much sympathy in the American press, revealed the customary pattern. The legislative powers of the Diet were abolished, ancient liberties were stifled, and bureaucracy was entrenched. The usual attacks were made on the Lutheran Church, on the Finnish language, and on judges who handed down the "wrong" decisions. The press was censored, malcontents were summarily deported to Siberia, spies and *agents provocateurs* swarmed over the land, and refractory Finnish youths were conscripted into the Russian army. American newspapers reported, in connection with the conscription riots of 1902, that mounted Cossacks whipped women and children through the streets. Two years later a Finnish patriot shot and killed Governor General Bobrikov. In 1905 the Finns staged a crippling general strike, and this demonstration, combined with the terrible disorders growing out of the Russo-Japanese War, forced Nicholas II to restore liberties as of 1899. After a breathing spell, a new wave of Russification was launched, and when the World War broke out in 1914 the Land of a Thousand Lakes was hardly more than a geographical expression.

When the "Reign of Terror" began in 1899, many determined Finns sought refuge in Sweden, and tens of thousands of others fled to the United States, particularly Michigan, Wisconsin, and Oregon, where they proved to be a not unimportant element in the mounting antagonism toward our erstwhile benefactor. In 1899 the legislature of Michigan passed a concurrent resolution protesting against Russification as a violation of imperial pledges, and urging President McKinley to make appropriate diplomatic representations at St. Petersburg.[12] Scandinavian groups in the United States, who felt a close tie with the Finns and who were distrustful of the overshadowing power of Russia, shared much of this bitterness.

The democratically minded Americans had special reasons for admiring plucky little Finland. The Finns, like us, were a Protestant people. They had adopted many liberal innovations, including women's suffrage, for which reformist and "muckraking" Americans were then agitating. We traditionally respected constitutional guarantees, the rights of the oppressed, and the aspirations of those who sought self-government. We were deeply touched by the cruel fate of a people who shared a not dissimilar tradition of freedom and whose struggle bore some resemblance to our glorious resistance to George III. Bullying the little fellow, punishing a loyal people, starving innocent subjects, changing some 3,000,000 supporters into bitter enemies, attacking the Protestant Lutheran Church, and turning back the clock of civilization—all this seemed savage and senseless, whatever its justification from the imperial point of view. And above all, Nicholas II's shameless violation of his coronation oath strengthened the stereotype that the plighted word of a Russian was worthless.

---

[12] *Cong. Record*, 56 Cong., 1 sess., p. 81 (Dec. 6, 1899).

6

As the century neared an end and as the Industrial Revolution belatedly begrimed the Czar's Empire, economic rivalry between Russia and the United States grew more intense. As early as the 1870's Russian wheat producers had complained bitterly that machine-grown grain from America was beating them out in competition for the markets of Europe. Yet in certain categories in which the Empire was backward, Russia welcomed imports from the United States, as she had for decades. By 1899 some four hundred Baldwin locomotives had been sold to the Russians, to say nothing of mining and agricultural machinery, including cotton gins, mowers, reapers, and binders. A photograph published in an American magazine in 1901 showed an American reaper in southern Russia being drawn by two camels.[13] Paradoxically, one third of the agricultural machinery outside the United States was being operated in the poorly mechanized Russian Empire.

A notable victory for American enterprise and dollar diplomacy was won in 1899, when the St. Petersburg government awarded to the Maryland Steel Company the contract for 80,000 tons of steel rails for the Chinese Eastern Railway. The United States had succeeded in elbowing out European competition only after vigorous representations by the Department of State.[14] In 1901 an American visitor rode out of Port Arthur on a train drawn by a locomotive manufactured in Philadelphia, over rails made in Baltimore, laid upon ties grown in the forests of Oregon. Trade follows the railroad no less than the flag, and American ingenuity was securing a huge slice of the Manchurian melon.

Even so, commerce between Russia and the United States in peacetime has never been of front-rank importance. In 1901 a New York journal noted that Denmark, with only 2,000,000

---

[13] *Century Magazine*, LXII, 504 (Aug., 1901).
[14] Hay to Hitchcock, Dec. 28, 1898, National Archives (Instructions); Tower to Hay, April 26, 1899, *ibid.* (Dispatches).

people, bought from us annually more goods than the Russian Empire, with 135,000,000 people. But official trade statistics are often misleading. In 1899 approximately one half of the American cotton imported by Russia was purchased in England, as was true in large degree of American machinery obtained through German middlemen.

Russia continued to emulate the protective tariff of the United States throughout the nineteenth century. Her policy not only paralleled that of the Republican dynasty in the United States, but in 1897 the Empire forsook silver for the gold standard, thus raising itself in respectability among that host of Republicans who in 1896 had voted against Bryan's free-silver heresy.

7

The towering tariff walls of the United States in the 1890's had no serious effect on amicable relations with Russia until 1901, when the Czar's government granted a subsidy to Russian sugar exporters. This was regarded by our officials as an export bounty, and under existing law the Secretary of the Treasury was forced to levy a countervailing duty on Russian sugar. St. Petersburg speedily countered with a "penal duty" of 50 per cent on our agricultural machinery and other products, thus dealing a discouraging blow to American business worth about $7,000,000 a year. As the retaliatory spiral mounted, petroleum and other items were included.

Informed Russians seemed to regard the action of their government as unduly harsh and precipitate, and the imperial Finance Minister, the able Sergei Witte, spoke to the American envoy in the friendliest terms. He denied that Russia had a genuine export bounty; he expressed regret that this unfortunate rift should have developed between old friends; and he insisted that retaliation was necessary lest Germany and other European nations be encouraged to discriminate against Russia. He promised that the moment the United States removed its countervailing duties, he would remove his—a proposition he would not make to any other nation in the world.[15]

Even though the diplomats spoke of this disagreeable economic warfare in conventionally friendly terms, the American press, as was so often the case, adopted an entirely different tone. Our people will stand for a great deal, but not for prohibitively high tariffs imposed by other nations. The New York *Evening Post* regarded the Russian restrictions as the most serious trade reprisal we had suffered since the War of 1812. A few newspapers were inclined to blame our own sugar trust, which had imposed its "sweet will" on the administration, but the most outspoken sheets complained that the punishment did not fit the alleged crime; only $300,000 worth of Russian sugar was involved annually, as compared with $7,000,000 worth of American manufactures.

Irate American editors served notice that this country would not back down under pressure. The Boston *Transcript* regarded the reprisals as casting a revealing light on the claim of Russia to "great friendship for the United States." The New York *Press*, interpreting the restrictions as connected with our attempts to preserve the Open Door in the Far East against Russia, referred to an "irrepressible" "conflict," and thanked the Czar's lackeys for having opened our eyes so that we could enter the controversy "without a remaining particle of the 'traditional friendship' myth which has so long beguiled so many of our people." "If the Russians are hunting trouble," the Pittsburgh *Commercial Gazette* snarled, "they are coming to the right place to find it." [16]

The tariff war was waged with much bitterness from 1901 to 1905, when Nicholas II, presumably out of gratitude for President Roosevelt's mediation in the Russo-Japanese War, lifted the retaliatory duties. Certain American observers remarked that this was done out of necessity rather than gratitude, for Russia urgently needed our agricultural machinery. Actually, in a number of important categories American exports to Russia had increased

---

[15] Tower to Hay, July 3, 1901, *ibid.* (Dispatches).
[16] *Literary Digest*, XXII, 775 (June 29, 1901).

even under the handicap of retaliation, though one may reasonably assume that the increase would have been larger had these fetters not existed. In any event, the whole unhappy episode, which has been curiously neglected by historians, further opened the eyes of our people to the tenuous nature of the century-old tie.

A Parting of the Ways

"To murder a Jew is to remove forty sins
from off one's soul."—Ukrainian proverb

I

THE woes of China did not end with her disastrous defeat by the Nipponese in 1894–1895. Having betrayed her weakness to the outside world, she was pounced upon by the European powers, who greedily extorted rich leaseholds and spheres of influence. The Germans, the Russians, the French, and the British were foremost among the imperialistic harpies, but the Russians, who pushed into Manchuria and secured Port Arthur in 1898, were perhaps the most conspicuous in the American public eye.

The rich prize of Manchuria was contiguous to the Czar's Siberian domains, and the Port Arthur lodgment suggested permanence, power, and expansiveness. American businessmen, who had been enjoying a boom trade in railway materials and other supplies, feared that Nicholas II would close these markets and slam shut the Open Door. American missionaries, whose solicitude for the heathen of this area was no less keen, joined with our merchants in exerting pressure on the State Department to halt the rapacity of the European imperialists, especially Russia.

There is no need to repeat the story of Secretary Hay's spectacular note of 1899, in which he urged the imperialistic powers to subscribe to the principle of the Open Door in their leaseholds and spheres of interest. Italy was the only nation to adhere unconditionally to the broad principle of a fair field and no favors in competition for the trade of China. (Italy had no leasehold, although she had recently made an unsuccessful bid for one.) The remaining addressees generally accepted Hay's proposal, although hedging about their replies with evasions or with the condition that all the other powers consent. The response of St. Petersburg is of special interest.

The Russian Foreign Office was clearly annoyed by the embarrassing American proposal, which was like asking all persons in a room who were not thieves to stand up. Nicholas II did not want to be jockeyed out of his long-coveted and hard-won outlet in Manchuria. Nor did he care to bind his hands in the future. The expression "Open Door" was odious to the Russians, who had never been devoted to liberal trade principles, and who quite correctly associated the phrase with free-trade Britain. The Czar's government was traditionally slow in making agreements of this nature, and, besides, the Hay proposal was not altogether clear. Nevertheless the American note was received courteously, discussed in a friendly spirit, and given a degree of attention which, in the words of the Foreign Minister, it would not have received if it had come from any other capital.[1]

The belated Russian reply on the surface appeared to consent to the Open Door, but actually it was evasive in content. This meant that all the other nations that had adhered conditionally were released from their commitment. But Hay, rather than press Russia and the others and run the risk of a flat refusal, blandly announced that the acceptances were "final and definitive." The St. Petersburg Foreign Office, which had an opportunity in advance to protest against this farfetched interpretation, strangely acquiesced in Hay's uncandid announcement.[2]

Henry Adams, a close if cynical friend of John Hay, observed

---

[1] Tower to Hay, Jan. 2, 1900, National Archives (Dispatches).
[2] Tower to Hay, Feb. 9, 1900, *ibid.*

that Hay had succeeded in embarrassing Russia very much, but that the agreement "binds no one to anything, and perhaps that is the reason why everybody assents." "No one," concluded Adams, "believes a Russian under any circumstances, but I am always interested in speculating why an oriental tells one lie rather than another. . . ." [3]

2

The Far Eastern cauldron began to bubble more violently when in 1900, the year after Hay's first Open Door note, the Chinese "Boxers" rose against the "foreign devils," and among other things attacked the Czar's outposts in Manchuria. This gave the Russians a good excuse to tighten their military grip there, and the other powers feared that the Russian armies would march into the adjacent Chinese provinces. Confronted by this threat, Great Britain and Japan joined hands in the alliance of 1902. The Japanese were worried primarily about Manchuria and Korea, on which they themselves had designs, while Britain was more concerned about the Russian menace to Turkey, Persia, Tibet, and China generally.

The Russians, responding to these outside pressures, negotiated a treaty with China in 1902, under which they bound themselves to evacuate Manchuria over a period of eighteen months. [4] If this pact had been kept in good faith, there probably would have been no Russo-Japanese War. The Russian troops partially and temporarily retired from Manchuria, and then returned, all the while pressing new and secret demands on Peking. A conservative group of Russian leaders favored economic penetration, at least at first; an aggressive group, which had the ear of the Czar, urged positive action in Manchuria and eventually a challenge to Japan in Korea.

Secretary Hay meanwhile had been laboring to bolster up the sagging Open Door in Manchuria. Russia responded with some vague assurances which American public opinion interpreted as

---

[3] W. C. Ford, ed., *Letters of Henry Adams, 1892–1918* (Boston, 1938), p. 281.
[4] For details see J. V. A. MacMurray, ed., *Treaties and Agreements with and concerning China, 1894–1919* (New York, 1921), I, 326–329.

assent, but Hay was distrustful. He believed that Cassini was a "lying diplomat," that Czardom had made "mendacity" a "science," and that Russia's promises were as "false as dicers' oaths when treachery is profitable. . . ." [5] Hay was prone to make extravagant statements, especially when crossed.

In 1904, when Japan with blazing guns challenged Russian dominance over Manchuria, the American public, while unwilling to join the fray, was prepared to sympathize with the Japanese. The half-dead friendship for Russia was not strong enough to overcome the painful impression created by the threat to the Open Door, combined with Russian evasion, procrastination, prevarication, and evident bad faith.

3

As if Russian manipulations in Manchuria on the eve of the Russo-Japanese War were not enough to prejudice American opinion against the Czar, another frightful outburst against the Jews in 1903 further undermined the few remaining pillars of the one-time cordiality.

The pogroms of the 1880's had tapered off in the 1890's, but with the turn of the century there were renewed outrages. The most spectacular came in 1903, when the populace of Kishinev, capital of Bessarabia, ran amok in a frightful orgy of burning, plundering, raping, and murdering. Babies were reportedly snatched from the arms of mothers and dashed to the pavement from upper stories. Statistics for such affairs are notoriously unreliable, but moderate estimates placed the number of murdered Jews at 45, the seriously wounded at 84, the injured at 500, and the destitute at 10,000.

The Kishinev pogrom was in some respects no worse than some of its predecessors, but peculiar circumstances compounded the enormity of the crime. The orgy of lust and bloodletting broke loose during the Easter season, at a time when the crucifixion of Christ by the Jews was fresh in memory. Greek Orthodox priests

---

[5] Tyler Dennett, *John Hay* (New York, 1933), p. 317.

allegedly preached sermons against the Jews and then led hordes of inflamed peasants against them. The riots were also incited by the one local newspaper, which enjoyed government support and which played up the ancient tale of ritual murders. The officials in Kishinev did not bestir themselves actively to curb or suppress the disorders; and in America the suspicion grew to a certainty that these local authorities, aided and abetted by the central government, unloosed the mob upon its victims. The bureaucrats of Nicholas II seemed nothing loath to drown out mounting revolutionary disturbances in the blood of defenseless Jews.

Ambassador Cassini issued a statement to the American press in which he blamed the Jews for having aroused the hatred of the peasants and for not being agriculturalists instead of merchants. A good many Americans happened to know that Jews were barred from agricultural pursuits, and the Russian envoy was further blackened as an inept liar. Secretary Hay cabled St. Petersburg that American friends of the Jews wanted to send succor, but the Russian authorities politely and rather haughtily rebuffed him. While appreciating the spirit of the offer, they stated that there was no suffering among the Jews in Kishinev and that the Russian government had the situation well in hand.[6]

An outcry of horror against these barbarities arose from all over the civilized world, not solely in the United States and by no means solely among Jews. Congress was not in session, but spontaneous meetings of protest mushroomed all over the United States. Altogether there were 77 public gatherings in 50 towns in 27 states. Most of the resolutions passed by these bodies condemned the massacres and besought Washington to use its influence to stop them. The press, whether religious or secular, was outraged. The Hearst chain was all for belaboring the bear with the bloody paws and insisted that, if Secretary Hay would not protest, Congress should do so. The Russians would then know that they were hearing from "the power that makes treaties and

---

[6] *Foreign Relations, 1903* (Washington, 1904), p. 712.

declares war." [7] Hearst seems to have been the only editor to hint at armed hostilities; the others were content to speak in terms of formal protest.

THE PERFORMER—"IT WAS UNINTENTIONAL!"

(From the St. Paul *Pioneer Express*, 1903, by permission.)

4

The Department of State again found itself in an awkward position. The Kishinev outrage was a purely internal one, like a large-scale lynching in Georgia, all the more so since our citizens had apparently suffered no injury to life and property. Uncle Sam could not come into court with clean hands, what with the blood stains of Indians, Negroes, Chinese, and more recently Italians and Filipinos. The press of Russia and western Europe satirically

---

[7] *Literary Digest*, XXVI, 775 (May 30, 1903).

181

reminded us of our inconsistencies. One Berlin cartoon had President Theodore Roosevelt remark to the Czar, "You cut up your Jews, I'll burn my negroes." [8]

Yet the Department of State did have one strong talking point. The pogroms had driven and were driving thousands of human derelicts to the United States, where they would have to be rehabilitated and supported. Tens of thousands of Russian Jews had reached our shores since the first trickle in the early 1880's, and they had come to be a powerful voice politically, particularly in the electorally important states of New York and Massachusetts. Washington obviously had to make some kind of vote-saving move, especially since "His Accidency" Theodore Roosevelt, President by virtue of the bullet that had killed McKinley, was desperately eager to be elected the next year "in his own right."

Thousands of earnest Americans appended their signatures to a petition, circulated under Jewish auspices, which condemned the Kishinev horrors and pleaded with Nicholas II for religious and racial toleration. Secretary Hay cabled the American envoy in St. Petersburg to inquire if the petition would be accepted by the Autocrat of All the Russias. The Foreign Minister replied that the government did not want to appear discourteous or unfriendly, but the document would not be received by either the Foreign Office or the Czar. The Emperor, whose will was the sole law of the land, needed no information from the outside world as to conditions within his domain or advice as to how he should manage his internal affairs.[9]

Everything was done politely and according to protocol, and essentially the same ends were served as if the petition had been presented. Nicholas II was informally apprised of its contents; the petitioners were aware that the State Department had done all it could; and Theodore Roosevelt's political boots were kept clean.

The trial in Russia of those persons accused of complicity in

---

[8] *Review of Reviews*, XXVIII, 269 (Sept., 1903).

[9] Riddle to Hay, July 16, 1903, National Archives (Dispatches).

the mass murders was duly concluded in 1903. Two culprits were sentenced to penal servitude for five and seven years respectively. The other twenty-two who were found guilty received sentences of from one month to two years. Twelve persons were acquitted, and forty-eight civil actions were dismissed. Many Americans regarded the sentences, which were ridiculously light by our standards, as a travesty of justice.

5

Kishinev was by no means the last of the anti-Jewish orgies, and the protests of the United States, whether informal or diplomatic, seem to have had no influence on the Russian Jew-baiters, even assuming that they knew of them. The general disorders accompanying the Russo-Japanese War evidently accelerated attacks on the Jews. In 1904 there was a horrible saturnalia at Smiela, and the next year another at Odessa took a toll of about a thousand lives. In 1905, after the war had ended, two frightful new outbursts occurred at Kishinev, one of which eclipsed the massacre of 1903. That at Bialystok in 1906, in which Russian troops allegedly took part, was unusually bloody and left a most unfortunate impression in America.

The members of Congress, some of whom had large Jewish constituencies, could not long remain silent. A half-dozen or so introduced resolutions expressing sympathy and abhorrence, or demanding inquiry. One of the prime movers was Representative Goldfogle of New York City, himself of the Jewish faith, who was indefatigable in supporting the interests of his coreligionists. In June, 1906, both houses of Congress overwhelmingly approved a resolution which stated that we were "horrified" by the massacres, and that the bereaved had "the hearty sympathy" of the American people.[10] Aside from earlier resolutions requesting information, this was the only legislation of its kind that passed both houses during the Czarist era.

The hollow-sounding ancient friendship entered conspicuously

[10] *Cong. Record*, 59 Cong., 1 sess., pp. 8919, 9004 (June 22, 1906).

into a discussion of the pogroms both in Congress and in the country as a whole. Some apologists argued that out of gratitude to the Russians for their past support we should not nag them about their Jewish troubles. Others replied that the ancient attachment gave us a moral right to present a polite protest, and that Nicholas II was endangering the century-old cordiality by driving so many of his embittered subjects to America, where they became an important and anti-Russian part of the body politic. American Jews expressed the hope that bankers of their faith would bring Russia to her senses by withholding loans, and Oscar S. Straus, a prominent Jew, went so far as to cast doubt on the Russian fleet legend.[11]

Until Kishinev our people had been led to believe that the Russians were a kindly folk, and that the Czar was a well-meaning man, who was just the prisoner of brutal bureaucrats. But when it became evident that the peasants were violently anti-Semitic, and that the bureaucrats in some cases connived at or encouraged the outrages, the American press was disposed to blame not only the officials but Nicholas II and his people as well. A cartoon in 1905 showed the Emperor, his ermine bespattered with the blood of Kishinev, piously remarking, "I wonder why I am not popular." [12]

The Russian spokesmen on their part bitterly resented our attempts to lay hands—hypocritical hands at that—on the Empire's peculiar problem. They referred time and again to their assistance during critical eras in the past, and reproached the American busybodies for ingratitude. There can be little doubt that when the Russo-Japanese War flared up in 1904, the vitality had already ebbed from the ancient friendship.

[11] O. S. Straus, "The United States and Russia: Their Historical Relations," *North American Review*, CLXXXI, 244–245 (Aug., 1905).
[12] *Literary Digest*, XXX, 771 (May 27, 1905).

XVI

The Russo-Japanese Debacle

"I like the Russian people, but I abhor the Russian
system of government and I cannot trust the word of
those at the head."—Theodore Roosevelt, 1905

I

THE deadline for the evacuation of Manchuria by the
Czar's armies came and passed in 1903, but still the resourceful Russians found excuses for staying. Their most
plausible argument was that conditions were still unsettled, and
that they could not expose their large interests without ironclad
guarantees from the Chinese government. The American public
was annoyed by all this shilly-shallying, and the New York
Nation cynically compared a genuine evacuation with an "evacuation *à la Russe*." [1]

The Japanese, who feared the Czarist threat to their ambitions
in both Manchuria and Korea, pressed St. Petersburg for a speedy
withdrawal, but the Russians, who were naturally dilatory, found
it profitable to play a stalling game. Time was on their side. The
trans-Siberian railroad was nearing completion, and formidable
naval and military reinforcements were being rushed to the Far
East. If the Mikado's men were going to strike at all, they had

---

[1] LXXVII, 219 (Sept. 17, 1903). Actually, the Treaty of 1902 stipulated a withdrawal of Russian troops "provided that no disturbances arise and that the action
of other Powers should not prevent it" (J. V. A. MacMurray, ed., *Treaties and
Agreements with and concerning China, 1894-1919* [New York, 1921], I, 327).

better do so before the Muscovite Atlas had gathered its full strength.

Early in February, 1904, on the initiative of Japan, diplomatic relations between Tokyo and St. Petersburg were broken off, and this alarming move was regarded in the United States as a certain prelude to shooting. Two days later, without warning and without a declaration of war, the Japanese fleet attacked Russian naval units at Port Arthur, inflicting some damage. A considerable number of American newspapers broke into praise of the clever and plucky Japanese, who under extreme provocation had shown that they were not bluffers, and who had caught the careless Russians asleep at the switch at a time when everyone knew that an attack was inevitable.[2]

Even though the American press had earlier expressed warm sympathy for tiny Japan, the Russians were shocked and angered by the chorus of commendation in the United States for the sneak attack. Russia was by far the largest white nation; and the white people ought to stand together. The Russians were combating the Yellow Peril: having driven out the Tartars during the fifteenth century in the interests of western civilization, they looked upon themselves as having a similar mission in the Far East. The task could not properly be left to the Nipponese, who were a half-civilized Oriental race with only a veneer of westernism.

The Russian Empire was a Christian nation, although Greek Orthodox, and even some Roman Catholic journals in the United States argued that if Russia won there was some chance of converting Korea, Manchuria, and China to Christianity. If she lost, the heathen Japanese would move in, and possibly all Asia would be barred to the Christian faith. Russian apologists also pointed out

---

[2] W. B. Thorson, "Pacific Northwest Opinion on the Russo-Japanese War of 1904–1905," *Pacific Northwest Quarterly*, XXXV, 305–322 (Oct., 1944). The parallels to the later Pearl Harbor attack are striking. In 1941 we were delaying, hoping to gather strength in the Far East, while our economic restrictions strangled the Nipponese. Time was on our side; the Japanese were under strong compulson to attack.

that the Czar had legitimate aspirations in the Far East, including the long-desired ice-free port, just as the United States had earlier cherished legitimate designs on Louisiana, California, Hawaii, and other desirable acquisitions.

The Russians in addition regarded the Japanese as the aggressors and themselves as peace-loving. Had not Nicholas II called the conference that had brought into being the Hague Court? The righteousness of the Russian cause was further bolstered by the fact that the Japanese had delivered an unethical punch below the belt while the two nations were still nominally at peace, and this dastardly act removed the fanatical yellow men from the roster of decent nations. The Russians also felt that the fickle Americans should be stirred by an elemental sense of gratitude for the favors conferred upon them in the past by the Czars. The time had come for the United States to pay off the long-overdue interest on the traditional friendship.

2

Lack of sympathy in the United States for Russia was compounded of two major ingredients: an increasing distaste for Czarism and a sentimental regard for Japan.

As for dislike of Russian despotism, enough has been said of ruthless Russification, of pitiless pogroms, of Siberian prisons, and of religious repression. Unfavorable impressions from these sources were heightened by the novels and short stories of Maxim Gorky, who enjoyed an extraordinary vogue in the United States from about 1900 to 1906. His pen portrayed Russian life under the Czars with the rawest of realism, and with emphasis on coarseness, brutality, debauchery, degradation, and viciousness.[3]

---

[3] Gorky came to America in 1906 to raise funds for the Russian revolutionists, and was meeting with considerable success when the news leaked out that he was accompanied by a Russian actress who was not his wife. Moralistic America dropped him with a thud. There is evidence that the Czarist Embassy in Washington contrived to discredit him by exposing his amours. See Alexander Kaun, *Maxim Gorky and His Russia* (New York, 1931), pp. 570–571.

American businessmen were also being alienated by new and onerous restrictions on their activities in Russia. They had been encouraged to erect factories, as was true of the Singer Sewing Machine Company, and then had been confronted with the prospect of being taxed out of existence.

Russian aggression in the Far East also troubled a multitude of Americans. While Czarist imperialism was not basically different from that of certain other powers, it was nevertheless marked by an arrogant disregard for the sovereignty of China and the rights of other nations, including Japan and the United States. Lucrative markets in Manchuria were in danger of being roped off by the Russians. To many Americans the menace of Czarist aggression was such that as between the existing Muscovite Peril and the problematical Yellow Peril, the Yellow Peril seemed to be the lesser of the two evils.

Distrust of Russia was further increased by a deepening conviction, strengthened by generations of British propaganda, that the Russians were incorrigible liars. Secretary Hay was distressed in 1903 to find that he had a copy of a Russian document, the existence of which the Russians themselves emphatically denied.[4] Count Cassini amply upheld this reputation for trickery, while complaining publicly of American ingratitude for the Czar's support in the past.

The American masses, despite an unmistakable preference for Japan, nevertheless still retained a substantial residue of attachment to Russia. Ancient legends die hard. The threadbare argument was again employed that the Russians were a splendid people cursed by an intolerably bad government. Even Nicholas II was a good man and a lover of peace, but he was surrounded by the "war party and crafty bureaucrats." A few adventuresome Americans actually sought to enlist in the Russian navy.

If the Czar had again been fighting the "unspeakable Turks" rather than the sturdy little Japanese, American sentiment would doubtless have been more cordial, though less so than in the nine-

4 W. R. Thayer, *The Life and Letters of John Hay* (Boston, 1908), II, 368.

teenth century. But Nippon was also our time-honored friend, and we could not openly sympathize with one belligerent without appearing to be hostile to the other.

Nor could we overlook the fact that Japan in a very real sense was the protégé of the United States. The American Commodore Perry in 1854 had forced her to open her doors, and we took genuine pride in the marvelous achievements of the little fellow whom we had helped to bring up. The Japanese were not Christians to be sure, but they were reasonably tolerant of foreign religions. Christian missionaries were permitted to proselyte freely, and there were a few Japanese Christians in high office. A good many religious journals in America argued that Protestant Christianity would fare better in Asiatic lands controlled by Japan than by Russia, whose illiberal policy toward proselyters, dissenters, Roman Catholics, and Protestants was notorious. In brief, to many Americans the non-Christian Japanese seemed more Christian than the Christian Russians.

Well-informed American observers also regarded the Japanese as more liberal politically. They had seemingly come up farther from medievalism, and in a much shorter time, than the backward Russians. George Kennan, as a distinguished war correspondent, again took up the cudgels. He pointed out that Russian prisoners were better off in Japanese prison camps than they would have been as Czarist exiles in Siberia. In a noteworthy article for *Outlook* entitled, "Which Is the Civilized Power?" he argued that the Japanese were superior to the Russians.[5] He concluded that he now preferred the Japanese people to the Russian people, although up to this time he had merely preferred the Tokyo government to that of St. Petersburg. In common with many other liberal Americans, Kennan greeted Russian disasters as good news. A breakdown of Czarism in both the military and civil branches seemed to be the only real hope of weakening the death grip of despotism and introducing some degree of popular control.

Most Americans looked upon Japan as fighting in self-defense,

[5] LXXVIII, 515–523 (Oct. 29, 1904).

even though she had sneakingly fired the first shot. Korea and Manchuria were pistols pointed at the heart of Nippon, and their control by a powerful and hostile foreign nation could not be tolerated. Tiny Japan, arrayed against gigantic Russia, was the underdog. It was a David and Goliath drama all over again, and the sporting instincts of the Americans went out to David. The Japanese soldiers aroused our respect and admiration. They proved themselves to be sober, disciplined, skillful, courageous, and fanatically willing to die on the battlefield for their God-Emperor. If Russia won, she would presumably close the Open Door in Manchuria; if Japan won, she would presumably keep it open for American and other foreign merchants. "Japan is playing our game," wrote President Roosevelt smugly if shortsightedly.[6]

American enthusiasm for the Nipponese during the early stages of the war was consequently spontaneous and sincere. The number of post offices named Tokyo rose to six, and several other places were named after the Japanese naval hero Admiral Togo— to our embarrassment after Pearl Harbor. Large sums of money were subscribed for loans to Japan, particularly by Jewish Americans, who were outspokenly and understandably anti-Russian. They even talked of raising funds with which to present a warship to Japan.

3

Even before the guns began to boom, the Russian press was expressing increasing bitterness toward the Yankee ingrates. The various journals, whether unofficial or semiofficial, were annoyed that we should have lionized Czarist exiles, swallowed the Kennan tales, taken up the cause of the Jews, erected tariff barricades, and sponsored the Open Door, which was obviously designed to jockey the Russians out of Manchuria and deprive them of their warm-water outlet. As if all this were not enough, the Americans had shamelessly rejoiced over the dastardly attack at Port Arthur,

---

[6] H. F. Pringle, *Theodore Roosevelt* (New York, 1931), p. 375.

and were expressing delight over continuing reverses to Nicholas II's armies.

Russian journals paraded the hoary tale of the Civil War fleets, and recalled that the generous Alexander II had sold Alaska to the ungrateful Americans for a pittance. The most influential newspaper in St. Petersburg (*Novoye Vremya*) accused the American trusts of having precipitated the war because they wanted to drive Russia out of Manchuria in order to exploit it and the rest of China by themselves. (This is a foreshadowing of the Stalinist charge that American dollar imperialists after 1945 were fomenting war.) In a scorching editorial entitled "Russia's Real Enemy," the same newspaper flatly accused us of having instigated the Japanese and then of having hounded them on. The semiofficial nature of this journal caused the Department of State seriously to consider an oral and informal protest.[7]

The Russian accusation of our having incited the Japanese, and of having formed a secret alliance with them, merits examination. Our position regarding the Open Door was roughly similar to that of Britain and Japan, and in this sense we supported the Anglo-Japanese alliance. On the eve of hostilities our strong pro-Japanese predilections, which to the Japanese seemed to promise neutrality and even financial support, undoubtedly encouraged the war spirit in Japan. (President Roosevelt, according to his own dubious tale, warned France and Germany to stay out of the clash at the peril of American armed intervention.) But the Russian allegation that our attitude tipped the scales in favor of war simply cannot be proved. The Russians did so much of the tipping themselves that the search for an American scapegoat seems childish.

The acid comments of the Russian press, together with repeated invocations of the historic friendship, touched off a new discussion in American newspapers as to the genuineness of that sentiment. There was an increasing disposition to look upon it with

---

[7] Meyer to Hay, April 18, 1905, National Archives (Dispatches), carrying a State Department notation.

suspicion. As for the "sealed orders" of Lessovsky's fleet in 1863, one critic declared that if any had existed they certainly would have come to light within forty years; anyhow the fleet was rotten. Another critic, pointing to Russian naval ineptitude in the current war, thought it fortunate that no one had called Lessovsky's bluff.[8]

Less cynical commentators conceded that Russian friendship had been genuine and useful up to a point, but that we had fully discharged our obligation in the famine relief shipments of 1892. Alexander II admittedly had sold us Alaska, but we had paid cash for it and no debt was involved. What sentimental kinship we had for Russia by 1903 had been fully washed away by the blood of the Jews who had perished at Kishinev. So ran the obituaries on the ancient friendship.

4

Russian resources, huge though they were, could not be effectively funneled into the faraway theater of combat in Manchuria. The Czar had formidable naval strength, on paper about twice that of Japan, but it was dispersed through four different fleets: the Baltic, the Black, the Caspian, and the Far Eastern. The Russian Empire was further handicapped by widespread civil disorders, culminating in open revolt; and the oppressed minorities, especially the Finns and Poles, grew ominously restive.

The Czarist armies fighting in Manchuria, anomalously on Chinese soil, were gradually beaten back with heavy losses. The monotonously rearward motion of these troops was the object of much ridicule in our newspapers; the Baltimore *American* referred to the Slavs as "of an exceedingly retiring nature." The Russian garrison at Port Arthur was trapped but held out doggedly for many months, exacting frightful losses from the attackers. American admiration was aroused; the siege was described as one of the great sagas of history, including that of Troy; and the commander, General A. M. Stoessel, attained the stature of a hero. But when the fortress finally yielded, inquisitive newsmen found im-

---

[8] See *Literary Digest*, XXVIII, 399 (March 19, 1904).

mense stocks of supplies and unbreached defenses, all of which indicated that the surrender had been premature, and hero Stoessel quickly became a fallen idol. (After a trial he was condemned to death by the Czar's government, but in consideration of his personal bravery his sentence was commuted to ten years' imprisonment.)

The tale of the sea was hardly less sorry. At Port Arthur the Russian ships not only were caught napping, but they ran into their own mines and fired upon one another. A powerful reinforcing fleet, commanded by Admiral Rozhdestvensky, was slowly gathered in the Baltic, amid much jeering in our press about its reluctance to depart, and green sailors were pressed into service. In wretched condition to undertake this unprecedentedly long voyage, the armada finally sailed. Emerging into the North Sea the lookouts spotted in the foggy night what were claimed to be Japanese torpedo boats. The fleet opened fire and maintained it for about half an hour, sinking one British fishing trawler, damaging others, killing two British sailors, wounding six others, and sailing on without attempting rescue.

The British public was outraged; the "rule Britannia" jingoes clamored for war. The Russians made matters worse by inept explanations. But saner counsels finally prevailed, and the dispute was referred to an international commission of five admirals, which reported the attack as not "justifiable," even though Rozhdestvensky had received false reports as to the presence of Japanese torpedo boats. St. Petersburg thereupon paid the British an indemnity of £65,000.

The most rational explanation of this irrational act seems to be that the Russians were in such a highly nervous state that they were seeing things in the fog. The American press further suggested that they might have mistaken their own torpedo boats for those of the Japanese and fired upon them, which was consistent with their conduct in the Far East. Less charitable was the explanation, advanced by the London *Punch*, that Admiral Vodka must have been in command that night. In any event our editors agreed that the Russians were "dangerous fools" who were so clumsy that they ought not to be allowed at large with lethal weapons.[9]

RUSSIA—"NEVER WILL I COMPROMISE MY DIGNITY FOR THE SAKE OF SECURING PEACE"

(From the Boston *Herald*, 1905, by permission.)

After this blundering beginning, the Russian fleet at length reached Far Eastern waters, only to be wiped out by Admiral Togo at the Strait of Tsushima. The odds against the invader on a tonnage and gunnage basis were not hopeless, about ten to nine, but his ships, operating at a suicidal distance from bases, by then had foul bottoms. The Russians were badly outmaneuvered and

[9] *Ibid.*, XXIX, 634–636 (Nov. 12, 1904).

outshot. The wounded Admiral Rozhdestvensky was gallant in defeat, and the London *Punch* thought that he deserved credit, after the attack on the trawlers, for having sailed his fleet out to the place of execution without further serious mishap.

The holocaust at Tsushima plummeted Russia from fourth to seventh place as a naval power, and without building another ship the United States jumped from fifth to fourth place, ahead of Japan and Italy, but behind Britain, France, and Germany. Witticisms appeared in American newspapers commending the peace-loving Nicholas II, who had summoned the Hague Disarmament Conference, for his very substantial contribution to disarmament. The war finally ended with Russia's navy crippled, with her armies shattered and in retreat, and with the country convulsed by civil war.

5

The unfavorable picture of Russia in the American public mind was darkened by other events. Stories drifted into the United States of the cruel treatment that Russian officers meted out to their men, especially to Jews. Tales of rape and other atrocities, circulated by unfriendly British news agencies, appeared in our press, although in every large war there are always atrocities on both sides. A writer in one British journal reminded his readers that the Cossacks, during the late war with Turkey, "practically lived on the blood of the Turks whom they had captured." [10] Russian officials aroused further ill will by arresting or otherwise restricting the activities of American newsmen in the Far East, as did the Japanese, but we heard more about Japanese tactics later.

The diplomatic front between the Potomac and the Neva was also troubled during the years of fighting. The Russian government protested to Washington that the Japanese were violating the laws of war, and that China was not maintaining her neutrality in dealings with the Japanese. Chinese unneutrality was no direct

---

[10] *Ibid.*, p. 916 (Dec. 31, 1904).

concern of the United States, but the St. Petersburg Foreign Office, speaking through Count Cassini, complained repeatedly about our failure to intervene. After the crushing defeat at Tsushima Strait, three of Rozhdestvensky's damaged ships sought refuge in Manila Harbor, but since they were in no condition to leave within the conventional twenty-four hours, they were interned for the duration of hostilities. Both the Russian government and press regarded this as straining international law in favor of Japan, and hence an unfriendly act. They were also grieved because a United States officer at Chemulpo Bay, Korea, had allegedly not extended humane treatment to Russian survivors of a naval battle, although the representatives of other powers did so. The American commander officially explained away or denied the charges in a report to his superiors, but so bitter was the feeling in Russia that large orders for American goods were canceled, including plumbing supplies amounting to 60,000 rubles for an institution under the patronage of the Dowager Empress.[11]

6

A curiosity of the war was the reversed role of St. Petersburg regarding freedom of the seas. Both the United States and Russia had traditionally seen eye to eye in opposing infractions of this principle by Great Britain. But in the Russo-Japanese War the Russians, seeking to choke off supplies from Japan, violated what we regarded as freedom of the seas, and as a result the United States and Britain, erstwhile antagonists on this issue, were drawn together by a common grievance.

American newspaper readers were annoyed by reports, whether true or not, that the Russians had been sowing floating mines in the open sea. The Czar's government arbitrarily and contrary to previous practice declared food, coal, and cotton contraband of war, and began to seize these commodities on neutral ships sailing for Japan. Washington protested against such unwarranted ex-

[11] McCormick to Hay, Feb. 25, 1904, National Archives (Dispatches).

tensions, particularly in the case of cotton, which our southern states normally exported in substantial quantity to Japan.

While enforcing these pretensions, the Czar's cruisers seized or detained a number of merchantmen, most of them British-owned, and confiscated American property that was capriciously defined as contraband. United States mail was also seized, searched, and delayed. Some of these cases were presented to the Russian prize court in Vladivostok, but the American plaintiffs were unable to defend their interests properly at such a distance and on short notice. The most famous incident involved the *Knight Commander*, a British ship under American charter that was carrying American property. Overhauled by a Russian cruiser near Tokyo, it was sunk on the pretext that it was carrying contraband, after the crew had barely had time to board a neighboring ship. The press of the United States branded this incident as an "act of piracy."

The protests of Washington against such seizures were vigorous, and noticeably lacking in the customary references to the ancient amity. The buttons were off the diplomatic rapiers. "It would be a blessing to the world," declared the Chicago *Record-Herald*, "if every one of Russia's war-ships were on the bottom of the ocean" and "if she should be bound over by the Powers never to build another until she had learned to understand and recognize the rights of other peoples." [12] Even making due allowance for the anger of the moment, one cannot avoid concluding that both at the diplomatic and popular levels the time-honored attachment had received another crippling blow.

[12] *Literary Digest*, XXIX, 635 (Nov. 12, 1904).

XVII

Berated Are the
Peacemakers

"Russia is so corrupt, so treacherous and shifty, and
so incompetent, that I am utterly unable to say whether
or not it will make peace, or break off the negotiations
at any moment."—Theodore Roosevelt, 1905

I

THE disasters to Russian arms in the conflict with Japan
quieted for some time the talk of a Muscovite menace.
As in the Crimean War, the bubble of Russian invincibility was pricked, and the huge Empire was so exhausted that
the Czar no longer carried the weight that he formerly had in the
European balance of power.

In the American mind old stereotypes were more sharply etched
or new ones emerged, even though some of them were less than
fair to Russia. Our newspaper readers came to believe that the
Russians could not fight, at least not effectively. Their generals
were stupid, constantly bungling and blundering; their armies had
only one gear, and that was reverse. Their sailors were not at
home on the sea, and their soldiers were drunken, stolid, and
stupid, so ignorant that they would shoot themselves in the
shoulder, so the incredible report ran, not knowing that they
should place the stock of the rifle rather than the muzzle there.

Their officers were braggarts before battle, boasting that they would make short work of the Japanese "monkeys," and apologists afterward, bleating excuses of childish inapplicability.

The Russian bureaucracy was likewise painted for the American public in unflattering hues. The agencies of the government moved only after exasperating delay; their promises were not binding on other branches; and they all seemed to work independently of one another, like the roving eyes of a mythological monster. After the unfortunate attack on the British fishing trawlers, the Russian Foreign Minister told the American envoy that he had no information about the occurrence from the Admiralty or elsewhere, and that the Foreign Office had no control over the actions of the Admiralty.[1]

Czarist censorship operated even more clumsily than usual. The news of the catastrophe at Tsushima was suppressed for three days, though known to all the world. When General Kuropatkin, who at one stage commanded the Russian armies in the Far East, later brought out his history of the war, it was confiscated by the government, though published in Germany. While paying tribute to the gallantry of his men, Kuropatkin laid naked the incapacity, negligence, and disobedience of his officers; the inexcusable unpreparedness of the War Minister; and the folly of working at cross-purposes. Even making due allowances for Kuropatkin's desire to justify himself, his story presented Czarism in an unlovely light.

The Russian commissariat fully upheld its already well-established reputation for corruption. The admirals signed receipts for coal that they did not receive, and shamelessly pocketed the bribe. The Grand Ducal cabal of peculators turned out to be "royal vultures." Yet in spite of this dreary and one-sided picture, which was presented time and again to the American public, there was abundant evidence that the Russian soldiers and sailors had fought bravely in arctic cold and blistering heat. "It is the system

---

[1] Eddy to Hay, Oct. 24, 25, 1904, National Archives (Dispatches).

that has failed, not the men," explained the American *Review of Reviews*.[2]

2

The underdog has traditionally appealed to the American spirit of fair play, and when war came we cheered loudly for the Japanese. But when the smaller dog got on top and began chewing up the bigger dog in a merciless fashion, we gradually developed more sympathy for the Russians, no matter how richly they may have deserved their distasteful rewards. American enthusiasm for the little men of Nippon cooled appreciably when we learned that they fought with satanic fury, and that they employed barbarous and allegedly uncivilized methods of warfare.

The sensational victories of the tiny yellow nation over the enormous white empire naturally went to the heads of the Nipponese. American observers, overlooking our tightened hatbands after the Spanish War only six years earlier, complained that our former wards were becoming intolerably cocky. Correspondents for American journals wrote bitterly of Japanese censorship, which, however justifiable from a military viewpoint, was tactlessly handled. A new and formidable power had now appeared in the global arena, and our people began to entertain fears for the American-owned Philippines. If the Japanese became dominant in the Orient, perhaps they would slam the Open Door in the face of the "foreign devils" from the Occident. Perhaps they were not "playing our game" after all.

The Slavic Peril was now deflated, but what about the Yellow Peril? The exploited masses of the Orient might rise under Japanese leadership and utter the heretical cry, "Asia for the Asiatics." One ex-Confederate colonel was heard to say, "We Southerners don't like to see a colored man licking a white man." [3] If Japan completely smashed the military might of Russia, the balance of power in the Far East would be destroyed. It seemed best from

[2] XXXII, 9 (July, 1905).

[3] *Literary Digest*, XXIX, 371 (Sept. 24, 1904).

the point of view of American interests to have the Czarist Empire left with sufficient strength to act as some kind of brake on Japanese ambitions. Yet even though our enthusiasm for Japan fell substantially and our sympathy for Russia rose appreciably, on the eve of the peace conference our sentiments were still strongly pro-Japanese and anti-Russian.

3

The Japanese were running short of men and yen by the late spring and early summer of 1905. Not wishing to betray their weakness to the Russians, they approached President Roosevelt secretly and suggested that he, acting ostensibly on his own initiative, mediate between the two belligerents. The Rough Rider had no real desire to reap the uncertain wages of an umpire, but he did not want either Russia or Japan to collapse, with a consequent imbalance of power and a threat to our own interests in the Far East, whether commercial, military, religious, or political. With grave misgivings, therefore, he accepted the responsibility.

The American ambassador in St. Petersburg at that time was George von Lengerke Meyer, a wealthy sportsman of the Rooseveltian stamp who got along well with the Russians. His reports, like those of so many of his predecessors, stressed the peculiar and oft-noted traits of the ruling class, ranging from mysteriousness to mendacity. He found the Foreign Minister, Count Lamsdorff, tricky and unreliable. The Russians had broken our diplomatic code, as was common even in that day, and knew the contents of our notes before they were presented, but even the Czar pretended to be ignorant of them.[4]

Roosevelt thoroughly distrusted Count Cassini in Washington. The Russian had made himself offensive by protesting against American neutrality, and impertinently scolding the President for seeing too much of the Japanese ambassador and the representatives of the neutral powers. Roosevelt suspected that Cassini was

---

[4] M. A. DeWolfe Howe, *George von Lengerke Meyer* (New York, 1920). p. 198.

afraid to relay disagreeable truths to his superiors, and even if he did Count Lamsdorff, who complained of being "hustled," could not be counted on to present them to the Czar. After his experience with Cassini, Roosevelt wrote: "What I cannot understand about the Russian is the way he will lie when he knows perfectly well that you know he is lying." [5]

Roosevelt consequently decided to deal directly with Nicholas II through Meyer, much to the dissatisfaction of the bureaucracy, which objected to being by-passed. After protracted negotiations, during which Russian officialdom revealed an astonishing but characteristic capacity to ignore misfortunes, arrangements were made for Japan and Russia to send representatives to a conference at the Portsmouth Navy Yard, near Portsmouth, New Hampshire.

The head of the Russian delegation was Sergei Witte, an energetic and amiable statesman of unusual ability. He was a self-made man, in the American tradition, and realizing the growing unpopularity of the Russians, he went out of his way to ingratiate himself with the newspaper men. In this he achieved some success, but his published memoirs lead one to believe that overnight he caused American public sympathy to swing from Japan to Russia. There was undoubtedly some swing, but to the very end of the conference a substantial majority of the American newspapers were still pro-Japanese.[6]

The Mikado's representatives at Portsmouth demanded all of the island of Sakhalin, among other things, and an indemnity for the war which they claimed that Nicholas II had forced upon them. But the Russians were adamant. They had already lost much "face"; and nations were not ordinarily expected to pay indemnities until their homeland was invaded. Besides, the island of Sakhalin commanded the mouth of the all-important Amur River, the Mississippi of eastern Siberia.

Roosevelt was vastly annoyed, and growled that the Russians

---

[5] J. B. Bishop, *Theodore Roosevelt and His Time* (New York, 1920), I, 392.

[6] W. B. Thorson, "American Public Opinion and the Portsmouth Peace Conference," *American Historical Review*, LIII, 439-464 (April, 1948).

were unable to make war and incompetent to make peace. With characteristic intemperance he called them "hopeless creatures" who acted with "Chinese or Byzantine folly," and who lied so much that they "got into the dangerous position of lying to themselves." They were "quibblers," "stupid," "unrealistic," "sly," "evasive," "insincere," "treacherous," "double dealing," "shuffling," and "corrupt." Even Czar Nicholas II, to whom Roosevelt appealed directly, was "a preposterous little creature." [7]

4

Prodded by Roosevelt, the Japanese suddenly and unexpectedly abandoned their demands for indemnity, and accepted the southern half of Sakhalin rather than all of it, thereby winning plaudits in the American press for their magnanimity. Yet in spite of their apparent diplomatic defeat, they had won an epochal victory and had vastly strengthened their position in the Far East.

Roosevelt guarded well his secret that the Japanese had been the first to propose mediation, and hence was unable to avoid the opprobrium usually showered upon the honest broker. His picture was turned to the wall in Japan, and during the Tokyo riots of protest against the peace terms some American property was damaged.

The Russian masses greeted the news of peace with characteristic stolidity, and presumably with a feeling of relief not devoid of gratitude to America. The liberals and radicals were not completely happy; many of them were hoping that continued defeat would lead to a full-blown revolution. Members of the war faction were deeply angered by Roosevelt's intervention. They still believed that they needed only one more campaign to turn the tide of defeat and redeem their tarnished honor. Petitions urging continuance of the conflict poured in on the government, some of them from the clergy. When the terms of peace were announced, the St. Petersburg *Novoye Vremya* commented bitterly, "America will get nothing but broken bones for the share she has

---

[7] H. F. Pringle, *Theodore Roosevelt* (New York, 1931), p. 385.

played." [8] The story was circulated in St. Petersburg among Jew-haters that Roosevelt was himself a Jew, his original family name having been "Rosenfelt," and that he had merely acted at the bidding of "the cosmopolitan race whose scepter is finance." [9]

Irate Russians not only falsely condemned the Jewish-American community for having induced Roosevelt to mediate, but in their efforts to excuse their failures they accused the Jews of having financed the Japanese to victory. There was some little truth in this charge, for the German-born Jew, Jacob H. Schiff, head of the powerful New York banking house of Kuhn, Loeb, and Company, raised some $200,000,000 through the sale of bonds. Jewish-American bankers would have been less than human if they had not sought satisfaction in striking back at the Russians for the brutal treatment meted out to their defenseless coreligion-ists. In recognition of his services Schiff was twice decorated by the Japanese government.

American ill feeling against Russia subsided in some degree with the passing of time. During the war Nicholas II had lightened the imperial yoke somewhat by at least nominal reforms seeking to improve the criminal code, to lessen censorship, and to ameliorate the lot of the peasant and the workingman. Most important of all was the Easter Day ukase, issued in April, 1905, granting religious liberty to all non-Greek Orthodox communicants, except Jews, and thus lifting disabilities from some 40,000,000 persons, includ-ing Greek Orthodox dissenters, Roman Catholics, Lutherans, Mo-hammedans, and others. This concession was hailed by wishfully thinking Americans as heralding the dawn of Russian liberalism. A happier atmosphere also developed in Washington when the wily Cassini was replaced by the more highly respected Baron Rosen.

Czar Nicholas II shook hands warmly with Ambassador Meyer in the spring of 1905, near the end of the fighting, and remarked,

---

[8] *Literary Digest*, XXXI, 335 (Sept. 9, 1905).

[9] *Review of Reviews*, XXXII, 427 (Oct., 1905). A story later revived against Franklin D. Roosevelt by the Nazis.

"Say to your President I certainly hope that the old friendship which has *previously* existed and united the two nations for so long a period will be *renewed*."[10] The words that are here italicized indicate that the Czar knew that the delicate structure of historic cordiality had been shattered. The truth is that two ancient friendships, one sealed by Commodore Perry in 1854 and the other by Admiral Lessovsky in 1863, died on the wind-swept plains of Manchuria during or shortly before the Russo-Japanese War. The United States, with its Philippines, was now a Far Eastern power; and both the Russians and Japanese, whom we had safely viewed from the distance as friends, were now rivals and potential enemies.

5

The Russian bureaucracy, among other handicaps, had been forced to fight a two-front conflict: one against the Japanese abroad and one against its own people at home. The government seemed to be able to mobilize mobs more easily than troops, and the grave disorders of 1904 developed into the revolution of 1905.

The frightful state of affairs in Russia during the war accounts in large part for the pro-Japanese feeling of millions of Americans. Massacres of Jews were in some places accelerated, allegedly to distract attention from governmental blunders. So-called Tartars fell upon Christian Armenians with horrible butchery. Poland was afire with strikes; martial law was proclaimed; and the Cossacks were ordered to crush hundreds with sabers and hooves. Finland, resisting suffocation with dying gasps, wrested sweeping concessions from the nervous Nicholas II.

Disorders were not confined to minority groups. Student revolts, despite rigorous repression, were still flaring up. Reservists fought regulars in pitched battles. Peasants murdered proprietors, burned sugar refineries, and fired the oil wells of Baku. Sailors and marines mutinied, and the crew of one ship in the Black Sea killed its officers and in a weird Odyssey sought refuge in a Romanian

[10] Howe, *George von Lengerke Meyer*, p. 162.

port. The mutineers returned for punishment after the police had allegedly threatened, with a now-familiar tactic, to maltreat their parents. Bomb throwings and assassinations of public officials took their deadly toll, including the Minister of the Interior, the brutal von Plehve. Other officials, among them Nicholas II, lived in daily fear of their lives. As the Los Angeles *Express* put it in 1905:

> Twinkle, twinkle, little Czar,
>   How I wonder where you are.
> Hope you're locked up good and tight,
>   In your bomb-proof for the night.[11]

"Bloody Sunday"—January 22, 1905—received its name when an immense crowd of St. Petersburg strikers, accompanied by wives and children and led by Father Gapon, attempted peacefully to present a petition to the Little Father. They were charged by their beloved Czar's soldiers, who killed or wounded hundreds of them. The American people, with their Anglo-Saxon reverence for the right of peaceful assembly and petition, were profoundly shocked, as were the Russian people themselves.

The very foundations of government were trembling when, in October, 1905, Nicholas II approved a constitution—Russia's first —conceding some civic freedom, an extended suffrage, a legislative Duma, and ministerial responsibility. American newspapers applauded these apparent gains for freedom, while expressing grave doubts as to their reality.

The high hopes entertained for the Duma were quickly dashed. The first one, meeting in 1906, was dissolved after a deadlock during which the liberals sought more power. The second one, that of 1907, suffered a like fate. The third Duma, 1907–1912, was reactionary, thanks to a new electoral law, as was its successor, that from 1912–1917. Although there were some reforms, concessions were withdrawn, disorders were suppressed, executions were increased, and from Finland to the Caucasus there was "universal silence in all languages."

---

[11] *Literary Digest*, XXXI, 733 (Nov. 18, 1905).

Prominent among those banished to Siberia was the gifted agitator Catherine Breshkovsky, the so-called "Little Grandmother of the Russian Revolution," who had already spent over twenty years in prison or exile. She was well known in the United States, having visited this country in 1904–1905, and her trial and

THE EDGE OF THE PRECIPICE

(From the Chicago *Inter-Ocean*, 1905.)

banishment in 1910 attracted a good deal of attention. In American eyes there was something basically wrong with a government that was fearful of the activities of a woman who seemed so gentle and inoffensive.

Editorial writers in the United States continued to extend warm sympathy to the Russian people in their struggle for a free government, while poking fun at the futile doings of the Duma. Many died but little was done. The autocratic Emperor, fearful of his people, was held in increasing contempt, and there was a growing unwillingness to accept the stereotype, already weakened by Kishinev, that the Czar was just a good man surrounded by bad bureaucrats. They all seemed tarred with the same brush. A swelling number of Americans were prepared to echo the poem of their own Edwin Markham, first published in 1905, "Russia, Arise!" [12]

---

[12] *Gates of Paradise and Other Poems* (Garden City, N.Y., 1920), pp. 68–69.

XVIII

Battling for Principle

"The flag knows no Jew."—New York *Evening Mail*, 1911

I

A CURIOUS by-product of the internal upheaval in Russia was the case of Jan Janoff Pouren, a non-Jewish Lettish peasant who had actively participated in the revolutionary disorders. Upon fleeing to the United States, he was sought by the Czar's government on charges of robbery, arson, and attempted murder. He was further accused of having stolen clothing, watches, and other personal property from defenseless peasants, and of having beaten women. Such crimes, in the eyes of the Russian officials, were nonpolitical and hence came under the extradition clauses of the Russo-American treaty of 1893. The Imperial Embassy in Washington therefore made a formal request for extradition early in 1908.

American feelings, already rasped by the postrevolutionary repression in Russia, were quickly aroused in behalf of this lowly and friendless man. Socialist groups and labor organizations, particularly the American Federation of Labor with Samuel Gompers as its spokesman, bestirred themselves. Mass meetings were widely held, including one in Faneuil Hall in Boston and another at the Cooper Union in New York. Strong pressure was brought to bear on the White House and the State Department by such groups as the Political Refugees Defense League and the Friends of Russian Freedom, whose letterhead carried some seventy distinguished names, including Jane Addams, Samuel L. Clemens, Senator Robert M. La Follette, Jacob A. Riis, Julius Rosenwald, Jacob H. Schiff, Ida M. Tarbell, Oswald Garrison Villard, Rabbi Stephen S. Wise, and George Kennan. The list was studded with the names of clergymen, editors, and writers, some of whom were Jews and many of whom were conspicuously identified with "muckraking" or other liberal movements.

Printed form petitions were widely circulated by various groups, with instructions to fill them out and send them to Washington. The most active organization was the specially constituted Pouren Defense Conference, which consisted of representatives of 210 different societies in New York. It presented to the State Department a trunkful of petitions containing 69,625 signatures from 311 cities in 42 states, over half of them significantly from New York City, whose large Jewish population represented an important congestion of Russophobia.

Meanwhile the extradition proceedings had been going forward in New York before a United States commissioner. The defense counsel for Pouren argued that his alleged offenses had been committed during a revolution, and hence were political, not criminal.[1] But no evidence was presented to prove that he was a member of a revolutionary party, or connected with the revolution, except that he had operated in revolutionary times. The commissioner therefore ruled, in October, 1908, that Pouren was guilty of four acts of burglary, three of arson, and two of attempted murder, as a consequence of which he was to be extradited. The legal experts in the State Department reviewed the case and concluded that the evidence warranted the ruling.

---

[1] One of the witnesses who identified Pouren received anonymous threats of death, and later an attempt was apparently made on his life. After appropriate representations from the Russian Embassy, the Washington authorities provided a guard to "shadow" the witness.

2

The decision to extradite Pouren, far from quieting the furor, inflamed public interest to such a degree that the Russian ambassador in Washington formally complained of the "violent agitation." [2] Pouren obviously would not receive a fair trial when he reached Russia, assuming that he would receive one at all. The Baltimore *Sun* asserted that the Czar's hangmen were busy enough as it was. We had long prided ourselves on being the haven of escaped revolutionaries of every race and clime, and to deport Pouren seemed like an attack on the very foundation stones of the republic. Scores of other Russian political refugees in America, who were allegedly under the scrutiny of Nicholas II's spies, would no longer be safe, and they were anxiously watching the outcome. [3] The only hope of toppling Czarist tyranny was by revolution; and to remove the once-safe American sanctuary would further dash Russian hopes for liberty.

Fortunately for Pouren, the American political cauldron was bubbling. Theodore Roosevelt's hand-picked successor for the presidency, William H. Taft, was in the final stretches of the campaign of 1908, and pressure converged on the White House. Among others, the eighty-nine-year-old Julia Ward Howe wrote to the President with wavering hand, protesting against returning refugees to Russia, where testimony was said to be extorted by torture.

Pouren's lawyers argued that they had new evidence from certain witnesses, who hitherto had been shielded for fear they would attract the Czar's agents. Responding to this argument, and presumably also to political pressure, Washington ordered a reopening of the case. Early in 1909 a different commissioner found Pouren guilty of the crimes as charged, but ruled that since the

---

[2] *Foreign Relations, 1909* (Washington, 1914), p. 519.

[3] It was estimated that the Czar had about five hundred secret agents in America (Gustavus Myers, "The Tsar's Spy System in America," *Harper's Weekly*, LII, 9–10 [Nov. 28, 1908]).

culprit had acted as a revolutionist and not from motives of personal gain or malice, his offenses were political and hence not extraditable. The Russian government, no doubt puzzled and angered by Anglo-Saxon standards of justice, was assessed the cost of the judicial proceedings.

The verdict was greeted in the United States with approval if not enthusiasm. Grave doubts were expressed as to the desirability of Pouren as a potential citizen, but the principle seemed sound. "To return a revolutionary to Russia," declared the *Outlook*, "whatever his offenses, is to return to his torturers a man who has been goaded by them into the crimes which he has committed." [4]

3

Concurrently with the Pouren proceedings in 1908, St. Petersburg sought the extradition of Christian Rudewitz on charges of murder (three), arson, burglary, robbery, and larceny. The case was heard before a United States commissioner in Chicago, who was without legal background and who ruled in December, 1908, that the defendant should be extradited. The accused had able lawyers, including Clarence S. Darrow, the champion of the friendless, and Professor Charles Cheney Hyde of the Northwestern University Law School, both of whom were reported to be serving without remuneration.

Public interest ran high, both before and after the decision, especially after. Most of the agitation for the release of Rudewitz centered in the area west of the Alleghenies, possibly because New York and the Atlantic seaboard were preoccupied with the Pouren case. Mass meetings of protest were held as far away as Stockton, California; and from Texas to Minnesota petitions poured into Washington, a large number of them scrawled on rough paper. Pamphlets were issued with the title, "Shall America Soil Her Hands in Blood?" The Cleveland *Press* struck a popular and widely echoed note under the editorial caption, "America Can-

[4] XC, 3 (Sept. 5, 1908).

not be the Czar's Partner." One petitioner demanded that we terminate the extradition treaty: we did not need it, and if our criminals escaped to Russia, that would be punishment enough for them.

Socialists were especially active for Rudewitz, and they and others coupled their appeals in his behalf with those for Pouren. Immigrant groups like the Poles and Lithuanians were also outspoken. Two huge mass meetings were held in Chicago, at one of which the name of the United States commissioner was hissed. Raymond Robins aroused his audience to tremendous cheering when he cried that the Wall Street bankers wanted Rudewitz extradited so that they could continue their profitable business of peddling bonds for the Czar. He called upon the ghosts of the victims of Kishinev to haunt the holders of the bonds, and pleaded for such a tidal wave of protest that no American banker would ever dare offer Russian securities for sale. Symptomatic of the embittered atmosphere in Chicago is the fact that the Russian consul and his legal counsel received anonymous threats.

Secretary of State Root, as was within his power, overruled the commissioner and refused to extradite Rudewitz.[5] The legal experts of the State Department agreed that this was clearly a situation involving political offenses. Rudewitz, unlike Pouren, had actually been a member of the revolutionary party, and it was never established that he had been at the scene of the crimes.

Early in 1909, a few weeks after the release of Rudewitz, the more sensational case of Yevgeni Azeff splashed across the headlines. Azeff was the leader of one of the committees of the social revolutionists, and as such was active in plotting bomb outrages. The word now leaked out that all this time he had been a secret agent of the Russian police and that he had used funds supplied by the government to prepare the bombs. His chief duty was apparently to encourage revolutionary-minded students and others

---

[5] Root to Rosen, Jan. 26, 1909, National Archives, 16649/9. Root received an anonymous letter threatening his life if he returned Rudewitz to "the butcher of Russia."

to commit overt acts for which they could be jailed—a practice that was completely revolting to our Anglo-Saxon ideals of fair play. Revelations of this sort indicated that the Russian autocracy had never intended to grant any real freedom, and the Little Father grew even smaller in our estimation.

The public outburst over the Pouren and Rudewitz cases showed that the spirit of liberty was still vibrantly alive among a people who had rolled out the welcome mat for revolutionists like Schurz, Sigel, Garibaldi, and Kossuth. Agitation increased for abrogation of the hated extradition treaty of 1893. Pressure techniques were perfected which were soon transferred to an additional campaign for a termination of the Buchanan treaty of 1832. The attempt by the long arm of Russian tyranny to snatch revolutionary refugees from under our noses brought the problem home to these shores, and further deepened distrust of Czarism.

4

The outcry in behalf of Pouren and Rudewitz, vociferous though it was, proved to be but a warming-up exercise as compared with the overwhelming public demand for abrogation of the commercial treaty of 1832.

The time-honored Buchanan pact provided for mutual privileges of entrance, sojourn, and protection. This seemed innocuous enough at the time, but two unforeseen complications ultimately arose. First, there was the heavy exodus to America of Jews, on whom the Empire had long placed severe restrictions. Secondly, Russia was one of the few unenlightened nations, like China and Turkey, that did not recognize the right of a subject to discard the cloak of his nationality and put on that of a foreign country. Russian law stipulated that persons who became naturalized without permission were subject to Siberian exile and the loss of all civil rights. A few cases developed of Russian subjects having been punished for the crime of becoming American citizens without permission.

By the 1880's the problem of Russian Jews naturalized by the

United States began to take on some diplomatic significance. A few of these expatriates, after having secured American citizenship, sometimes fraudulently, would return to Russia and demand business and other privileges that their less fortunate fellow Jews did not enjoy. Some of them also involved their adopted land in controversy when they sought to use their new nationality as a shield for escaping military service. The United States minister, Andrew D. White, expressed annoyance in 1893 over this "attempted prostitution of American citizenship." [6]

Several points must be stressed. American Jews were not the only Jews discriminated against by Russia; Jews of other nationalities, including British, were also denied visas. Non-Jewish Americans might also be barred if they were revolutionaries or otherwise objectionable. A Jew might be refused admittance for political reasons alone. In 1911 the State Department reported that for the previous five years it had found only four cases of Jews who had been denied Russian visas on grounds of race or religion.[7] The St. Petersburg government had actually shown unusual deference to the United States. According to a Russian government journal, eleven American Jews in 1910 had requested visas, and only three of the group had been disappointed.[8] At all events the actual numbers were small, but they do not take into account the much larger group of potential applicants who were deterred from applying because of the known antipathy of Russia.

The Czarist officials, their nerves shattered by bursting bombs, were naturally nervous about admitting Jewish socialists, anarchists, or revolutionists. They contended that they could not permit foreign Jews to enjoy privileges not extended to their own. Suppose that Russian Negroes were to come to our shores and, invoking an ancient treaty, demand rights in the South not enjoyed by our colored citizens. The spokesmen for Nicholas II also pointed out that our immigration laws excluded certain classes

---

[6] *Foreign Relations, 1893* (Washington, 1894), p. 542.
[7] Knox to Parsons, Aug. 8, 1911, National Archives, 711.612/44.
[8] Guild to Knox, Dec. 14, 1911, *ibid.*, 711.612/78.

of people whom Americans deemed undesirable, including Mongolians, of whom there were many millions under the imperial flag.

Russian apologists further argued that there was no breach of the treaty, which plainly stated that Americans might enjoy reciprocal privileges "on condition of their submitting to the laws and ordinances there prevailing. . . ." If the Czar's government wanted to discriminate against American Jews in the same manner that it lawfully discriminated against its own, this could scarcely be regarded as a violation of the pact. Also, if Russia admitted American Jews, she would have to admit other foreign Jews, and before long the barriers erected against Jews for the presumed safety of the Crown would crumble away.

5

From 1882 to 1908 a dozen or so resolutions were introduced in Congress making inquiry about discrimination against American Jews in Russia, or protesting against their mistreatment. Increasing pressure for action was no doubt partly due to revulsion against the Kishinev massacre of 1903, and to the growing political power of the large body of Jews already here. In 1909 Representative Goldfogle of New York presented a joint resolution requesting a renegotiation of the treaty of 1832, and his proposal was passed by both houses of Congress with little discussion and signed by President Theodore Roosevelt on his last day in office.

The wheels of diplomacy were meanwhile grinding slowly. This problem had been hanging fire for over forty years, and the Russian government, traditionally dilatory and ungoaded by a large bloc of Jewish voters, was unwilling to make haste. The Department of State, recognizing that Congress was beginning to get out of hand, hoped for some quiet concession, but the Foreign Office was unmovable. Russia regarded the existing anti-Jewish policy as so vital to her internal security that she was not prepared to give it up, even to salvage the shattered fragments of the ancient friendship.

Early in 1911 the first resolution calling for termination of the existing treaty was introduced in Congress, and before the year ended about a dozen of similar intent were presented. The Democrats had recently won control of the House of Representatives, and with an eye to putting their nominee in the White House the next year, they were not loath to embarrass the Republican administration of President Taft. They charged that Republican Secretaries of State had dallied too long with the preservation of American rights, and now it was time for the Democrats to take the bull by the horns. (They later claimed credit in their national platform of 1912 for having forced the Republican President to correct this remissness.)

Pressure groups of various kinds now swung into action. A termination of the existing treaty would be harmful to our citizens doing business with Russia, and spokesmen for abrogation accused the government of being more interested in shielding the Almighty Dollar than in standing up for American rights. There were now about two million Jews in the United States, and they showered Congress with demands for abrogation. On December 11, 1911, Senator Henry Cabot Lodge alone presented more than seventy resolutions from various Jewish groups in Massachusetts,[9] and other Senators followed with similar appeals from such widely separated states as Connecticut, Virginia, Minnesota, Rhode Island, and Wisconsin.

The Jews themselves undoubtedly contributed much in the way of money, organization, and leadership to the anti-Russian crusade, especially in its earlier stages, but in the end such pressure groups were almost drowned out by the outcry from the great mass of our aroused citizenry. Freedom of religion, traditionally a sacred American principle, was involved. Protestant Americans or even Catholic Americans, if not preachers or priests, might hope to go to Russia without undue difficulty, but not Jewish Americans. The sanctity and dignity of United States citizenship, which meant the honor of the flag, were likewise involved. In Russian

---

[9] *Cong. Record*, 62 Cong., 2 sess., pp. 181–182.

eyes there were first-class American citizens who might come and second-class American citizens who might not. While we have long treated the Negroes and other groups as second-class citizens, we are quick to resent such discrimination by a foreign power.

A relatively few voices urged that arbitration be used before abrogation, and that diplomacy be given an opportunity to exhaust all hope. But had not diplomacy been dallying for decades with the issue? Could red-blooded Americanism endure forever this intolerable insult? Something like a wave of hysteria swept the country in behalf of the sacredness of American citizenship, equality before the law, and freedom of religion.

Enthusiastic meetings favoring abrogation were held from Massachusetts to Mississippi, from California to New York. The immense gathering at Carnegie Hall, in December, 1911, was presided over by William G. McAdoo. Among the dozen or so prominent speakers were William R. Hearst, Andrew D. White, Champ Clark (Speaker of the House), and Woodrow Wilson, governor of New Jersey, who was repeatedly hailed by the crowd as the next president.[10] Congress was inundated with proabrogation memorials from numerous bodies, including the legislatures of Connecticut, Illinois, Massachusetts, Montana, Wisconsin, New York, and California. Some of these states, it will be noted, had no potent body of Jewish voters. Our people were crusading for American and not Jewish principles.

6

The joint resolution that ultimately passed the House of Representatives came up for final debate on December 13, 1911. It arbitrarily and undiplomatically charged Russia with having violated the treaty, declared the pact terminated, and instructed President Taft to give formal notice to that effect. About fifty members spoke for the resolution, and a number of others vainly sought the floor, presumably for the same purpose. A few Representatives urged that the wording be made less accusatory, but an amend-

[10] New York *Times*, Dec. 7, 1911.

ment to remove the blunt charge of treaty violation was shouted down, 183 to 115. Only one member, Representative George R. Malby of northern New York, opposed the resolution, and he did so on the grounds that it would do the Jews no good and our businessmen positive damage. Then, injecting a note of unreality, he argued that summary abrogation would harm the "friendly relations which have so long existed between the two countries." [11]

After a warm debate the resolution, brusque wording and all, passed by the lopsided count of 301 to 1, and was then sent to the Senate. Malby was the sole dissenter. A vote so overwhelming could not be partisan or sectional or racial: it was a ringing manifestation of grass-roots Americanism.

The hysteria of Congress was not shared by the officials in the State Department, who were hoping to solve the problem by quiet negotiation. They were also disposed to feel—especially the legal experts—that St. Petersburg was right in insisting that there had been no violation of the treaty.[12] They deemed it unwise to endanger American trade and other economic ties with Russia over the denial of visas to several Jews each year. If the treaty was summarily abrogated, our commercial relations with the Empire would be thrown into a "state of nature," governed by such uncertain rights as we might claim under international law and comity from an aggrieved nation. We would weaken our position in dealing with Russia in the Near East and Far East; we would undermine our claim to exclude Mongolians and other undesirables; and we would make things more difficult for our own Jews and those in Russia.

President Taft, fully aware of these objections, was forced to move rapidly in the hope of heading off the imminent congressional insult to Russia. He sought from the St. Petersburg Foreign Office a joint statement, to be issued within twenty-four hours, to the effect that the old treaty was being ended in the hope of

---

[11] *Cong. Record,* 62 Cong., 2 sess. (Appendix), p. 17 (Dec. 13, 1911).

[12] State Department Memorandum, April 22, 1911, National Archives, 711.612/55.

speedily negotiating a new and modern one. But Foreign Minister Sazonov, who was angered by the whole affair, refused to be stampeded into any such pronouncement. He could not understand why the Americans would sacrifice a valuable trade to the interests of a few Jews. Our Ambassador replied that we were an idealistic and not a materialistic people. Sazonov remarked seriously and not cynically that he was willing to consider an arrangement by which all Jews might be transferred from his country to the United States. He insisted that Russia as a self-respecting power could not be hurried into taking action that would seem to be a public confession of wrongdoing.[13] Sazonov's decision left no alternative but outright abrogation.

President Taft, who preferred a less offensive diplomatic notification to the more offensive congressional resolution, caused a quiet and formal notice of termination to be given on December 17, 1911, effective a year later, December 31, 1912.

The Senate thereupon shunted aside the House resolution, which was now unnecessary, and passed a tactfully worded resolution approving Taft's course. The House promptly and overwhelmingly endorsed the action of the Senate. Thus it was that Taft, although forced to move with undignified haste, won his point by fending off a joint resolution couched in harsh language. The Russian officials unfortunately did not clearly understand or fully appreciate what he had done for them.

7

The insulting action of Congress aroused the articulate portion of the Russian public against the United States to an unprecedented degree. The Nationalists of St. Petersburg convened a mass meeting that was reported to be the first public gathering of protest ever sanctioned by the government. A bill was introduced into the Duma, with the signatures of 120 of the 420 members, stipulating that duties on American imports be increased to 100

---

[13] *Foreign Relations, 1911* (Washington, 1918), p. 697. Guild to Knox, Dec. 22, 1911, National Archives, 711.612/82.

per cent and that all Jewish-Americans be excluded from Russia. Fortunately for already embittered relations, this retaliatory proposal did not pass. The Russian press, which began to cartoon Uncle Sam with the features of a Jew, played up the political power of the Jewish pressure groups, from whom Yankee politicians were allegedly soliciting campaign funds. The leading St. Petersburg newspaper, *Novoye Vremya*, charged that "the Jewish bankers have become the real lords of America." [14]

Widespread boycotts were organized in Russia against American goods. New and more severe restrictions were clamped down on Russian Jews, and American Jews in Russia were treated with far less consideration. A leading Jewish-American merchant in St. Petersburg, who had earlier told our ambassador that he wished Russia to be given a "slap in the face" regardless of the consequences, now came to the Embassy with a plea that the government "do something" for him as an American citizen and force the Russians to buy his goods. [15]

The absence of a treaty, with its most-favored-nation clause, temporarily created a partial paralysis of American exports. Shippers wrote anxiously to the State Department inquiring about consuls, trade-marks, visas, and similar problems. American goods were now automatically subject to a tariff increase ranging from 26 per cent to 46 per cent. A number of the Senators and Representatives, who only a few weeks before had passed the abrogation resolution with a whoop and a hurrah, now forwarded to the State Department anxious letters from their constituents. British and German competitors were hastening to fill the vacuum caused by the exclusion of American products.

European diplomats gleefully fished in troubled waters, hoping for a breach in Russo-American relations. In the Far East the Russians were given a further push in the direction of an agreement with Japan. St. Petersburg, perhaps as an expression of pique, at first refused and then belatedly consented to send an exhibit to

---

[14] *Literary Digest*, XLIII, 1214 (Dec. 30, 1911).
[15] Guild to Knox, Feb. 24, 1912, National Archives, 711.612/101.

the Panama Pacific International Exposition in San Francisco during 1915.[16]

The expiring Taft administration, finding St. Petersburg receptive, secretly put out feelers for a *modus vivendi* to operate when the treaty formally died at the end of 1912. But our Jewish pressure groups made it clear that they preferred to have no pact at all rather than one which did not concede their demands. In 1916, after the Russian Foreign Office had again shown interest, President Wilson sent Ambassador David R. Francis to Russia for the primary purpose of negotiating a new commercial treaty. The administration evidently hoped to score a diplomatic victory that would influence Jewish voters in the election of 1916. But the Russian Foreign Office decided to postpone all negotiations pending the outcome of an inter-Allied economic conference in Paris. The next year came the outbreak of revolution, and with it the dashing of our commercial hopes.

8

Abrogation accomplished few of its avowed objectives. The Jews in Russia were worse off; the Jews in America were worse off; American trade, though increasing somewhat in certain categories, was worse off; relations with Russia were worse off.

All these liabilities had been clearly foreseen by the officials in the Department of State. Then why should Congress and public opinion have been so blind? First of all, we did not anticipate that the Russians would react so unfavorably to pressure tactics. Secondly, we misjudged the intensity of feeling in Russia regarding the Jews, just as outsiders misjudge the intensity of feeling in the South regarding the Negro. Finally, the election of 1912 was approaching, and few men in public life wanted to stand out against the sanctity of American citizenship, especially where the powerful Jewish bloc was involved. "Apparently," remarked the Chicago *Tribune*, "the Russian vote in this country is negligible." [17]

---

[16] Guild to Knox, June 21, 1912, *ibid.*, 711.612/136.

[17] *Literary Digest*, XLIV, 8 (Jan. 6, 1912). Interest in the mistreatment of

But this does not explain the near-hysterical tidal wave of public pressure that swept the country and dragooned the President into acting against his will. The basic answer appears to be twofold. First, we responded to an accumulation of indignation against Czarism, compounded of prisons, pogroms, and other persecutions. Second, America of 1911 was in an evangelical mood. The Progressive movement was nearing flood tide, and some of the leading liberals, including Woodrow Wilson, identified themselves actively with the abrogation crusade. Trade with Russia, although normally comprising slightly more than one per cent of our total, nevertheless accounted for some $40,000,000 a year. We were willing to jeopardize these profits while standing firm for the sanctity of American nationality and for the termination of a treaty which perpetuated the odious doctrine of inalienable allegiance.

9

While the abrogation controversy was running its course, a revolution was occurring on the diplomatic front. After generations of bitter rivalry, and in disregard of Kipling's immortal warning, the British made a truce with the bear in the memorable Anglo-Russian entente of 1907. Russia and Britain divided Persia into northern and southern spheres of influence; Britain agreed not to alter the political status of Afghanistan; and both nations pledged themselves to respect the territory and sovereignty of Tibet. One result was to quiet talk in the United States, much of it British-inspired, of the Slavic threat to southern Asia. But this was not true of eastern Asia.

The victories of Japan over Russia, as it turned out, served to dislodge the Russians only from southern Manchuria. A series of agreements between Tokyo and St. Petersburg, notably a secret

---

Russian Jews continued in America until the very eve of 1914. Mendel Beilis, a Jew accused of the ritual murder of a Christian boy, was acquitted in 1913 after two years' imprisonment. The case called forth petitions, mass meetings, and a resolution sponsored in Congress by Senator Lewis of Illinois (*Cong. Record*, 63 Cong., 1 sess., p. 5735 [Oct. 22, 1913]).

pact in 1907, divided China's Manchuria into two spheres of influence. Japan, with her South Manchurian Railway, was dominant in the south; Russia, with her Chinese Eastern Railway, was dominant in the north. The Open Door seemed in grave danger of being shut.

Secretary of State Knox, seeking to break the Russo-Japanese stranglehold, blundered forth late in 1909 with a scheme designed to jockey both Russia and Japan out of Manchuria. He proposed that foreign financial interests lend China the money with which to buy the Manchurian railroads and thus regain her former ascendancy. Knox's ill-considered proposition merely resulted in driving Russia and Japan, only recently bitter enemies, closer together in brotherly embrace. They not only sharply rebuffed the American Secretary, but the next year signed an agreement further clarifying their commercial grip on Manchuria. Referring to Knox, the St. Louis *Post-Dispatch* grumbled, "He never meddles but he muddles." [18]

The railroads of Manchuria meant little to the American on Main Street, and the Knox note made no great splash in the United States, except as a political stick with which to belabor the foundering Taft administration. But the Russian government and press, to whom Manchuria meant a great deal, were wrathfully aroused.

Irate Russian editors, clearly with the blessing of the Czar's censors, accused the United States of seeking to take advantage of the Empire's weakness growing out of the Russo-Japanese War. We were trying to kick Russia while she was down; we would not dare make such a proposition to a first-class power.[19] The charge was repeated that we had selfishly backed Japan against Russia in 1904–1905, and now we were greedily backing China against Russia so as to establish a new commercial empire for ourselves in North China.

Russian wrath cooled with the passage of time and with Ameri-

[18] *Literary Digest*, XL, 214 (Feb. 5, 1910).
[19] *Ibid.*, XL, 271 (Feb. 12, 1910); 338 (Feb. 19, 1910).

can semiacquiescence in the Russo-Japanese agreement regarding Manchuria, but in St. Petersburg Uncle Sam was portrayed as an uncommonly disagreeable fellow. When in 1913 the controversy between Japan and California boiled up to the danger point over alien land legislation, the Russian press hoped that the little yellow men would stand up to the bullying Yankees.[20] A clash between America and her Oriental protégé would be a godsend: Russia could work her will in Manchuria while the two nations that seemed most intent on stopping her would fight to the point of exhaustion. The Russians thus paid us back for our sympathy for Japan on the eve of Port Arthur, and although their reaction was both natural and understandable, it was hardly conducive to a revival of the ancient attachment.

10

The bad taste left by the Knox blunder of 1909 and the treaty abrogation of 1911 was in some small degree sweetened by the North Pacific sealing convention of 1911. The United States, faced with the destruction of its once magnificent Pribilof seal herd, induced Russia, which had a smaller herd, to join in a pact with Japan and Great Britain to eliminate indiscriminate killing.[21]

But such slight gestures were eclipsed by a renewed fear of Russian imperialism. The chastened Muscovite titan had recuperated slowly from the wounds of the Russo-Japanese War and had been forced to sit back in impotent fury when, in 1908, Austria-Hungary snatched Serb-speaking Bosnia and Herzegovina from the outstretched hands of Serbia, a sister Slav nation. But gradually the Russian giant regained its strength, and began to assert itself with greater vigor in the Balkans and in Persia.

The Anglo-Russian entente of 1907, as earlier noted, divided Persia into a Russian northern sphere and a British southern sphere. In 1911 the Persian government, whose finances were in wretched

---

[20] *Ibid.*, XLVIII, 750 (April 4, 1914).
[21] T. A. Bailey, "The North Pacific Sealing Convention of 1911," *Pacific Historical Review*, IV, 1-14 (March, 1935).

shape, employed an American expert, W. Morgan Shuster. The energetic Shuster plunged into his task with efficient zeal, and promptly made himself objectionable to Russia, allegedly because of his interference with Russian property, but presumably because

THE ADVANCE OF CIVILIZATION

Russian atrocities in Persia. Note the characteristic Cossack whip.
(From the New York *World*, 1911, by permission.)

the Czar's interests would be best served by keeping Persia in a weakened condition. St. Petersburg presented two ultimata to Teheran, the second of which demanded Shuster's dismissal. When he was retained, the Russians invaded Persia with a force that reportedly butchered some five hundred women and children at Tabriz. With the foe nearing its capital, the Persian government was forced to yield, and on Christmas Day, 1911, Shuster and his colleagues were dismissed.[22]

[22] For Shuster's own story, see W. Morgan Shuster, *The Strangling of Persia*

This unhappy incident, which broke into the headlines almost simultaneously with the abrogation of the treaty of 1832, made a deep impression in the United States. An American was involved, and Russian imperialism was revealed in all its brutality and ruthlessness. Presumably Nicholas II would not stop until he had taken over all Persia. Shuster became something of a hero in the United States for having stood up against the mighty bear, and our editors branded Russia in such terms as "barbaric, brutal, blasting Tartar." [23]

Fears as to Russian designs on central Asia were not entirely erased when, in 1913, a Russo-Chinese declaration recognized the autonomy of Outer Mongolia under the suzerainty of China. The Czar continued to build up his vast army, and to rehabilitate the navy, which had been so badly mauled in the Russo-Japanese War. In 1908 he had been forced to back down when Serbia had been confronted by Austria-Hungary; in 1914, when the Archduke Francis Ferdinand was murdered in the Bosnian town of Serajevo, he was prepared to back Serbia to the hilt. He did, and that fateful decision, among other factors, helped touch off the long-dreaded but long-awaited world conflagration. The days of the Romanov dynasty were numbered.

(New York, 1912). The present writer is advised by the publisher that this volume sold over 5,000 copies in the United States.

[23] *Literary Digest*, XLIV, 1 (Jan. 6, 1912).

XIX

Days That

Shook the World

"The treatment accorded Russia by her sister nations in the months to come will be the acid test of their good will. . . ."
—Woodrow Wilson, Fourteen Points Address, 1918

I

WHEN war erupted in the summer of 1914 autocratic Russia, by virtue of binding alliances, found herself in the camp of the democracies, principally Britain and France, fighting militaristic Germany and Austria-Hungary.

The presence of despotic Russia in the democratic fold was greeted in the United States with mixed feelings. We were well aware that the semi-Oriental Russian absolutism, which claimed dominion over both body and soul, was perhaps the most oppressive in the western world. A few of us vaguely feared that in the event of an Allied victory a partly civilized and imperialistic Russia might be as dangerous as a victorious Germany. Had not the Czar contributed substantially to the coming of the current war by his ill-timed mobilization?

But American sympathies were overwhelmingly on the side of the western democracies, and autocratic Russia rose in respectability by keeping good company. The oft-heralded Slavic Peril, which had faded after the Russo-Japanese War, on the whole seemed tame when compared with the vibrant militarism, navalism, imperialism, and jingoism of Germany under Kaiser Wilhelm II. The long-moribund ancient friendship, submerged under decades of unpleasantness, was in some degree again revived. We were favorably impressed by Russia's contributions to the Allied cause, especially her self-sacrificing invasion of East Prussia, which diverted German troops from France on the eve of the battle of the Marne and probably saved Paris. The embattled British, who naturally embraced the traditionally hostile Russian a good deal more enthusiastically than did the neutral Americans, further colored our outlook by sending us news with a pro-Russian slant.

Nicholas II also improved his standing in the United States by interdicting, as a war measure, the sale of alcoholic liquor. Countless thousands of American prohibitionists rejoiced. If Alexander II in 1861 had freed over 20,000,000 serfs from the grip of their masters, Nicholas II in 1914 had freed some 160,000,000 people from the grip of demon vodka. What unenlightened Russia had done, enlightened America might also do.

American immigrants were likewise pleased by the prospect of a new day in Russia for persecuted minorities, even though there was no real faith in Czarist promises. "Russia has made pledges before and broken them," scoffed the Springfield *Republican*.[1] Specifically, the Russian army issued a manifesto which rather vaguely held out hope of a reunited and self-governing Poland under Czarist auspices. The Jews were also assured of better treatment, which as it turned out was not satisfactorily forthcoming. Jewish-Americans, still flushed by their abrogation victory of 1911, were perhaps the one group in America most outstandingly anti-Russian, as a consequence of which they appeared to be, whether correctly or not, pro-German. The German-born Jewish banker, Jacob H. Schiff, declined to participate in a huge Allied loan, even though it would have brought substantial profits to his firm. The Russian officials were well aware of Jewish hostility and deeply resentful of it.[2]

---

[1] *Literary Digest*, XLIX, 401 (Sept. 5, 1914).
[2] Francis to Lansing, June 16, 1916, National Archives, 711.612/249.

At the outset of the war the United States and Russia were drawn more closely together, especially by American exports. Partly to fill the vacuum caused by the withdrawal of German goods, and partly to supply some of the Czar's military needs, exports from America increased from some $27,000,000 annually to almost $500,000,000 in 1916—a volume never previously attained, and not again to be attained until the lush days of lend-lease in the 1940's. Russian bonds, bearing a high interest rate indicative of the risk, were floated in the United States to the extent of some $86,000,000.

Yet unpleasant reports from the realm of the Romanovs continued to discolor this rather roseate picture. There were accounts of German agents and saboteurs, of bureaucratic stupidity and mismanagement, of Grand Ducal cowardice and bungling. After initial successes, the Russian armies were driven back by the Germans and yielded huge chunks of territory. As in the Russo-Japanese War, the American newspapers poked fun at this constant rearward motion, while expressing admiration for the Russian capacity to absorb punishment, lose enormous numbers of prisoners, and still keep up the fight. "About the only thing the Russians have consistently beaten during the war is a retreat," sneered the Philadelphia *North American* in 1915.[3]

As additional disasters befell Czarist armies, it became evident that the stories were true about soldiers being sent into wintry combat without proper shoes, clothing, blankets, and even rifles. They were supposed to pick up arms and boots from fallen comrades, all of which pointed to continuing graft and incompetence. Other tales credited the ignorant and lecherous priest Rasputin with exercising a malign influence over the Czar and the Czarina. His assassination on the eve of the 1917 revolution caused many of our citizens to feel more kindly toward the Empire.

---

[3] *Literary Digest*, LI, 340 (Aug. 21, 1915).

2

In March of 1917 the news reached the United States that
Nicholas II, unable to stem the tide of revolution, had been forced
to abdicate. A provisional government was formed and took steps

BREAKING INTO THE BIG LEAGUE

(From the St. Louis *Republic*, 1917, by permission of the St. Louis
Globe-Democrat.)

toward long-awaited political and social reforms, such as freedom of assembly, extension of the suffrage, the abolition of restrictions on race and religion, and the granting of privileges to minorities, including independence for Poland and virtual independence

for Finland. Tens of thousands of political exiles were reported streaming back from the mines of Siberia.[4]

These momentous changes were greeted with genuine enthusiasm in the United States. Russian democracy had at long last broken through the hard crust of despotism—or so it seemed. The Romanovs were removed; perhaps the contagion would spread to the lands of our potential enemies, Hohenzollern Germany and Hapsburg Austria-Hungary. "The Czar has abdicated. Next!" gloated the Philadelphia *Press*. Washington, after a wait of only a few days, hurriedly recognized the new provisional government —the first among the great powers to do so.

The satisfaction of our people, aside from their traditional devotion to democracy and hatred of monarchy, sprang partly from the imminence of our war with Germany. We had recently broken relations with Berlin and were about to embark upon a frenzied crusade to make the world safe for democracy. But our slogans would ring hollow if the blackest autocracy in the world were on our side. As if to prove that the United States was arrayed with righteousness, Providence (and the Russian revolutionists) removed this embarrassing incubus only three weeks before Congress formalized hostilities. In his war message President Wilson referred eloquently to the essential democracy of the Russian people, and to the Germanic character of their autocracy. "Here," he exulted, "is a fit partner for a League of Honour." We were now more than the friends we once had been; we were allies dedicated to a common cause.

American rejoicing was also inspired by the naïve supposition that Russia, now that she was a democracy, would continue the war with renewed zest. The purging of pro-German influences from the Czarist clique would eliminate an element that was in-

---

[4] Among them was the well-known Catherine Breshkovsky, the "Little Grandmother of the Russian Revolution," who favored the provisional government, but who turned against the Bolsheviks and toured the United States in 1919. See her "From the Land of the Living Death," *Atlantic Monthly*, CXIX, 686–697 (May, 1917).

efficient, corrupt, disruptive, and treasonable. Democracies, knowing the ideals for which they fought, were, we fondly believed, invariably more determined fighters. We had actually little or no appreciation of the terrible sacrifices in blood and treasure that the Russian people had already been called upon to make.

Powerful and vocal groups of hyphenates in America were likewise overjoyed, especially the Jewish-Americans. Their anti-Russianism had brought down upon them vehement accusations of pro-Germanism, and now they could support the Allied cause wholeheartedly. Poles, Finns, and other racial minorities hailed the dawn of a new era, and hundreds of former Russian subjects began the long journey from the United States back to the Old Country. American businessmen talked optimistically of a revived commercial treaty; bankers spoke hopefully of new loans. All lovers of free worship gave thanks to their God, and even the Roman Catholics, with the apparent promise of a vast new field for their faith, were prepared to bury their age-old animus against the anti-Pope Czar and his schismatic Greek Orthodox Church.

The amateurish and purblind American ambassador in the Russian capital [5] was a sixty-seven-year-old Missouri grain merchant by the name of David R. Francis. Lacking any real knowledge of Russia, he egregiously misled Washington as to the prospects of the provisional government. President Wilson, acting upon such misinformation, dispatched a special mission for the purpose of encouraging the Russians to keep up the fight. It was headed by the wealthy and conservative elder statesman, Elihu Root, who was distasteful to the liberal and radical elements of Russia and who, repelled from intimate contact with them, could not bring back a full-length picture of what was happening. The new provisional government on its part sent a war mission to the United

---

[5] The Germanic name of St. Petersburg was changed to Petrograd in 1914 and to Leningrad in 1924. The Bolsheviks moved the capital to Moscow in 1918, partly to secure greater defense in depth against potential enemies.

States. The visitors were enthusiastically received by both the House of Representatives and the Senate, and succeeded in persuading our government to advance some $187,000,000, none of which was ever repaid.

3

In the summer of 1917 the provisional government launched a new offensive against the Austro-German forces which, after early victories, collapsed miserably. The radicals meanwhile had been weakening the will of the masses to fight. Conspicuous among the agitators were Nicolai Lenin, whom the German High Command, hoping to produce dissension, had permitted to cross Germany from Switzerland in a sealed railway car, and Leon Trotsky, who had only recently been the editor of a radical sheet in New York City. The slogans of the Bolsheviks—"Loot the Looters," "No annexations, no indemnities," "Peace, Land, and Bread," and "All Power to the Soviets"—proved pervasively disruptive.

The lid blew off when, in November, 1917, the Bolsheviks seized power, with Lenin and Trotsky in leading roles, and with the virtually unknown Stalin in a secondary post. Sweeping changes were instituted, some more rapidly than others. The peasants were given the land (which was soon nationalized), and the workingmen were given control of the factories (which were later nationalized). Banks were nationalized and private accounts were seized. Churches and church property were confiscated, religious instruction in the schools was abolished, and God was exiled. The debts of the Empire and the provisional government were completely repudiated, partly as a gesture of defiance to bourgeois capitalism, although somewhat later the Bolsheviks indicated a willingness to discuss a mutual scaling down of claims. Secret treaties were exhumed from the archives and published, in an effort to expose the wickedness of the Czar and his imperialistic allies.

The Bolshevik revolution burst upon the outside world with staggering force. Conservative and capitalistic America, repelled

234

by even mild socialism, was scandalized by Communistic methods and programs. Wealthy Americans, dedicated to the sanctity of private property, were shocked by the brutal seizure of land, factories, and other agencies of production. Our bankers and tax-payers were alarmed by the cavalier repudiation of financial obligations, a considerable amount of which was held by American investors. Religionists were shocked by the fate of the churches, all the more so when lurid stories arrived relating how the "godless" Bolshevik "Jews" had enthroned atheism and turned temples of worship into houses of ill fame. The New York *Tribune* condemned the revolutionists as "embittered paranoiac adventurers," while a correspondent of the New York *Times* wrote of the "nightmare in a lunatic asylum." George Kennan, who had welcomed the March revolution, branded the Bolsheviks a "usurping gang," and soon was urging that we send troops to Russia to help overthrow the new despotism.[6] Perhaps the only influential segment of the press that reacted sympathetically to the Bolshevik "democracy" was the Hearst chain, but for various reasons Hearst ultimately reversed himself and became one of the most implacable foes of the "Reds."

The Bolsheviks were not only a menace to capitalistic society but more immediately they were a threat to the success of what they condemned as the "imperialistic" war then being waged by the Allies. Almost simultaneously with the Russian revolution, the Italian front began to collapse under the German-Austrian sledge hammer. If the Bolsheviks withdrew Russia from the conflict, thereby releasing several hundred thousand German veterans for the western front, the democracies might be overwhelmed. The vast resources of Russia would then be available to Germany, which would be able to prolong the struggle by billions of dollars and millions of lives. "The Bolsheviki," exclaimed the Houston *Chronicle*, "are as dangerous to organized government as are the Hohenzollerns and Hapsburgs, and probably more so."[7]

---

[6] *Outlook,* CXXI, 218 (Feb. 5, 1919).

[7] *Literary Digest,* LV, 16 (Dec. 8, 1917).

Hostile though the American people were to the Bolshevik revolution, they were not so deeply interested as they should have been in these faraway and confused events. The belief was current in the United States that the usurpers were such violent extremists that they would soon kill themselves off with crazy ideas, and thus make room for a genuinely democratic growth. They were so negligible a minority—they *were* a minority—that they would soon fall from power. When the liberty-drunk Russian masses sobered down, their essential "democracy" would reassert itself and they would soon be back in the war. We did not think too kindly of the defunct provisional government anyhow. It had courted its own death by dealing too mildly with the radicals. It had been somewhat socialistic, and we were suspicious of socialists. "Socialism," remarked the Detroit *Journal* in 1919, "is Bolshevism with a shave." [8]

The delusion was also current that the revolution had been cooked up by the German High Command, which was merely using Trotsky and Lenin as tools, and as a result the whole Bolshevik edifice would soon collapse of its own weight. This partly explains why our press and people took so little notice of the sensational secret treaties, which our allies had earlier made with one another for dividing up the spoils of battle, and which the Bolsheviks had so rudely published. Was not this exposé only a German-Bolshevik hoax designed to sow dissension between us and our allies?

4

If the Washington government was deceived by the on-the-spot misrepresentations of Ambassador Francis, the American people were no less completely deceived by their own press. Our conservative newspapers deliberately or unconsciously slanted their news columns against the usurping regime. The New York *Times*, according to a study made by Walter Lippmann and Charles Merz for the period from November, 1917, to November,

---

[8] *Ibid.*, LXIII, 20 (Nov. 29, 1919).

1919, referred to the probable fall of the Bolsheviks no fewer than ninety-one times.[9] If such was the practice of so distinguished a daily, one can well imagine the tactics of less reliable journals. In addition, anti-Bolshevik propaganda in the United States was

SVENGALI

(From the Newark *News*, 1917, by permission.)

being disseminated by disillusioned or conservative Russians, many of whom were traveling or remaining in America for their "health." Conspicuous among them was the orphaned Russian ambassador, whom we continued to recognize for more than five years after the fall of the provisional government.

---

[9] *New Republic*, XXIII, 299 (Aug. 11, 1920).

The Washington administration cautiously withheld recognition from the Bolsheviks, in glaring contrast to its open-armed welcome of the March revolutionists. Wilson himself was a strong noninterventionist and self-determinist, and not unwilling to let the dust settle in the hope that a triumphant democracy would emerge. If one could assume, as many Americans did, that Leninism was but a passing phase, the United States would merely prejudice good relations with the succeeding government if it opened premature negotiations with the Bolsheviks.

Thus from the very beginning every instinct of our administration and people was to turn against the new gang of revolutionaries. The argument is now used, especially in Communist circles, that *because* of this unfriendliness the Bolsheviks *developed* a strong enmity for the United States. The fact is that even before the fugitive Lenin and other Communists reached prostrate Russia, they had in their writings and speeches declared ideological warfare on the capitalistic world, of which the United States was rapidly becoming the most powerful pillar. Before leaving New York to undo the provisional regime, Trotsky urged his followers to keep on organizing until they were able "to overthrow this damned rotten capitalistic government." [10] All this was before Washington had an opportunity to declare itself, or to support counterrevolutionary movements.

In December, 1917—a month after the Bolsheviks seized power —the new Communist clique appropriated 2,000,000 rubles for the use of its agents abroad in promoting world revolution.[11] In other ways—and many months before American armed intervention—the Bolshevik directorate proclaimed its undying hostility to the decadent capitalistic world. Significantly in 1919, less than two years after the Leninist coup in Russia, the Communist party of the United States, with well-established Moscow connections, sprang into being. From such tiny seeds was destined to grow an enormous crop of ill will.

[10] *World's Work*, XXXIX, 477 (March, 1920).
[11] *Trends in Russian Foreign Policy since World War I* (Washington, 1947), p. 2.

XX

The Red Specter
of Bolshevism

"Bolshevism is merely czarism in overalls."
—Dexter (Missouri) *Statesman*, 1918

I

THE Bolsheviks first sought a general armistice, and failing to secure one, attempted to withdraw from the war singlehandedly. Unsuccessful in this also, they were finally compelled at bayonet point, in March, 1918, to sign with Germany the humiliating treaty of Brest Litovsk, by which they lost about a fourth of their population and much of their most valuable territory.

The Allies and the United States, left to continue the conflict alone, were shocked and angered by what they regarded as an act of perfidy. The legend took quick root, in ignorance of their immense sacrifices, that the Russians were cowardly quitters. "Trotsky might get the ignoble peace prize," jeered the Raleigh (North Carolina) *News and Observer*. Hearst's Baltimore *American* castigated the work of "a group of lewd fellows of the baser sort: filthy pocket-pickers and despicable degenerates of lucre." With a strong suggestion of sour grapes, the Kansas City *Star* rationalized: "Well, if Russia is lost to us, all right. We never did want to make the world safe for the Bolshevik kind of democracy anyway." [1]

American public opinion warmly supported the decision of President Wilson neither to recognize nor to have dealings with the Bolsheviks. We still sympathized with the unfortunate Russian people, and there was some little demand for armed inter-

WHAT'S THE DIFFERENCE?

(From the St. Louis *Post-Dispatch*, 1918, by permission.)

vention to help them throw from their backs this new and more terrible tyranny. We were also neck-deep in a desperate war with Germany, and since relations with Moscow were secondary to victory, we were under strong compulsion to assist the counter-revolutionists in the hope of keeping Russia in the conflict. At all costs those powerful German divisions had to be pinned down

[1] *Literary Digest*, LVI, 14 (Jan. 12, 1918); LVIII, 16 (Sept. 28, 1918).

on the eastern front. A few Americans even entertained the thought that we might have to fight a second conflict, once we had disposed of the Kaiser, this time to make the world safe against Bolshevism.

After the surrender at Brest Litovsk, the confusion in Russia thickened. There were separatist movements on the periphery, civil wars within (Reds versus Whites), interventions from without, and assaults on the flanks, including invasion from Turkey. The central core of the nation was attacked from every point of the compass: north, south, east, and west. At one time, when Bolshevik fortunes were at lowest ebb, Russia was reduced to approximately the size of medieval Muscovy.

From the north an Allied expedition operating out of Archangel marched to within some 400 miles of Moscow (January, 1919). From the east (Siberia) a White army under Admiral Kolchak came within some 500 miles of Moscow (May, 1919); from the south a White force under General Denikin advanced to within about 175 miles of Moscow (October, 1919); and from the west a White detachment under General Yudenich penetrated to a point seven miles from Petrograd (October, 1919). This complicated picture does not take into account the subsequent invasion by Poland from the west or that by the White General Wrangel from the south.[2]

2

Two of these foreign interventions involved the United States. An Allied expedition occupied Murmansk and Archangel, in northern Russia on the Arctic Ocean, in the summer of 1918. The primary objectives were initially to encourage local resistance to the Germans and to keep huge quantities of military supplies from falling into German hands. Later the invaders co-operated with the counterrevolutionaries (Whites) against the Bolsheviks

---

[2] F. L. Schuman, *American Policy toward Russia since 1917* (New York, 1928), p. 181.

(Reds), thereby drawing upon themselves the wrath of Moscow.

The United States contributed some 5,000 troops to the Arch-angel intervention, upon assurances that they were to guard military stores and to render such aid as was acceptable to the Russian people without interference in their internal affairs. The American press at the outset seems to have been rather favorable to the enterprise, although some fear was expressed that a foreign invader would rally the people behind the Bolsheviks. But armed support of the Whites inevitably led to clashes with the Reds, in which American boys lost their lives. A regiment from Michigan was frozen in at Archangel, and the confused doughboys sent home "gripe" letters, some of which were published in the local newspapers. One of them wrote:

> It's the land of the infernal odor,
> The land of the national smell,
> The average United States soldier
> Would rather be quartered in L.[3]

The United States had gone to war to fight Germany, not the Bolsheviks, and indignation meetings were held in Michigan against Wilson's undeclared and unauthorized war in North Russia. The junior United States Senator from Michigan, Charles E. Townsend, reported that he was receiving hundreds of letters and telegrams from outraged parents. Following a minor mutiny and other difficulties, the American troops were finally withdrawn, in July, 1919, after having suffered more than 500 casualties. The Allies felt betrayed, the Bolsheviks were embittered, and the Americans were bewildered.

3

Wilsonian intervention in Siberia was undertaken on a considerably larger scale and involved about 9,000 United States troops. For the ostensible purpose of rescuing a marooned contingent of some 45,000 Czecho-Slovak soldiers who could be used

---

[3] *Literary Digest*, LX, 99 (Feb. 8, 1919).

in France, as well as keeping military supplies from falling into Bolshevik hands, a joint Allied intervention was undertaken in 1918. Wilson joined the enterprise with extreme reluctance, and partially for the purpose of restraining the Japanese, who were clearly taking advantage of the European conflict to promote their imperialistic ambitions at the expense of Russia.[4]

Strange as it may seem, the ill-starred Siberian expedition received considerable public support in the United States. For one thing, the unfortunate Czechs, who had many cousins in the United States, caught the popular fancy. Some Americans actually criticized the administration for not starting sooner, on a larger scale, and with less ambiguous objectives.

Determined though Wilson was not to side with the Whites against the Reds, American troops were gradually sucked into the morass. One of our main objectives was to protect the trans-Siberian railroad, in the interests of succoring the Czechs, but keeping open this line meant that we were ensuring supplies for the White Admiral Kolchak, who was the most serious threat to Red Moscow. Bolshevik bands attacked American guards, killing thirty-six, and the guards shot back. The Reds were angry because we were indirectly helping their enemies; the Whites were bitter because we did not help enough; the Allies were displeased because we had such limited objectives; and the Japanese were suspicious because we so obviously were trying to hamper their ambitions. Actually, by opposing Japanese designs we were promoting the territorial integrity of Russia.

After the Allied Armistice with Germany in November, 1918, the Siberian expedition simply failed to make sense. The Czechs had been evacuated; military supplies could no longer help the Germans. Why continue to fight unknown enemies for unrevealed reasons? The parents of the American boys, who had been drafted for other purposes, brought great pressure to bear on their

---

[4] The anti-Japanese purpose of the intervention could obviously not be made public at the time. See Pauline Tompkins, *American-Russian Relations in the Far East* (New York, 1949), pp. 47 ff.

representatives in Congress to bring the lads home. Republican partisans, who were accelerating the postwar drift toward isolation, lambasted the Democratic Woodrow Wilson for his unconstitutional private war. The last American contingent was withdrawn from Siberia in 1920, while a Japanese band, reflecting the satisfaction of the Tokyo imperialists, played, "Hard Times Come Again No More."

The objectives of the United States in the Archangel and Siberian expeditions were not avowedly anti-Bolshevik. But in the case of Admiral Kolchak, whom the Allies backed as the principal White hope, the story was different. After extracting pledges from him that he would work for the freedom of the Russian people and recognize foreign debts, Wilson joined the Allies in a program of economic support and military supplies for Kolchak. The United States also co-operated with the Allies in sending food and munitions to the Poles during their war with Russia in 1920.

Wilson's unofficial and backhanded clashes with the Bolsheviks weaken the allegation that Russia is the one great power with which we have never had an armed conflict. Some American newspaper editors freely stated that by participating in intervention we were actually waging war on the Bolsheviks. Spokesmen for the new revolutionary government were not backward about echoing the same charges.[5]

At all events, the active intervention of the Allies, rather feebly seconded by the United States, enabled the Russian Communists to raise the cry of capitalistic encirclement, and call upon patriotic citizens to repel the invader of Russian soil. Fearful that imprisoned Nicholas II would be released by the foreign-supported White invaders, the Bolsheviks cold-bloodedly murdered him and his family in July, 1918. His death caused no great sorrow in the United States, where we have usually applauded the abrupt termination of royal dynasties. Yet if we were indifferent to the passing of Nicholas II, the Bolsheviks were not indifferent to the armed intervention of the Allies and the United States. We were

---

[5] See *Literary Digest*, LVIII, 9 (Sept. 21, 1918).

savagely condemned, along with our associates. But both we and our comrades in arms had already been liberally condemned before becoming involved in any of these dubious enterprises, and our actions merely served to intensify and justify a hatred that had existed before the beginning of the Communist experiment in Russia.

THE GOVERNMENT OF RUSSIA

(From the New York *World*, 1918, by permission.)

4

In August, 1918, a female revolutionist wounded Lenin with her revolver and touched off the full-blown Red Terror, which was accelerated by the nervous tension resulting from beleaguered Russia's desperate plight. Hundreds of persons, chiefly from the upper and middle classes, were done to death. Kill a thousand today, ran the Bolshevist philosophy, so as to ensure the happiness of thousands tomorrow. Lurid reports reaching America told of streets running with blood and of a new electrically driven guillotine capable of decapitating 500 persons an hour. A corresponding White Terror accounted for the butchering of uncounted Bolshevik adherents, but American prejudices were so violently anti-Red that little account was taken of these atrocities, even when they were mentioned in our conservative press, which they often were not.

At the Paris Peace Conference in 1919 Wilson sought to secure Russian representation, but no agreement could be reached as to what faction represented the entire nation. Still wedded to nonintervention, Wilson resolutely resisted French and other schemes to crush what Winston Churchill called "the foul baboonery of Bolshevism." Wilson himself finally came to believe that the new dictatorship in Russia was just as selfish, ruthless, and pitiless as that of the Czars, but his heart went out to the ill-starred masses.[6] He did co-operate with the Allied blockade against the Bolsheviks to the extent of an embargo, which appears to have commanded public support in America and which was not substantially lifted until 1920. This, in a very real sense, was waging economic war on Bolshevist Russia.

A disquieting element was injected into an already dynamite-laden situation when in March, 1919, the first congress of the newly formed Communist (Third) International—the so-called Comintern—met in Moscow and proclaimed a program of world revolution. "Down with the Imperialistic Conspiracy of Capital!" was its clarion call to the workers of every land. The Comintern attempted to maintain the fiction of independence, but its leaders were also the leaders of the Communist party in Russia and of the government of Russia. Lenin, the most important member of this interlocking directorate, had merely to change hats to discharge his different functions.

---

[6] R. S. Baker and W. E. Dodd, *The Public Papers of Woodrow Wilson, 1917–1924* (New York, 1927), II, 70 (Sept. 9, 1919).

During the turmoil of revolution and terror, and even later, the American press continued to be conspicuously unfriendly to the Bolsheviks, and to give unquestioning credence to forged documents and other propaganda emanating from Russian exiles. The most noteworthy exceptions were the New York *Nation* and the *New Republic*, both leading liberal journals without large circulations. Both of them believed that hostility rather than cordiality toward the new regime was merely accelerating undesirable trends. But leading socialists, like John Spargo, were distressed by the Communist betrayal of socialist ideals. A writer in the conservative *Saturday Evening Post* spoke of "despotism by the dregs," while the British correspondent E. J. Dillon wrote for American readers that "Bolshevism is Tzarism upside down." [7] Other commentators found that Ivan the Terrible was a kindly character compared with these "beasts drunk from a saturnalia of crime." The press continued to write in shocked terms of the alleged "nationalization of women" and "the Bureau of Free Love." Such stereotypes were further strengthened by a somewhat sensational senatorial investigation of communism in 1919.

5

Fear of Bolshevism among patriotic Americans found a spectacular outlet in the Great Red Scare of 1919. An epidemic of strikes then sweeping the country, many of them the natural result of skyrocketing prices, was commonly referred to as Moscow-inspired, especially the spectacular outbursts in Seattle and Boston. In the spring of 1919, while Hungary was going Bolshevik, a number of packages containing infernal machines were discovered in the New York post office bearing the addresses of prominent personages, and subsequently a series of explosions occurred in different cities, including a blast that wrecked both the home and nerves of Attorney General Palmer. This official, known as the "Fighting Quaker," undertook vigorous repressive measures,

---

[7] See Meno Lovenstein, *American Opinion of Soviet Russia* (Washington, 1941), p. 35.

which included exclusion of a Socialist newspaper from the mails. "Too many persons in this country are enjoying the right of free screech," agreed the Brooklyn *Eagle*.

Most conspicuous of Palmer's activities was the rounding up of hundreds of so-called Reds. A popular song caught the spirit of the hour, "If you don't like your Uncle Sammy, then go back to your home over sea." In 1919 a total of 249 undesirables were loaded onto an American transport, satirically known as the "Soviet Ark," and bundled off to the Russian "paradise." Prominent among them were the veteran anarchists Emma Goldman and Alexander Berkman, who added notoriety to what one newspaper called the "unholiest cargo that ever left our shores." Enthusiastically applauding the "deportation delirium," Guy Empey wrote, "My motto for the Reds is S.O.S.—ship or shoot. I believe we should place them all on a ship of stone, with sails of lead, and that their first stopping place should be hell." [8]

One prospective deportee was an emissary from the Soviet government, L. C. A. K. Martens by name, who had established offices in New York City for the ostensible purpose of opening trade relations. Snubbed by Washington, he issued statements designed to paint a more roseate picture of Russia, as a consequence of which he was accused of disseminating Communist propaganda. In imminent danger of deportation following an adverse ruling in December, 1920, he left voluntarily rather than involuntarily. (His experience in some respects was even less pleasant than that of Francis Dana at St. Petersburg, 1781–1783.)

The Red Scare was primarily a domestic disease, and more important as a manifestation of the overwrought emotionalism of the war than as an incident in Russian-American relations. But it further seared into the American public mind the familiar stereotype of a bloodthirsty, bewhiskered, bomb-throwing, free-loving Bolshevik.

The position of the Wilson administration, as emphatically set

[8] Quoted in Foster R. Dulles, *The Road to Teheran* (Princeton, 1944), p. 164.

forth in a note by Secretary of State Colby, was that the United States would have no official traffic with the Communist regime. Though a minority, they had usurped and destroyed popular gov-

ON THE THRESHOLD!

A typical Red Scare cartoon. (From the Los Angeles *Times*, 1920, by permission.)

ernment. They had repudiated their lawful debts. Openly boasting of bad faith as an instrument of national policy, they were not only a menace to our institutions but to law, order, and the sanctity of international dealings. They were committed to unceasing international propaganda for world revolution through their diplomatic establishments, and also through the subterfuge of the Comintern. Such was the pronouncement of Secretary Colby in 1920.[9]

The general feeling in America, among both officials and citizenry, was that the masses of Russia had merely changed chains, and that after a few fitful glimpses of liberty they had been betrayed and enslaved by a despotism more diabolical than anything conjured up by the Czars. They had never known real democracy; one form of autocracy had just slipped into another. The New York *World* branded the new Russia as "the Judas of the nations." The Czar had been objectionable, but whatever his shortcomings, he had not launched a militant and revolutionary attack upon the institutions of free people everywhere.

[9] *Foreign Relations, 1920* (Washington, 1936), III, 463–468 (Aug. 10, 1920).

XXI

Reds Become Pinker

"If Uncle Sam didn't know Russia, he
might recognize her."—Toledo *Blade*, 1923

I

THE electoral tidal wave of 1920 swept the Harding
administration into office, and the Moscow government,
hoping for more cordial treatment from the victorious
apostles of normalcy, again sought to open diplomatic and commercial relations with the United States. But Secretary of State
Charles Evans Hughes spurned the Russian overture, baited
though it was with the prospect of business profits. His view was
essentially that of the preceding administration and every succeeding administration during the twelve years of Republican
supremacy. He insisted that we would have no truck with the
Bolshevik faction as long as it repudiated its lawful debts, refused
to make reparation for confiscated American property, and
abused the hospitality of friendly nations by sending abroad
agents to foment a Communist revolution.

Patriotic American editors vigorously applauded Secretary
Hughes as he broke his lance for international morality and
decency. "Thus we stand four square for liberty and justice,"
declared the Grand Rapids (Michigan) *News*. "The United
States refuses to sell its honor for a ton of Russian gold." [1] The

---

[1] *Literary Digest*, LXIX, 12 (April 9, 1921).

Soviets risked another rebuff in 1923, and received it in even more emphatic language. Again Secretary Hughes was rewarded with a chorus of commendation, especially for the "ring of righteous wrath." The Philadelphia *Enquirer* remarked that it was bad enough to countenance confiscation and repudiation, but "to ask us to embrace such brigands and murderers when we know that they are seeking to stab us in the back is to go upon the assumption that the American people are both blind and feeble-minded." [2]

Secretary Hughes again snubbed the Russian government when he omitted it from the list of powers invited to the highly publicized Washington Disarmament Conference of 1921–1922. Moscow promptly filed notice that it would not be bound by any decisions reached at that conclave. But at the Washington Conference the United States did help to ease Japan out of Siberia, in pursuance of our policy of not countenancing the dismemberment of a once great Empire. We actually held off recognizing the formerly Russian Baltic states until after the Allies and Russia herself had done so.

The Soviet regime had meanwhile taken a giant stride toward respectability. Confronted with the breakdown of Communistic methods, Lenin in 1921 adopted the New Economic Policy, which was confessedly a "strategic" retreat, over socialistic paths, toward hated capitalism. While this was avowedly a temporary maneuver, many of the devices and incentives of capitalism were adopted, including private trade, private property, and the abandonment of wage fixing. The true significance of this partial surrender was not fully recognized by the American people, then or later, and the comforting thought found lodgment in some quarters that before too long the prodigal Russians would be back in the capitalistic fold.[3]

---

[2] *Ibid.*, LXXX, 11 (Jan. 5, 1924).

[3] The theory of the Soviet leaders was that once they had attained socialism they could move on to communism.

2

In the spring and summer of 1921 a terrible famine again descended upon Russia, centering in the rich Volga area and threatening some 30,000,000 people with a lingering death. Many Americans regarded the catastrophe as divine retribution for Bolshevist crimes. A searing drought was no doubt the precipitating cause, but hardly less important was the chaos wrought by war, revolution, intervention, blockade, nationalization, and runaway inflation. "Russia," declared the Louisville *Post*, "appears to have abolished about everything except hell and hunger." [4]

Conditions became so desperate that in July, 1921, the well-known Russian writer Maxim Gorky, presumably acting at the behest of the Moscow government, appealed to "All Honest People" in Europe and America for aid. "Give bread and medicine," he pleaded.[5] We detested Bolshevism and all its works, but our sympathies still went out to the Communist-ridden Russian people. The bewildered masses, especially the children, were not responsible for the sins of the Communists, and we responded with some enthusiasm to the elemental dictates of humanity.

Many of our more calculating citizens concluded that since Russia was now turning to capitalism and democracy, we had a heaven-sent opportunity to accelerate this desirable trend through famine relief, and at the same time revive the historic friendship. Still others thought that on the ground of self-preservation alone we ought to help; Bolsheviks driven to desperation might go berserk and seek diversion in foreign wars. On the other hand, a small group of suspicious Americans feared that famine relief was designed to trick us into granting recognition, while one Socialist paper complained that we were unfairly exploiting the opportunity to conquer communism with kindness.

Lenin and his cohorts were at all events placed in a humiliating

---

[4] *Literary Digest*, LXX, 17 (Sept. 10, 1921).

[5] H. H. Fisher, *The Famine in Soviet Russia, 1919–1923* (New York, 1927), p. 52.

position by having to solicit aid from the hated transatlantic republic. To permit Americans to disburse alms in Russia would advertise the fact that under capitalism we were wallowing in abundance, while under communism the Russians were perishing in destitution. The Moscow government also feared that any American agency distributing food would adopt Communist tactics and discriminate in favor of antirevolutionary elements, thus conniving at the downfall of the Great Experiment. The foreign loaf was more to be feared than the foreign sword. The Russian leaders could not comprehend why we would dispense charity to their people while refusing to recognize their government. Surely there was some ulterior motive—at least this was the understandable reaction of pathologically suspicious minds.

Secretary of Commerce Herbert Hoover, world-famed for his large-scale benefactions in Belgium and elsewhere, was authorized to handle the problem under the American Relief Administration. His well-known anti-Bolshevik bias did nothing to quiet the distrust of the Russian rulers, who then and decades later accused him of having deliberately doled out food to anti-Communist elements.

The Kremlin was in a poor position to bargain, so an agreement was finally worked out for the gigantic American Relief program, similar to that used elsewhere in Europe. Moscow was to release the eight or so Americans then held prisoners, and provide facilities and full co-operation for the necessary work, including freedom of movement. On its part, the Relief Administration agreed to engage in no propaganda and to dispense aid impartially to all classes and sections.[6]

President Harding, after appealing to the ancient friendship, secured from Congress an appropriation of $20,000,000. The American farm bloc, nothing loath to dispose of embarrassing grain surpluses, supported the relief program with enthusiasm. A total of $66,300,000 was raised, counting private benefactions. Among these were contributions by Communist organizations in

---

[6] See text of the agreement in *ibid.*, pp. 507–510.

the United States, who labored zealously to see to it that their efforts helped the "cause." About 90 per cent of all relief going to Russia came from the United States, in all nearly one million short tons of food, to say nothing of clothing for the tattered and

HARD TO HELP

American sympathies were with the Russian people rather than with their leaders during the famine. (From the Philadelphia *Evening Ledger*, 1921.)

medicines for the victims of cholera and typhus. The lives of an estimated 10,500,000 persons were saved, many of them children who later indirectly and unwittingly repaid their debt to America by halting the German invader at Stalingrad and elsewhere.

Famine conditions persisted from 1921 well into 1923, when the American Relief Administration closed up shop. The Russian masses were undoubtedly grateful for our succor, when they were able to recognize its source, which they could not always do because of the tactics of the Soviet officials. Among other things, numerous posters of the Relief Administration were mysteriously torn down. The Communist dictators remained distrustful to the very end, and charges were freely made on both sides that the original agreement had been broken. The Soviets later accused us —and there was some truth in the charge—of having helped them because we had to shore up our sagging economy by exporting surpluses.

A new element of friction entered the picture in 1923 when, in the midst of starvation, Moscow began to export considerable supplies of grain, even from the famine-stricken Volga area.[7] The American press was severely critical of what it regarded as characteristic double-dealing by the Bolsheviks, while the Soviets alleged that transportation deficiencies forced them to export surpluses from certain areas and with the proceeds import supplies or farm equipment into others. At any rate the American public had done its somewhat distasteful duty—the Dallas *News* spoke of sending "soup to nuts"—while the Soviet hierarchy had even more ungraciously accepted the "tainted" charity.

3

A great-power conference was held at Genoa in 1922, and the machinations of the Soviet delegation did nothing to allay American distrust. The Moscow representatives expressed a willingness to discuss the Allied claims amounting to $13,000,000,000, in return for a consideration of counterclaims for $60,000,000,000 growing out of the Allied blockade and intervention—a sum which the Soviets indicated they might scale down to $25,000,-000,000. No meeting of minds was possible in the face of such preposterously inflated estimates, and the conference broke down in failure, but not until Moscow had negotiated a sensational treaty with Germany at Rapallo. If the two great outcast nations pooled their strength, they might menace the world. The New

[7] New York *Times,* Feb. 21, 1923.

York *Herald-Tribune* referred to the pact as "an alliance of hatreds."

The menace of communism seemed to weaken perceptibly when in 1924 Lenin died. American editors greeted his death with such unflattering phrases as "another Scourge of God," "the Judas of the real Russian revolution," and "one of the great wreckers of history," who had attained "the very eminence of infamy." [8] Joseph Stalin—silent, smiling, sinister—gradually wrapped the mantle of succession about him, and on the whole his advent seemed to Americans an agreeable change in the direction of moderation. Willing to achieve his objectives patiently and in Russia first, he broke with the wildly radical Trotsky in 1926 and in a public speech said, whether sincerely or not, "We have had enough of that idiotic slogan, 'The World Revolution.' " [9]

Nervousness in America regarding the Soviet Union continued to wane in the late 1920's, despite lurid reports of Communist gains in China, despite the spectacular break in relations between Britain and Russia over Communist infiltration, and despite the attempts of Secretary of State Kellogg to blame our troubles in Latin America on Bolshevik agents. These were the days of booming Coolidgean prosperity, and communism could have no possible appeal to a well-fed proletariat who rode to the factories in shiny new automobiles.

Maxim Litvinov, speaking for Moscow at a meeting of the League of Nations preparatory committee on disarmament in 1927, exploded a "peace bomb" when he urged immediate and complete disarmament. The Red army was rapidly becoming the largest in the world, and many Americans viewed the Soviet proposal with distrust, just as they had Nicholas II's Hague call in 1898. "We have learned," remarked the Montgomery *Advertiser*, "to look at the tonsils of every gift horse in their stable." A large number of American editors applauded the theory of disarmament, but there was a general feeling that the Russians,

---

[8] *Literary Digest*, LXXX, 8 (Feb. 2, 1924).
[9] *Ibid.*, XCI, 8 (Oct. 30, 1926).

knowing that the scheme would prove completely unacceptable, or if accepted would leave the other nations at their mercy, had made the proposal so that their propagandists could point to the warmongering designs of the capitalistic powers. "Soviet Russia's disarmament gesture," opined one Oregon newspaper, "somehow carries the suggestion of a dove hatched in a buzzard's nest." [10] The same response generally greeted similar Moscow proposals during the next two decades or more.

In 1928, with the avowed objective of achieving socialism first in one country, the Soviet Union announced the first of its gigantic Five-Year Plans, plans that were designed to raise the industrial level and physical well-being of the nation. "Overtake and pass America," became the slogan of the hour, as the tractor replaced the ikon in Russian worship. These significant developments seemed to be a further veering away from world revolution —an interpretation that was further confirmed by the expulsion of Trotsky in 1929. Subsequent claims by Moscow as to the success of its huge industrial program were received in the United States with the skepticism that usually greeted Soviet statistics. Doubts were further deepened by the liquidation of the prosperous land-owning kulaks in 1928–1933, with a brutality and ruthlessness that brought death to countless thousands and dispossession to millions.

Secretary of State Kellogg administered a slap to Russia when in 1928 he failed to invite the Soviets to become signatories of the somewhat naïve Kellogg-Briand peace pact. Communist promises had proved worthless; besides righteous Uncle Sam would make no treaties with "bandits." Soviet Russia became a signatory anyhow. In 1929, when Secretary of State Stimson attempted to invoke the pact during the undeclared war between the Soviet Union and China over the Chinese Eastern Railway, he was stingingly rebuked by the Moscow Foreign Office for presuming to give advice to a government that we would not even recognize.[11]

---

[10] *Ibid.*, XCV, 12 (Dec. 17, 1927); XCVI, 15 (March 17, 1928).

[11] Actually, the State Department was sympathetic toward the Soviet case. See

4

The troubled events of the early 1930's did little to remove American distaste for the Soviet experiment, even though we were taking it more and more for granted. Herbert Hoover, the Great Engineer in Politics, was striving desperately to pull the country out of the quicksands of depression. The Soviet press sneered at his despairing efforts to salvage the corpse of capitalism, pointed gleefully to the absence of unemployment under the Five-Year Plan, and loudly recommended Marxism as the inevitable solution. American commentators found some solace in the retort that there is no unemployment in a penitentiary, and that the serfs of the Czars had become the slaves of the Commissars.

The civilized world was puzzled and to some extent startled when in 1930 the Soviet government brought to trial eight professors and engineers, on grounds of sabotage and connivance at foreign military intervention. This was the first treason trial ever broadcast by radio; and all the defendants glibly confessed their guilt in open court, thus evoking satiric admiration in America for the efficacy of Communist third-degree methods. There was a widespread feeling that the whole affair was a "frame-up," perhaps for the purpose of finding a scapegoat for the ultimate failure of the Five-Year Plan. Referring pointedly to President Hoover and the depression, one American newspaper observed, "The Russians blame all of their troubles on eight engineers instead of one." [12]

In 1930–1931 there was a tendency among our conservatives to attribute some of our depression ills to unfair Communist trade practices. Operating through the Amtorg Trading Corporation of New York, the Soviets were exporting considerable quantities of low-priced products to the United States, including wood pulp. Angry charges were made that the Russians were driving

Pauline Tompkins, *American-Russian Relations in the Far East* (New York, 1949), p. 245.
[12] *Literary Digest*, CVIII, 11 (Jan. 31, 1931).

American business to the wall by dumping convict-made goods below cost. Washington responded to such agitation by clamping a temporary embargo on wood pulp. The American press published horrifying accounts of how millions of persons were forced to work in convict camps for sixteen to eighteen hours a day, and

THE RUSSIAN WORKMEN'S GOVERNMENT

(From the St. Louis *Post-Dispatch*, 1920, by permission.)

of how "many" of them hacked off their hands to escape this form of torture. Soviet spokesmen vehemently denied that there was dumping by enslaved labor; besides, western capitalists had better give thought to the millions of colored peoples "enslaved" in their colonial systems.

Tales from Russia continued to black-eye the Soviet dictatorship, what with famine, theft, graft, and the spy trial of six British engineers, energetically prosecuted by Andrei Y. Vishinsky. But as the withering hand of depression continued to lay hold of American economic life, the thought of establishing formal ties with the Soviet Union became more attractive. "A 'dangerous Red,'" quipped the El Paso *Herald*, "is any Russian who appears in America without placing an order for machinery." [13] The Moscow Communists took another stride toward rectitude when in 1931 Stalin, in a sensational speech, indicated that the Soviets were turning even more sharply toward capitalistic methods.[14] These were seemingly blessed with success, for in 1933 the Soviet Union announced, with deafening fanfare, the premature completion of the first Five-Year Plan.

But by 1933 the international crisis, hardly less than the economic crisis, was causing the United States to see Soviet Russia in a less reddish hue. In 1931 the Nipponese imperialists had broken loose in Manchuria; in 1933 Adolf Hitler had strong-armed his way into power in Germany. Now was the time for all peace-loving nations to join hands against the aggressors or would-be aggressors.

In the United States the political overturn of 1932 had cleared the tables for a New Deal. Herbert Hoover, who disliked the Soviets and who was cordially hated by them, despite his famine relief succor of 1921–1923, was swept aside in favor of the more liberal Franklin D. Roosevelt, who as a Democrat was not committed to either the prejudices or policies of his Republican predecessors. The stage was set for recognition.

---

[13] *Ibid.*, CVI, 11 (Aug. 16, 1930).
[14] *Ibid.*, CX, 11 (July 18, 1931).

XXII

The Right Hand

of Recognition

"If this country recognizes Russia, it should also take steps to recognize the difficulty of getting along with Russia."—San Diego *Union*, 1933

I

TO THE bitter end a powerful body of Americans, though apparently not a majority, opposed official recognition of the Soviet Union. What in brief were their grievances? Repudiation of debts by the Bolsheviks still rankled. To welcome Russia into the family of nations would merely put the seal of our approval on her flouting the sanctity of contracts that are well recognized by international law. Even though the Soviet government did not pay in full, it should at least recognize the principle of its obligation as evidence of good faith and as a basis for future bargaining.

Bolshevist seizures of private property owned by American corporations and businessmen, amounting to an estimated $300,-000,000, could not be lightly brushed aside. Why should we open formal diplomatic and commercial intercourse and risk the danger of additional confiscations?

Soviet propaganda still inspired fear. Communist agents were sleeplessly active throughout the world. Both China and Great Britain, after having extended recognition, had broken relations with Moscow because of objectionable Communist propaganda. The Communist party in the United States, though small in numbers, was insidious in tactics, seeking to secure control of key labor unions and paralyze industry.

AREN'T WE HAVING ENOUGH TROUBLE WITH THE MACHINERY WITHOUT LETTING SOMEBODY THROW A MONKEY WRENCH INTO IT?

(From the Chicago *Tribune*, 1933, by permission.)

The technicality that the Communist Third International was not directly connected with the Russian government deceived few observant Americans. The Comintern was but one of the three masks worn by the Moscow clique. To extend formal recognition to the U.S.S.R. would merely enable the Russians to open an embassy and consulates from which to disseminate their poisonous ideology. Any avowal of abandoning world revolution was merely designed to lull us into a false sense of security; when Soviet Russia had strengthened herself sufficiently at home she would renew her campaign. To recognize her would merely encourage her; to lend her money would merely finance further subversive activity in the United States. Nothing could be more foolish than to build up a government dedicated to tearing down the very principles of democracy for which we stood.

The disestablishment of the Greek Orthodox Church and the enshrining of godlessness continued to shock millions of religionists in America. Our press reported in 1923 that, during atheistic celebrations in Moscow, young men dressed as devils and clergymen danced around burning effigies of Moses, Mohammed, and Jesus.[1] The bitterness of Roman Catholics in the United States deepened after the execution in 1923 of the Roman Catholic Monsignor Butchkavitch, following alleged tortures.

2

Other grievances still rankled with a considerable body of Americans. Many of our citizens, cherishing the remnants of the century-old sympathy for the oppressed Russian masses, regarded the existing hierarchy as an unconstitutional usurpation of the peoples' rights. The Bolsheviks had never held a free election; they had dissolved the last fairly elected constituent assembly when they found themselves in a minority. They had established not a dictatorship *of* the proletariat, but a dictatorship *over* the proletariat, by a relatively small Communist oligarchy. This was not government by the consent of the governed, in the tradition of the Declaration of Independence, and to recognize Moscow would merely blast the hopes of those liberals in Russia who were nursing the flickering flame of democracy.

The faithlessness of the Bolsheviks had become a byword among nations. "Soviet lies have made Russia's word as good as

[1] *Literary Digest*, LXXVII, 7 (April 14, 1923).

her bond(s)," observed the New York *Herald-Tribune*. The Communists were dedicated to the principle that the end justifies the means; they not only tossed overboard such bourgeois virtues as honesty, truth, and decency, but shamelessly boasted of doing so. Any agreement restricting their propaganda was not worth the paper it was written on, as other nations had learned to their sorrow. We would keep our own skirts clean and avoid inevitable squabbles by continuing our well-justified policy of nonrecognition.

To grasp the blood-stained hands of the Bolsheviks in recognition would retroactively put the stamp of our approval on all their foul deeds: the crushing of liberties, the Red Terror, the extermination of the kulaks, the slave camps, and the perversion of much that our western civilization held dear.

And how would recognition benefit the United States economically? American trade with Russia in the period before the war of 1914–1918 had risen to only a little more than one per cent of our total. To expect more was to pursue a mirage. A considerable commerce, larger than that before 1914, had sprung up even without recognition; and even this was creating friction over dumping and convict labor. A trade agreement with Moscow, like any other kind of agreement, would be violated if it proved burdensome to the Soviets. As for the loans that the anticapitalistic Communists wanted from our capitalistic coffers, who in his right mind would expose himself to further repudiation? "Lending money to Russia," said the Wall Street *Journal*, "would be borrowing trouble." [2]

Why bother to recognize the Soviet Union? The government would soon disappear when the topsy-turvy economic system collapsed, and to accord official recognition would merely prolong the agony. Besides, recognition was a serious step. Once granted, it was not easily withdrawn.

Such in general were the chief complaints of those Americans who were unfriendly to Russia. Prominent among them were

---

[2] *Ibid.*, XCVI, 17 (March 10, 1928).

Roman Catholics, and to a less embittered degree other denominations. They were joined by ultraconservative publications like the *Saturday Evening Post* and the Chicago *Tribune*. The rights of the worker had largely been swallowed by the state in Russia, and influential labor elements, notably the American Federation of Labor, would have no dealings with the Soviets. No less determined were business groups like Chambers of Commerce, to say nothing of veterans' organizations like the American Legion and patriotic societies like the Daughters of the American Revolution. Among individual opponents of recognition were the leading conservatives, such as Herbert Hoover and Hamilton Fish. Also unfriendly to the Soviet dictatorship was a growing group of disappointed radicals, including Emma Goldman, who after some unpleasant firsthand experiences, published *My Disillusionment in Russia* (1923).

3

By 1933 some of the arguments against recognition had lost much of their weight.

The depression had forced several nations, including France, to default on their debt payments to the United States, and in addition Great Britain and Italy were making only token payments. These debtors were not openly repudiating their obligations, but they were seeking renegotiation with a view to scaling them down. The Moscow government had also sought to scale down its obligations, notably at Genoa in 1922, but had likewise been rebuffed.[3]

The insistence of the Kremlin on the payment of counterclaims was difficult to parry, because United States troops in Siberia and North Russia had unquestionably caused some damage. The American debts repudiated by Moscow, amounting in all to some $650,000,000, in both public and private claims, seemed somewhat

[3] The government of the Soviet Union had established an excellent reputation for honoring its financial obligations (*The Prospects of British and American Trade with the Soviet Union*, monographs 7 and 8, published by the School of Slavonic and East European Studies in the University of London [London, 1935], p. 33).

secondary when compared with the six billion or so dollars lost by other nations. If the British and French, who were much heavier losers than we, could recognize Russia, why could not the United States? The Soviet Union moreover was faced with an insuperable obstacle. If it agreed to reimburse us in full, it would be hounded by other creditors to pay sums far beyond its capacity. Besides, any attempt to do so would alienate the Russian people, who had been strongly indoctrinated against bourgeois private property.

But by 1933 Bolshevist confiscations of American holdings rankled much less than formerly. Not only were our losses far smaller than those of some other major powers, but a number of our corporations, in negotiating new contracts for exports, had privately worked out a reasonably satisfactory adjustment of their claims.

The prevalence of Communist propaganda in the United States was undeniable, but no one had proved conclusively that the crimson thread ran back directly to the Kremlin. The era of militant, world-revolutionary communism had evidently passed; some form of capitalism in Russia seemed on the way back. Non-recognition in any event would not stop Communist propaganda, and our unfriendly attitude tended to encourage Soviet hostility. The Communist party in America, with a large foreign element in its membership, was ridiculously weak. Revolutions cannot be carried in suitcases. In our free society with its free press, democracy apparently had nothing to fear from communism; to think otherwise was to betray a lack of faith in our basic institutions. If Russia was moving away from communism toward state capitalism, the United States under Roosevelt's New Deal was moving away from capitalism toward socialism. We had less to fear from Communist propaganda than formerly.

The Greek Orthodox Church had undeniably been disestablished, but it had stupidly courted its cruel fate. It had been so inextricably a part of Czarist tyranny as to bring down upon itself the wrath of the revolutionaries, and its surgical separation from the Romanov state had proved fatal. The Communist campaign in behalf of atheism, while still continuing, had evidently lost some of its militancy.

4

Additional arguments of perhaps a less fundamental nature were mustered by those Americans favoring recognition. The rights of the Russian people had no doubt been usurped, but much water had gone down the Dnieper since 1917. The masses now tolerated or supported the government, regardless of how it had come into power. Nothing we could do would undermine its stability, and we might as well face the fact that it was becoming accredited by time.

Nor did recognition necessarily mean sanction of Bolshevik wrongdoing. We had often recognized regimes that had come into power by murder, especially in Latin America, simply because formal recognition facilitated diplomatic intercourse.

Trade was so persuasive an argument as to be, in certain American quarters, much more potent than communism. During the drear decade of the depression, which began roughly in 1929, American exports to Russia fell off sharply. The following table shows the trend for the peacetime years of the 1930's.

1930	$114,399,000	1935	$24,743,000
1931	103,717,000	1936	33,427,000
1932	12,641,000	1937	42,892,000
1933	8,997,000	1938	69,691,000[4]
1934	15,011,000		

American industrialists, not fully realizing that Soviet trade was state-controlled, hoped not only to recapture the lost business but to gain what they optimistically regarded as an enormous potential trade. The Soviet Foreign Minister in 1933 talked of placing

---

[4] Figures taken from the official *Foreign Commerce and Navigation of the United States*, published annually by the Government Printing Office, Washington, D.C. Although Russian trade with the United States declined after 1931, so did Russian trade with other countries, for reasons connected with the depression.

orders abroad for $1,000,000,000. Our British and French rivals, who had extended recognition, would presumably get in on the ground floor. Not only would increased business with Russia

JUST ANOTHER CUSTOMER

(From the Dallas *News*, 1933, by permission.)

profit our merchants and manufacturers, but many new jobs would be created for the tens of thousands of unemployed Americans then burdening government relief rolls. A lucrative trade was going on anyhow, and it might as well be assisted by consular offices that could be established once recognition was granted.

The current aggressions of Japan and the potential aggressions of Hitler were in themselves potent arguments for recognition.[5] As in the nineteenth century, when Russia and the United States had faced the same enemies, the two nations were being drawn together by a common fear of Germany and Japan. The traditional friends were potential allies in the rear of potential enemies. Why not extend the Good Neighbor Policy to Russia as well as to Latin America? Working together in close accord through regularly established diplomatic channels, we might be able to achieve the common goal of peace by halting both Hitler and Hirohito.

Recognition, so its proponents argued, would have a soothing effect on Soviet Russia; it would quiet her extremists. Our policy of ostracism had merely given the Bolshevik leaders a rallying cry, and had conceivably saved the regime. Hostility to the United States had increased. But once recognition was accorded, prophesied Russophiles like Senator Borah, the Communists would moderate their aims. "The less we meddle," the Baltimore *Sun* had declared, "the sooner Russia will throw her pirates overboard." [6]

No one could rightly challenge the stability of the Moscow government. "One of the most annoying things about Soviet Russia," confessed the *Ohio State Journal*, "is that she's still managing to get along." [7] The most backward major power in Europe, cursed with the chaos of war and other overwhelming catastrophes, had within sixteen years undertaken to accomplish essentially what had been achieved during several centuries by the Reformation, the French revolution, the industrial revolution, and the agricultural revolution. The regime had weathered terrible storms and was clearly able to maintain order and silence dissent. We had already recognized many governments in the past,

<hr>

[5] For the view that Japan was a minor consideration as compared with the depression, see Pauline Tompkins, *American-Russian Relations in the Far East* (New York, 1949), p. 263.

[6] *Literary Digest*, LXVIII, 7 (Feb. 5, 1921).

[7] *Ibid.*, XCIII, 15 (June 25, 1927).

notably in Latin America, that did not measure up to the government of Russia in stability.

The traditional, though not invariable, policy of the United States had been to recognize established governments, regardless of their antecedents or ideology. We had been the first to welcome the provisional government of Russia in 1917; now that all the other great powers had recognized Communist rule—and some of them had more serious grievances than ours—we were inconsistently holding back.

The position of the United States was gradually becoming absurd. The Soviet Union and the American Union were the two most populous white nations; their representatives sat around the same conference tables; they signed the same treaties, notably the Kellogg-Briand peace pact of 1928. The United States was handicapped diplomatically by not having formalized relations with Moscow, as Secretary Stimson discovered when he attempted to thrust his hand into the Sino-Russian hornets' nest. The Soviet Union was of great and growing importance, and since it was bound to wax stronger with or without our blessing, our position would become increasingly ridiculous if we persisted in closing our eyes to the realities of international life.

Among those who favored recognition were leaders of a liberal stripe, notably Franklin D. Roosevelt and Alfred E. Smith (who did not see eye to eye with his fellow Catholics). They were joined by liberal journals like the New York *Nation* and the *New Republic*, which had been pro-Russian since 1917. Also active were various intellectuals, shading into "parlor pinks," who were impressed with Soviet social objectives and who, perceiving the inperfections of American democracy close at hand, found that distant fields looked the greenest. Starry-eyed devotees of the ancient friendship, who did not know that it had been ruptured long before 1917, were eager to bridge the chasm. Less idealistic were industrialists and exporters, especially those like the southern cotton growers who were cursed with a surplus. No doubt the most vocal champions of recognition were the left-wing labor groups, the socialist organizations and newspapers, and the Communist press and the Communist party. Altogether this was a motley assemblage.

5

Soviet Russia was far from a burning issue when Franklin D. Roosevelt took the inaugural oath in 1933, during the most alarming days of the depression. Recognition had not figured as a major issue in the recent campaign, and although there was considerable agitation pro and con, no great amount of pressure seems to have converged on either the White House or the State Department. One poll of the press in 1933, the results of which are rather questionable, indicated that editors were about 60 per cent favorable.[8] There was a general assumption that the liberal Roosevelt would extend recognition, and a rather general resignation to its inevitability. We were not enthusiastically in favor of such a step, but we would tolerate it as a kind of necessary evil.

In October, 1933, Roosevelt communicated directly with President Kalinin of the Soviet Union in a letter that adverted to the traditional friendship and suggested negotiations looking toward recognition. The Kremlin forthwith sent to America as its emissary the genial and rotund Foreign Minister Maxim Litvinov, who had shown a greater friendliness to us than most of his Communist colleagues. After protracted discussions, a series of letters was exchanged between Roosevelt and Litvinov in November, 1933, setting forth what had been agreed upon.

In return for formal recognition, Moscow agreed, among other things, to grant freedom of worship to Americans residing in Russia, and promised to discontinue Communist propaganda directed at the United States. Soviet claims for damages growing out of the Siberian expedition of 1918–1920 were dropped (but not those for North Russia), when Secretary Hull showed Litvinov the

---

[8] Meno Lovenstein, *American Opinion of Soviet Russia* (Washington, 1941), pp. 139–146.

documents which proved that the United States had gone into the enterprise for the primary purpose of restraining Japan.[9]

The most serious stumbling block was the question of debts. Roosevelt assured Litvinov that he could persuade Congress to accept a figure as low as $150,000,000, while Litvinov expressed a willingness to recommend that his government go as high as $100,000,000.[10] No final agreement then being possible, further discussion was put off until a later date.

The press of the United States generally greeted recognition with quiet satisfaction, in contrast with the raucous applause of the Socialist *New Leader* and the Communist *Daily Worker*. Business and financial journals were pleased with the prospect of more trade. The opponents of recognition usually quieted down when confronted with a disagreeable reality, although many of them presciently predicted the disappointments and broken agreements that were bound to ensue. Die-hard conservatives went down with colors nailed to the mast; Representative Hamilton Fish spoke of the betrayal for "thirty pieces of silver," while the *National Republic* ran two articles entitled, "Reds Win as U.S. Holds Bag" and "Profits Stained with Blood."

At all events, the two powerful nations were now on official speaking terms with each other. The general view in America was a mildly skeptical, "Let's see how it all works out." [11]

---

[9] *The Memoirs of Cordell Hull* (New York, 1948), I, 299.
[10] *Ibid.*, p. 303.
[11] *Literary Digest*, CXVI, 13 (Dec. 2, 1933).

XXIII

A Descent into the Abyss

"The Soviet Union . . . is run by a dictatorship as absolute as any dictatorship in the world."—Franklin D. Roosevelt, 1940

I

THE months following the establishment of formal relations with Soviet Russia were barren of the promised results. Those optimists and wishful thinkers who had predicted friendship, co-operation, and trade found their hopes cruelly dashed, amid a chorus of "I told you so's" from hidebound conservatives.

The debt negotiations finally bogged down in complete failure during 1935, with nothing accomplished. A complication had been injected the year before when Congress passed the Johnson Act, which forbade our government to lend money to those nations in default to it. The Soviets earnestly desired loans and credits from the opulent Uncle Sam, and when they perceived that such largesse would not be forthcoming, they dropped the debt settlement with a quiet thud. Soviet officials charged that they had been assured of loans and that Washington had broken its promise. Unsympathetic Americans retorted that the Kremlin had no intention of honoring its commitments regarding debts, once it had tricked us into recognition. The Ohio *State Journal* expressed a grass-roots opinion when it sneered that Soviet Russia was "willing to do anything within reason about her war debts except pay them." [1]

Expectations of a depression-dispelling trade were likewise disappointed, partly because the credits expected by the Soviets were not forthcoming. In 1935 Secretary Hull negotiated a trade agreement which extended to the U.S.S.R. the tariff benefits granted other nations; Moscow in return was to purchase $30,000,000 worth of American goods in the next twelve months. This, incidentally, was the first commercial treaty with our former friend since the abrogation of the Buchanan pact in 1911. But because of various obstacles, most of which could have been foreseen by any discerning observer, Russian-American trade prior to 1939 never attained the peak of the years before recognition. Critics of the Soviets renewed their accusations of bad faith.

Ceaseless Communist activity in the United States, apparently directed from Moscow, was a constant source of annoyance if not alarm. The terms of the Roosevelt-Litvinov agreement of 1933 were as plain as the English language could make them:

[Russia is] not to permit the formation or residence on its territory of any organization or group—and to prevent the activity on its territory of any organization or group, or of representatives or officials of any organization or group—which has as an aim the overthrow or the preparation for the overthrow of, or the bringing about by force of a change in, the political or social order of the whole or any part of the United States, its territories or possessions.[2]

Flouting this unequivocal pledge, the city of Moscow played host in 1935 to the All-World Congress of the Communist International. The offense was rendered all the more flagrant by the presence of American Communists, who concerted measures for strengthening their party in the United States. Secretary Hull, his Tennessee mountain temper aroused, lodged a resounding protest against this flagrant breach of a solemn agreement. But the Kremlin rejected his protest and coolly asserted that it "cannot

---

[1] *Literary Digest*, CXIX, 24 (Feb. 16, 1935).
[2] *Foreign Relations, 1933* (Washington, 1949), II, 806.

take upon itself and has not taken upon itself obligations of any kind with regard to the Communist International." [3] Hull was criticized by American liberals for having made too big a fuss about the weak Communist party in the United States, but our conservatives were more convinced than ever that we had traded recognition for a sorry mess of broken pledges.

In retrospect it seems clear that Soviet Russia profited more in a direct way from recognition than did the United States. Although she did not obtain the coveted credits, she did strengthen her diplomatic hand against both Japan and Germany. In some respects she gained even more in increased prestige at home and abroad. This view is supported by an editorial in *Izvestia* (Moscow), which asserted that the growth of Soviet Russia's economic and political importance had "compelled" the United States to recognize her. [4] The last great capitalistic fortress standing out against recognition had capitulated.

2

Russia was further dignified when, the year after American recognition, she was accepted by the League of Nations as worthy of membership. The Russian Communist leaders betrayed some little inconsistency in embracing an organization which had been branded by the Communist International as "the holy alliance of the bourgeoisie for the suppression of the proletarian revolution." But once in the League, and needing peace for the fulfillment of the successive Five-Year Plans, the Soviets became one of the most vocal champions of disarmament, collective security, and joint action against aggressors.

As Russia emerged from her isolationist cocoon to espouse international co-operation, the United States during the late 1930's retreated deeper and deeper into the storm cellar of neutrality.

---

[3] *The Memoirs of Cordell Hull* (New York, 1948), I, 305. Robert P. Browder, in his doctoral dissertation being prepared at Harvard University, shows that the American negotiators did not mention the Comintern in the recognition agreement for fear that the Soviets would later change its name.

[4] Paraphrase in *Foreign Relations, 1933*, II, 821.

Distasteful though the choice was, a majority of Americans regarded fascism as less of an evil than communism, and Fascist propaganda as less dangerous propaganda than that of the Communists. Hitler, Mussolini, and Hirohito might have voracious designs on their immediate neighbors, and perhaps at some distant day on us, but they possessed certain redeeming virtues. They showed much more respect for private property, they did not enshrine atheism, they were not preaching world revolution, and they did not maintain a branch of the Comintern in our country for the purpose of fomenting dissension and ultimate dominance. When the House Special Committee on Un-American Activities was set up in 1934, it was far more concerned with Communists than with Fascists. Our depression-cursed people, even with the foundations of capitalism groaning under the burden of some 10,000,000 unemployed, showed little desire to follow the pied pipers of communism.

The Kremlin meanwhile continued its ardent support—at least verbally—of disarmament and collective security. For the six years prior to 1934 the Russian participants in the disarmament discussions of the League of Nations had strongly advocated complete or progressive disarmament. As on earlier occasions, the western world expressed grave doubts as to Soviet sincerity, especially in view of the impracticability of total disarmament, in view of the Soviet Union's secrecy as to its own military might, and in view of the continued activity of the Moscow-inspired Comintern in those countries that were being invited to demolish their defenses.

But in 1934 Foreign Minister Litvinov, speaking at Geneva, caused a sensation when he swung over to the French view that security must precede disarmament.[5] Hope was expressed in America that this indicated an abandonment of the ideal of world revolution. The Soviets again surprised the western powers, and caused them no little embarrassment, when in 1935 they urged stronger action against Mussolini's rape of Ethiopia than the

[5] New York *Times*, May 30, 31, 1934.

League of Nations dared take, and when in 1936 they advocated vigorous measures against Hitler's audacious reoccupation of the Rhineland.

But whatever credit the Soviet Union may have grudgingly received in the United States for its zealous espousal of collective security was largely wiped out by the sensational purge trials of 1937–1938. Scores of Russian citizens, both in administration and army, were accused of conspiring with Germany and Japan to bring about the overthrow of the Communist dictatorship. There were startling confessions, mass trials, and wholesale executions, including three of the most distinguished revolutionists and eight leading generals. If the accusations were true, then there was a degree of rottenness in the Soviet Union that had been completely blotted out by a smoke screen of propaganda. If not true, then the defendants had been hounded into confessions by third-degree methods beside which Czarist cruelties seemed like fraternity initiations. All this did violence to our traditional conceptions of justice and fair play. Even such thick-and-thin champions of the Soviet system as the New York *Nation* and the *New Republic* were critical of the purge trials.

3

The Red Peril took on a deeper hue as a result of the Spanish Civil War of 1936–1939, a struggle that was both a proving ground and a dress rehearsal for World War II. Hitler and Mussolini semiopenly backed the reactionary dictator Franco as he attempted to overthrow the leftist government of the Loyalists in Madrid. Stalin no less openly provided men, aircraft, and other assistance for the Loyalists, although in far smaller quantities. The rank and file of our citizenry, bogged down in the depression and hypnotized by the neutrality fixation, were neither pro-Franco nor pro-Loyalist. But the more militant Roman Catholics in the United States, their worst fears confirmed by the intervention of Russia in behalf of the anticlerical Loyalists, condemned the Kremlin. The Hearst press, which customarily headlined the

Russian-supported Loyalists as "Reds," damned the Madrid government and its Communist followers. In 1937, after Japan's invasion of China and Hitler's Jewish pogroms, a *Fortune* poll showed that among our people Russia ranked along with Japan, Germany, and Italy as the most disliked nation.[6]

The fateful year 1938 brought multiplying rumors of war, as the world teetered on the brink of the precipice. The climax came when Hitler pressed his demands on Czechoslovakia for the German-inhabited Sudetenland. War was narrowly averted when representatives of Britain, France, Germany, and Italy met in Munich, where, in flagrant defiance of French obligations to the Czechs, an agreement was signed that heralded the ultimate extinction of the ill-starred republic. This was the price that the western democracies were willing to pay for peace and for time in which to bolster their defenses against Hitler.

On the eve of Munich, Moscow asserted and reasserted its willingness to defend Czechoslovakia. But for various reasons, including doubts as to Soviet ability or desire to provide adequate aid, this offer was ignored by Britain and France. More than that, the representatives of Russia were not even invited to the Munich conference, where decisions were made that mightily affected the destiny not only of the Soviet Union but of the entire world. The American people, in their gratitude for having escaped a global conflagration, took little notice of Soviet efforts to support the Czechs, and seemed unconcerned over the resounding rebuff administered to the U.S.S.R. at Munich.

4

Fear and uncertainty continued to spread throughout the western world, while the conviction deepened that the pact of Munich was but a truce. If Hitler was bent on war, as seemed likely, would it not be better to turn him against Stalin than against the western democracies? The two titans would grapple on the steppes of Russia, bleeding each other to death, while the

[6] XVI, 109, 174 (Oct., 1937).

civilized world would be saved from the menace of both German National Socialism and Russian communism. Such was the view of many outspoken conservatives in western Europe, especially in Britain, and such also was the view of many Americans, who hoped, in the words of William H. Chamberlin, that the "two systems of streamlined neobarbarism" would swallow each other.

These wishful thoughts were not lost on the Soviet leaders, who in the late summer of 1939 were negotiating with France and Britain for mutual defense against Hitler. Unable to secure sufficiently sweeping assurances, Moscow astounded the world, in August, 1939, by signing both a trade agreement and a nonaggression treaty with Nazi Germany. (By a secret protocol that was captured from the Germans and published by the United States in 1948, Poland was divided into German and Russian spheres pending a final settlement. Lithuania was to be in the German sphere, while Finland, Esthonia, and Latvia were reserved for the Russian sphere.) [7]

The news of the fateful Russo-German pact, even without the secret protocol, burst like a bombshell upon the United States and the rest of the world. A few of our newspaper editors hoped that the agreement would postpone war, but the great majority were unsparing in their condemnation of Stalin. He had given Hitler a green light for the invasion of Poland; he had "knifed" the British and French in the back while carrying on negotiations with them in presumed good faith. Instead of devitalizing himself in a herculean struggle with Hitler, he had calculatingly reversed the tables and was turning Hitler against the democracies. By the terms of his trade agreement with Germany he would provide his new-found friend, Adolf Hitler, with oil and other sinews of war. While the Nazi "fascists" and the "bourgeois democracies" were locked in lethal embrace, he would accelerate his defense program; and when the rest of Europe sank back into a peace of

---

[7] R. J. Sontag and J. S. Beddie, eds., *Nazi-Soviet Relations, 1939–1941* (Washington, 1948), p. 78.

exhaustion, he would bestride the continent and impose the Soviet system on its prostrate people.

Communist editors in the United States, with scant advance news of the agreement with Hitler, were inveighing against the Nazis when the news of the Berlin-Moscow pact arrived.[8] Slavishly following the "party line" dictated by the Kremlin, they soon broke into praise of the Nazis and assailed the "imperialistic war" which had been provoked by the designing democracies. This was the "line" until the men in the Kremlin again changed it, also without warning.

Apologists for Stalin argued that he had double-crossed the western Allies for perfectly valid reasons. He suspected, so the defense ran, that Hitler would inevitably attack him and, emulating the British and French at Munich, he was buying time with which to build up his defenses. When Hitler attacked Poland from the west, a week after signing the fateful pact, Stalin invaded from the east and seized a large portion of Polish soil. Defenders of Stalin claimed that he had reacted defensively so as to keep his potential enemy, Hitler, as far as possible from his door, while at the same time recovering Russian territory inhabited mainly by non-Polish groups.

(The publication in 1948 of the secret protocol of 1939, which proved that Stalin and Hitler, with every appearance of friendship, had cold-bloodedly divided Poland *a week before the war began*, caused Soviet motives to appear in a somewhat less favorable light.)

But the American people, even with their limited knowledge of what was happening, were profoundly distressed by the conduct of the Soviet Union. Had not Stalin, with an act of betrayal, given Hitler a free rein to start this terrible world conflict? Had he not treacherously attacked Poland from the rear while scavenging for his share of the loot? Had he not, after this seizure and by formal

---

[8] See New York *Daily Worker*, Aug. 23, 1939, which began to prepare its readers for the announcement which it printed the next day.

agreement with his "partner in crime," partitioned Poland—ironically the fourth partition since 1772?

In the United States old memories of Czarist persecutions were revived, especially among our increasingly influential Polish-American group. These people were joined by millions of Roman Catholics who, fearing for their coreligionists in Poland, intensified their already bitter attacks on the Kremlin. Stalinist Russia sank to a new low in American esteem.

5

After Hitler had erased Poland from the map and attained his immediate objectives, he proposed that the fighting stop. But Britain and France, who could now perceive that appeasing Hitler was merely postponing a showdown under even less favorable circumstances, spurned the olive branch. The government-controlled press of Russia burst into praise of Hitler's magnanimous offer, and Stalin issued a statement accusing the two western democracies of being responsible for the war with Germany.

Moscow next turned its unwelcome attentions to Finland, whose territory stretched strategically to almost within cannon shot of Leningrad, the former capital and second city of the U.S.S.R. The Soviet leaders were evidently nervous over the possibility that the Finns might join hands with Hitler in a forthcoming attack. The Kremlin accordingly requested a mutual assistance pact, the cession of some territory around Leningrad ("the lost gates"), and a naval base on the shores of the Gulf of Finland. But the Finns resolutely rejected these demands, and late in 1939 the Red army lumbered into motion, while the Russian air force was bombing Finnish civilian centers.

American sympathies, as in the days of the Czars, were overwhelmingly with the courageous little republic. The Finns were sturdy democrats; they performed prodigiously at the Olympic games; they paid their debts fully and on time (which could not be said of certain wealthier nations); they were hopelessly outclassed; and they had been attacked by a power that was not only a bully but a Communist bully at that. In American public opinion polls Soviet Russia was second only to Nazi Germany as the "worst influence in Europe." [9] Washington proclaimed a moral embargo on the shipment of aircraft to Russia, and President Roosevelt, in a public address loudly booed by Communist auditors, condemned the Soviet Union as a dictatorship as "absolute" as any in existence. [10]

Countless Americans, in support of Finnish relief programs, danced, knitted, orated, bingoed, or banqueted for "brave little Finland." Congress made available a total of $30,000,000 in loans, all restricted to *nonmilitary* supplies. We favored the Finns but, gripped by the neutrality fixation, we were determined not to be sucked into the war. The House of Representatives came within three votes of severing relations with the Soviet Union by denying appropriations for the upkeep of the Moscow Embassy. Ex-President Hoover, writing for *Collier's,* demanded the immediate recall of our ambassador and insisted that the recognition of Russia had been a "gigantic political and moral mistake." The League of Nations expelled the Soviet Union from its membership as a thing unclean.

Britain and France went to the very brink of war with Russia in their attempts to aid Finland. But all their efforts failed, as the Soviet steam roller gained momentum after earlier reverses, and in 1940 the flattened Finns were forced to come to terms. The unexpected moderation of Moscow's demands by no means erased the memory of Communist aggression, while Soviet condemnation of our inept interference brought official relations to a dangerously disagreeable level.

6

The totally unexpected collapse of France in the spring of 1940 proved disastrous to Stalin's presumed strategy. Far from domi-

---

[9] *Fortune,* XXI, 102 (March, 1940).
[10] R. E. Sherwood, *Roosevelt and Hopkins* (New York, 1948), p. 138.

nating the two exhausted sets of belligerents, he was in grave danger of being dominated by a fresh and victorious Germany. In obvious fear, and not content with his recently won Polish and Finnish bastions, Stalin turned an acquisitive eye to the strategically important Baltic states of Lithuania, Latvia, and Esthonia, with all of which the Soviet Union had negotiated mutual assistance pacts in 1939. In mid-June, 1940, while France was still falling, Moscow presented demands to these three tiny nations which resulted in their complete absorption by the Soviet Union.

Both Washington and Berlin reacted unfavorably to this aggressive move. The United States government, opposed in principle to territorial gains by force, promptly froze the assets of the Baltic states in America, and not only continued to recognize their orphaned diplomatic representatives but supported them with frozen funds. The German government, by the secret protocol of 1939, had assigned Latvia and Esthonia to the Russian sphere of interest, but not Lithuania, and on this point friction developed that contributed to the final break.

Scarcely more than a week after the Baltic coup, Moscow forced Romania to yield Bessarabia and northern Bukovina. Unlike Bessarabia, northern Bukovina had not been allotted to Stalin in the secret protocol, and additional ill feeling was generated between Hitler and Stalin over this issue. Northern Bukovina, though preponderately Slavic, had never been Russian, unlike the recently reclaimed areas in Poland, in Finland, in the Baltic states, and in Bessarabia. Although the absorption of the Romanian and Baltic territories was defended by Russian sympathizers on the ground that Stalin wanted to place further defensive space between himself and his good friend Hitler, Under Secretary of State Sumner Welles issued a ringing denunciation of Soviet aggression.[11] Molotov in a public reply told the United States in effect to mind its own business, and characteristically accused us of imperialistic designs on Latin America.

The bitterness of our people toward Moscow continued to

---

[11] *Department of State Bulletin*, III, 48 (July 27, 1940).

mount. In April, 1941, the Soviet Union, obviously seeking to concentrate on Hitler, exploded another bombshell by signing a five-year neutrality treaty with Japan. Just as the Stalin-Hitler agreement of 1939 had turned the Germans westward against the democracies, so this pact was regarded by many Americans as an attempt to turn the Japanese southward toward the Philippines. Washington responded by freezing Russian funds in the United States and withholding further licenses for exports to Vladivostok.

The Hitler-Stalin love feast meanwhile had not been blessed with perfect accord. The German dictator, having overwhelmed France, presumably wished to crush the Communist menace on his flank before trying to beat the British to their knees. As was revealed by captured German documents published by the United States in 1948, Hitler attempted to bring the U.S.S.R. openly into the war on his side by promising a large share of the spoils, but he gagged on certain Soviet demands, particularly those relating to the Balkans. The Russians were especially insistent upon dominance over Bulgaria and the Dardanelles.[12] To Hitler the only safe alternative seemed to be a full-dress invasion of the Soviet Union, and this he was confident could be engineered in a matter of weeks.

7

In the spring of 1941 the press and radio of the United States were seriously concerned with the possibility that Russia might enter the war on the side of Hitler, with frightful consequences for human freedom. A world already accustomed to sensations was completely unprepared for the astounding news that on June 22 Hitler had turned upon his partner of the nonaggression pact and launched an all-out attack on the "Mongol halfwits." The Communist newspapers in the United States were again caught off guard, but like good Moscow-trained soldiers they forthwith reversed themselves. On June 21, the war to them was an "imperialist" conflict, wantonly precipitated and greedily prosecuted

[12] Sontag and Beddie, *Nazi-Soviet Relations*, pp. 226–254.

GRINDING IT OUT

The New York *Daily Worker* thus belittled rumors of an attack by Hitler on Russia the day before the attack was launched. (From the *Daily Worker*, June 21, 1941, by permission.) This paper was a Communist mouthpiece.

by the capitalistic democracies under the lash of Wall Street; the next day it was a just and holy war against "German fascism," in which the freedom-loving democracies, including Communist Russia, were fighting together.[13]

[13] New York *Daily Worker*, June 20, 23, 1941.

The neutrality-minded Americans on the whole welcomed Stalin into the democratic camp, if not with unbounded joy, at least with considerable satisfaction. Our good fortune seemed almost incredible. Locked in deadly embrace, the two menaces would eventually "claw" out each other's "guts" on the frozen steppes of Russia, and America would not be drawn into the war —that is, if the Red army stood fast.

But there were disquieting fears. American Catholics were in no haste to embrace the new bedfellow of democracy. "I have no more confidence in Stalin than I have in Hitler," declared Archbishop Curley of Baltimore. And if Stalin did win, certain isolationists were saying, how much better off would we be? What would it profit us to substitute a Communist menace for a Nazi menace? Many of such skeptics rather hoped that Russia would collapse, but the great majority of our people prayed that Hitler would suffer the icy fate of Napoleon. It was a prayer, rather than a hope, for most Americans, in common with the best military minds here and abroad, feared that the Red defenders would collapse in some six or nine weeks. The Soviets on their part were annoyed by our low estimate of their ability and courage.

President Roosevelt, recognizing the imperative necessity of keeping the U.S.S.R. in the war, unfroze Russian credits, refused to invoke the Neutrality Act against arms shipments to the Soviet Union, extended loans, and on his own initiative undertook to supply an enormous quantity of lend-lease equipment, under a broad interpretation of the lend-lease act that had been passed nine months before Pearl Harbor.[14] Some of these moves were made in the face of vigorous opposition from our isolationists, who insisted that the munitions be kept at home for the defense of our own shores and out of the hands of Hitler. But Roosevelt, who preferred to have American weapons kill Germans on the

[14] On October 1, 1941, as a beginning, the United States formally pledged about a billion dollars' worth of supplies during the next nine months. Within the next two months twenty-eight ships sailed from the United States carrying over 130,000 tons of cargo (E. R. Stettinius, Jr., *Lend-Lease: Weapon for Victory* [New York, 1944], pp. 126, 203).

Dnieper rather than on the Potomac, was under strong compulsion to gamble, and during these anxious months before Pearl Harbor the United States became a virtual ally of the Soviet Union. War, no less than politics, makes curious bedfellows.

XXIV

The Strange Alliance

"The truth is that they [the Russians] want to have as little to do with foreigners, Americans included, as possible. We never make a request or proposal to the Soviets that is not viewed with suspicion."—General John R. Deane, 1944

I

THE sneak attack at Pearl Harbor plunged the United States overnight into the vortex of war. Henceforth we could assist the Russians openly and regularly, unhampered by the hypocrisy of neutrality. By the Declaration of the United Nations, dated January 1, 1942, we entered into a formal military alliance with the Soviet Union, and as a consequence our sympathies for the valiant Russians rose markedly. We were all in the same leaky boat together, and both Communists and democrats would be well advised to forget ideological bickerings and pull lustily at the oars.

The blunt truth is that while the western American giant and the eastern Russian giant were in the conflict on the same side, they never became full-fledged allies either in spirit or in deed. The events since the Bolshevik revolution of 1917 had bred into the peoples and governments of both nations a distrust that would not easily melt away, even under the white heat of Hitlerism. We were much less suspicious of the Russians than they were of us, and considerably more willing to let bygones be bygones. But between the two countries hung a thick black curtain of misinformation. The Russian masses, with anticapitalistic propaganda dinned unceasingly into their ears, were a great deal more ignorant of us than we were of them, and with perhaps better excuse. Even though we could partially justify ourselves by saying that the Soviets denied us access to the facts, our ignorance of them, growing largely out of indifference or preoccupation, was at best deplorable.

Numerous public opinion polls during the war years revealed that the bulk of our citizens still entertained mistaken ideas about their new ally. In the few cases where these misconceptions were not held by a majority, they were held by a strong minority, and in all cases there was a distressingly large number of "Don't Knows." A survey in 1944 concluded that only one American in ten was even reasonably well-informed about the Soviet Union.[1] Few experts on Russia would have rated our comprehension nearly so high.

The precise nature of the Moscow government was generally misunderstood. Most of our citizens attributed to Stalin absolute dictatorial powers; some went to the other extreme and regarded him as dominated by the Politburo. An enormous number of our people thought of Russia as enjoying the dubious benefits of communism, not realizing that since 1921 the Soviet regime had abandoned Marxist communism and had gradually veered over to a system of state socialism, not realizing that Marxist-Leninism had been transformed into what might be called Stalinism, and not realizing that only a few million of the Russian people—carefully sifted and highly disciplined—belonged to the ruling Communist party. We were unaware, in short, that Russia was ruled by Communists who had long since ceased to practice communism as defined by the Bolshevik revolutionists.

---

[1] *Public Opinion Quarterly*, VIII, 522 (Winter, 1944–1945). The analysis of American opinion herewith given is based on all the national polls during the war and postwar years.

Most Americans did not know that there was some freedom of expression in the U.S.S.R., particularly with regard to criticizing the workings of the economic structure. And although most Americans feared Stalin's expansionist ambitions in one form or another when the war was over, many of them did not know that an avowed objective of the Communists was world revolution.

American misunderstandings sprouted partly from the fact that during the war the Soviet leaders, for the purpose of stimulating a last-ditch defense, had stressed patriotism and nationalism rather than socialism and the Third International. Less excusable was our failure to perceive that directives from Moscow, whether from the Comintern or the Kremlin, controlled the Communist party in the United States. Most Americans wishfully believed that the Soviet system, whatever it was, could not long endure, and some of us were inclined to regard the existing type of government as best for the Russian people.

2

No less pronounced was American ignorance of the Soviet economic system. Millions of our people still did not know that workers received different wages, according to their skills and capacities; that a speed-up system of piecework was in effect; that the individual citizen might hold private property, whether house or land, provided he did not exploit others; that he might transmit such property through inheritance; and that he might hold securities and receive interest on them. A vast body of Americans believed that Soviet Russia had attained only negligible industrial development, unaware of the tremendous strides under the successive Five-Year Plans, which in tempo eclipsed our own industrial revolution. We erroneously supposed that what little industry there was had all been established since the days of the Czars (actually Russia before 1917 had made considerable industrial progress); that the few manufacturing centers were to be found entirely in western Russia (actually the important trans-Ural development enabled the Soviets to resist Hitler); that negligible mechanization was to be found in Russian agriculture; that the economic resources of the U.S.S.R. were rather modest; and that, far from the fact, there was no opportunity in the Soviet Union for able young men to go far. With these false ideas fixed firmly in mind, the self-centered American naturally believed that Russia received the bulk of her war materials from the United States under lend-lease, rather than the 10 per cent or so that actually arrived.[2]

Countless Americans still envisaged the Russian social structure in terms of bomb-and-whisker Bolshevist stereotypes: sexual promiscuity; easy and cheap divorce (twenty cents); the encouragement of abortion; the abandonment of babies; the weaning away of children by the state; and the encouragement of defiance among the younger generation. All this had been markedly or completely changed since early Leninist days. We were generally unaware that the church to some extent had been rehabilitated, after a violent but unsuccessful effort to stamp it out. The Soviet rulers now felt more secure, the church had been divorced from Czarism, and the weary masses perhaps needed the solace of religion. Besides, Greek Orthodoxy might be used as a tool to promote Soviet aims in those countries that worshipped according to the same faith.

A host of ill-informed Americans still referred to Russia as having a classless society, not knowing that a bureaucratic ruling class had replaced the old nobility and enjoyed unusual privileges. Many of us were unaware that the Soviet system provided for large-scale social security, and that it had made surprising progress in wiping out the shameful illiteracy under the Czars. But to great numbers of our citizens the Russians were still ignorant, stupid, and uncouth beasts.

Those relatively few Americans who gave the scroll of history any scrutiny continued to confuse the provisional government of

---

[2] *Foreign Affairs*, XXVI, 82 (Oct., 1947). The Russians claimed that all their wartime imports, including lend-lease, were only 4 per cent of their total industrial output (New York *Times*, Dec. 12, 1949).

1917 with the Bolshevist regime of Lenin and Trotsky. Most of us had no recollection of the Archangel and Siberian interventions, though Soviet spokesmen belabored these skeletons constantly. Most of us could not recall, if we ever knew, that the United States was by a wide margin the last major power to recognize the Soviet Union. A large number of Americans, including some in high places, still spoke reverently of the ancient friendship, as though it had existed in full vigor before the advent of the Bolsheviks. As late as 1945 more than seven out of ten of our citizens could think of nothing the United States had done since 1917 to cause the U.S.S.R. to doubt our friendship! [3] Most of us could not remember that Russia had been an outspoken champion of disarmament and collective security in the 1930's, and that she had at least verbally upheld Ethiopia at the time of the Mussolini rape, and Czechoslovakia at the time of the Munich betrayal.

3

American ignorance of Russia correlated strikingly with hostility toward Russia. Most of the unfriendliness to the Soviets was concentrated in the educationally underprivileged groups, which broadly speaking were also the economically underprivileged groups—ironically the proletariat to which communism is supposed to appeal. The explanation seems to be that we have no class solidarity, we cling to our age-old traditions of freedom, and we still cherish the American dream of "striking it rich," which we could not achieve under a completely planned economy. Even our Negroes, who are the bottom rung of the social and economic ladder, have not swallowed the Communist "line" in alarming numbers.

Roman Catholics in the United States, with their well-founded distrust of the Stalinist system, were likewise profoundly suspicious. Not until 1942 would a majority of the American people say that they preferred communism to fascism, and they did so

---

[3] *Fortune*, XXXII, 234 (Sept., 1945).

under the shadow of the Pearl Harbor disaster. During the heyday of Soviet-American co-operation, our public opinion surveys indicated that one voter in three still did not trust Russia.[4] A vast and confused body of our more ignorant citizenry dismissed the Land of Contradictions as a hopeless enigma.

If ignorance was the mother of suspicion, knowledge was the mother of trust. The opinion polls likewise showed that the better educated were considerably more sympathetic toward Soviet Russia than their less well informed brothers, and also more hopeful of current and future co-operation, especially in world organization. If the proletariat paradoxically rejected communism, the wealthy and conservative groups no less paradoxically were somewhat more favorable to it. The explanation appears to be that the well to do had the money to secure a superior education, and increased tolerance often flows from an increased understanding.

Jewish-American groups, welcoming the immeasurably improved status of the Jew in Russia, were conspicuously more friendly to Moscow than our own rank and file. They were joined by wishful thinkers, apostles of world organization, champions of a planned economy (which included many New Dealers), and the intelligentsia, who, like others, often view distant pastures through a red-hued cloud of idealism. Someone has said that communism is the opiate of the intellectuals.

But one fact overshadows all others in any analysis of American sympathy or antipathy for the Soviet Union during the war years. The decisive factor was education—not class, religion, political preference, occupation, or race.

4

The tragic events at Pearl Harbor and elsewhere largely silenced the outcries of our isolationists against sending lend-lease shipments to Russia. The Soviets were precariously holding the Germans at bay, and since we were then in no position to engage Hitler's armies, the next best thing was to supply our Slavic allies

---

[4] *Public Opinion Quarterly*, VIII, 522 (Winter, 1944–1945).

with weapons. President Roosevelt, seeing clearly the over-all picture, gave Russia top priority in war materials, even above the pressing requirements of Britain, China, and our own armed forces.

Roosevelt's policy toward the Soviet Union was in the nature of a gigantic gamble. Not recognizing fully the ideological implications of Marxism, he evidently believed that the Russians were suspicious and unco-operative largely because the western nations had first encircled them and then treated them as outcasts. He appears to have concluded that if we were to give the Soviets all they wanted, generously and without demur, they might be weaned away from their dangerous ideas of world revolution and co-operate wholeheartedly in the common enterprise of building a better tomorrow.] He was eager to meet the Soviet leaders and talk things over with them, for he was confident that the force of his personality, combined with the powerful position of the United States, would cause them to be more reasonable.[5]

Roosevelt's countrymen on the whole were in a mood to support his be-kind-to-Russia policy. The United States was then engaged in a death struggle with a common foe; and from the days of the French alliance in 1778 we have invariably warmed toward those nations, however disagreeable our previous relations, who were fighting directly or indirectly on our side. The Red army was tying up Hitler's mechanized might, and if the Allies were going to win, every effort would have to be bent toward bolstering up Soviet resistance. The amazing Russians, confounding the prophets of a six-week collapse, were the only foemen that had halted the seemingly invincible German panzer divisions; they were the only people who were decimating the Hitlerian hosts by meat-grinder fighting; and they were exhibiting a degree of bravery in defending their native soil that will live

---

[5] *The Memoirs of Cordell Hull* (New York, 1948), II, 1249. An article setting forth Roosevelt's views regarding dealings with Russia, and generally believed to have been inspired by the White House, is Forrest Davis, "Roosevelt's World Blueprint," *Saturday Evening Post*, CCXV, 20–21, 109, 110 (April 10, 1943).

forever in the saga of Stalingrad. The heroism of the Russian people was providing a graveyard for German man power on the frostbitten steppes, and if great numbers of Russians continued to lose their lives killing Germans, fewer American boys would lose theirs when we at length came to grips with Hitler. Somehow or other we subconsciously subscribed to the silly notion that the Russians were fighting, secondarily if not primarily, for the preservation of American democracy. But at all events Russian co-operation was imperatively necessary if a new and viable world organization was to emerge from the fiery furnace of World War II.

American mistrust was further quieted by several interesting developments. In the month of Pearl Harbor, Joseph E. Davies, former United States ambassador to the U.S.S.R., published a best-selling book, *Mission to Moscow*, which on the whole gave a rather favorable picture of the Communist order. His story was made into a moving picture of the same name, and proved to be a highly successful vehicle for Soviet propaganda. In 1943 the Comintern was formally dissolved, presumably by the Moscow hierarchy, and presumably also as a sop to western opinion. Although this maneuver was generally hailed as a friendly gesture, a good many doubting Thomases in America branded it as "another clever Communist trick," and not without reason, for the circumstantial evidence is strong that the Comintern merely went underground. The Communist party in the United States, apparently responding to the voice of its Moscow manipulators, went out of existence in 1944, to be replaced by the Communist Political Association. But in July, 1945, significantly the month after Hitlerism was crushed, the Communist party of the United States was again formally reconstituted.

5

The Rooseveltian policy of appeasement, as all the world knows, did not work out happily. The officials in the Kremlin were hard bargainers, firmly attached to the principle of not giving anything without receiving an equivalent, and of not receiving anything without expecting to be asked for something in return. On occasion the United States was so generous in its offers of material aid as to arouse Soviet suspicions as to what we were up to. The Communist mind, already highly distrustful, recoiled instinctively from gifts borne by the one great nation which over the years had been most conspicuously unfriendly. We not only dispensed lend-lease with lavish hand, but at times we were forced into the curious and humiliating posture of giving as suppliants.[6] This handicap not only weakened us but further inspired mistrust in the Kremlin.

In all fairness one must concede that Soviet suspicions were far from baseless. The Communist leaders remembered the hostility of the outside world during the precarious years of the civil war and intervention. If the western democracies did not believe that Russia had abandoned world revolution, neither did Russia believe that the western democracies had abandoned capitalistic encirclement. The Kremlin could also not forget the hope that had been freely voiced in the western world, on the eve of the Stalin-Hitler pact of 1939, that Russians and Germans would cut one another's throats. The Roman Catholics in America were outspokenly bitter against Moscow, so much so that Roosevelt felt obliged to send a personal representative to the Vatican, Myron C. Taylor, with the object of holding them in line. The lend-lease aid that the United States poured out was clearly for the primary purpose of keeping our Communist ally in the war and saving American lives.

The rulers of Russia were further disturbed by the loud talk among irresponsible Americans about the inevitability of war with the Soviet Union, and about the desirability, once Hitler was crushed, of turning our fresh divisions upon the exhausted Russians and having done once and for all with communism. American mistrust of Stalin's motives increased as the Soviet steam roller shifted from reverse gear and rolled nearer and nearer Berlin.

---

[6] John R. Deane, *The Strange Alliance* (New York, 1947), p. 297.

Some of us feared that it would stop at the Russian border; others that it would roll to the English Channel. The Russian press objected to a headline in Hearst's New York *Journal-American*, "Red Wave Threatens to Drown Christian Civilization," and to one in the Chicago *Tribune*, "Soviet Union Is Only Aggressor in the World."

Hardly less irritating to the Soviets were the critical comments on conditions in the U.S.S.R. which were published in America by hasty visitors. Conspicuous among them was William L. White, who, on the basis of a six-week sojourn among the Soviets, wrote a book entitled *Report on the Russians* (New York, 1945), which was widely read in America as a best seller and as a capsuled article in the *Reader's Digest*. While it appears that White was not attempting to be maliciously unfair, he nevertheless angered his war-ravaged hosts by reporting many unflattering truths, some of which were distorted by his inadequate background.

Distrustful though Soviet officialdom was, the Russian people were conspicuously friendly, at least before the crushing of Hitler and before the Moscow propaganda machine began to pour out its poison against the United States. When the American GI's broke through German lines to meet Red troops on the Elbe, in April, 1945, they were greeted as *Amerikanskie tovarishchi* (American comrades). When the news of the German surrender reached Moscow, in May, 1945, immense crowds gathered in front of the United States Embassy to cheer every American who appeared at the windows, and to toss about, in a manner reminiscent of the Fox mission of 1866, every American who emerged.[7]

6

High on the list of specific Russian grievances stood the delay of the Allies in opening a real second front, especially after repeated promises and repeated postponements.

The Soviet view was that Russia alone was fighting the war, while the Allies, in the scornful phrase of the Moscow *News* in

[7] *Ibid.*, pp. 180–181.

1942, were "mere bystanders." The fact is that the great bulk of all the battle casualties sustained on the Allied side during *the entire war* were Russian.

The proposition was self-evident that the more German divisions the Allies could divert to a second front in France, the fewer German divisions would be ravaging Russia. The Soviet leaders strongly suspected that the western democracies were deliberately holding back, in pursuance of their bleed-each-other-white policy, and when columnist Drew Pearson made this charge, he was publicly branded a liar by Secretary Hull and President Roosevelt.[8] The traditionally suspicious Russians were no doubt disturbed by the knowledge that if they had been in Allied shoes they would have been strongly tempted to stand back and watch Germans and Russians slit one another's throats. The German air force showered the Red troops with propaganda leaflets proclaiming that this was the purpose behind the Allied delay.

Russian needling of the democracies for action continued in some degree until the attack on the French coast was finally launched. Allied substitutes for a second front produced sneers rather than cheers in the Soviet press. The spectacular invasion of North Africa and Italy, although knocking Italy out of the war, engaged only some ten German divisions, as compared with nearly 200 "Fascist" divisions bogged down in the U.S.S.R. The aerial second front, which turned German cities and factories into rubble heaps, was brushed aside by Soviet spokesmen as of negligible value. Our large-scale operations in the Pacific against Japan were dismissed in Moscow as of no consequence to the main European theater. The growing dissatisfaction of the Kremlin gave rise to fears that the U.S.S.R. might make a separate peace, and such disquieting thoughts spurred on our preparations for a second front.[9] The Soviets on their part suspected us of negotiating with Germany for a separate peace.

The Americans had their point of view, and they were irritated

---

[8] *Department of State Bulletin*, IX, 154 (Sept. 4, 1943).

[9] R. E. Sherwood, *Roosevelt and Hopkins* (New York, 1948), p. 734.

by the failure of the Soviet leaders to appreciate it. On the day of Pearl Harbor many of our tremendous war plants were not even in the drawing-board stage. After Pearl Harbor we were mired down in a morass of priorities and cross-purposes; one wag said that the real second front was established in Washington when the bureaus began battling with one another. Lend-lease to Soviet Russia, moreover, was absorbing much material needed by our own forces.

A cross-channel invasion of France was a tremendous operation and not, as certain Russian generals seemed to think, a mere crossing of the Vistula River. Nothing could be more foolhardy than to attempt an all-out second front operation before there was a reasonable prospect of success. A disastrous failure, even though it might suck German divisions from the Russian front temporarily, would postpone or prevent the day of a successful invasion, with a consequent prolongation or even loss of the war. The United States also had to grapple with the Japanese in the Pacific, while an alarmingly vocal body of our citizenry were demanding a policy of hanging Hirohito first. Not only were there these embarrassing public pressures, but within the Allied camp Churchill and other British leaders were vehemently opposed to an invasion of France, thinking it wiser to strike Hitler elsewhere in the "soft underbelly" than to turn the English Channel into a "river of blood."

When the Normandy sun set on D day in June, 1944, the Russians were pleased but not exuberantly grateful. They regarded the invasion of France as no more than their due, and unforgivably belated at that. The American General John R. Deane went for a walk in Moscow, expecting to be overwhelmed with the cheers of men and the embraces of women, but to his chagrin he passed unnoticed.[10] On the whole the Soviet leaders felt that they should have received fewer promises and more performance.

---

[10] Deane, *The Strange Alliance*, p. 151.

7

Second-front friction had a counterpart in the Far East. If the Russians were angered by our failure to get into the war against Germany, great numbers of Americans were angered by the failure of the Russians to get into the war against Japan. This was especially true of an ignorantly vocal group who, burning with indignation over the punch below the belt at Pearl Harbor, were demanding a concentration of effort in the Pacific, to the neglect of the main European ring. But public opinion polls showed that an overwhelming majority of our people, regardless of their views as to who should be chastised first, believed that the U.S.S.R. "owed it to us" to enter the Far Eastern cockpit, sooner or later,[11] and a smaller majority of our citizens had faith that she would ultimately do so.

The brutal truth is that the Russians had their hands more than full with the German invader. They were almost blasted out of the war in its early stages, and only by a supreme effort were they able to turn back the tide of conquest. If the Japanese had attacked the Russians from the rear, the Red armies probably would have collapsed under the double sledge-hammering. One of the major mysteries of the war is why Japan did not stab the Soviets in the rear, while they were reeling in 1941, rather than attack the United States and arouse the half-sleeping western giant. If the war lords of Nippon, instead of turning southward for easier and richer pickings, had first of all crushed the Russian forces in Siberia, the East Indies would doubtless have been plucked off just as easily and a good deal more permanently. The United States, without even an indirect Soviet ally, would then have been in a more desperate position than it was after Pearl Harbor.

The Russian High Command perceived all these things a good deal more clearly than our own citizens, especially those of the get-Hirohito-first stamp. The Soviets, who were quite content to see the tide of Japanese imperialism swirl toward the East Indies,

---

[11] *Public Opinion Quarterly*, IX, 249 (Summer, 1945).

went to extreme lengths to avoid any provocative act. The wisdom of their policy was later acclaimed by their bitterest foe, Adolf Hitler, who, while his Thousand-Year Empire was crashing down about his head, blamed his defeat on the failure of the Japanese to attack the U.S.S.R. in the rear.[12]

The persistent neutrality of Japan was actually a godsend to the Allied cause. Russia was saved from collapse. A substantial part of her Far Eastern army could be detached for service against the Germans. The remainder of this force immobilized hundreds of thousands of Japanese troops in the Kwantung army who otherwise could have been deployed against us, at least in large part. More than 50 per cent of all the crucially important lend-lease that Russia received from the United States was shunted over the trans-Siberian railway through the port of Vladivostok, and this vital stream of supplies, ironically carried on Russian ships past Nippon's back door, would have been pinched off had the Russians attacked the Japanese. American aviators from the Marianas, whose craft were damaged in the bombing of Japan, could land on Soviet soil without fear of being beheaded. Scores of these men were nominally interned by the Russians, as a gesture of neutrality toward Japan, but were secretly permitted to escape and bomb another day.[13] The B29 bombers were kept and copied.

Unthinking Americans, who were solely concerned with shortening the war and saving the lives of our boys, demanded that the Russians turn over to us bombing bases in Siberia from which to destroy Japan's bamboo cities. The get-Japan-first group, many of whom were former isolationists, insisted that Russia owed us at least this much for all the lend-lease she was getting from our taxpayers' pockets.

The unpalatable truth was that the establishing of American bases on Soviet soil would have been a flagrant violation of neutrality, and the Japanese, at least in the earlier stages of the conflict, would undoubtedly have attacked the U.S.S.R. as a matter

[12] New York *Times*, March 9, 1945.
[13] Deane, *The Strange Alliance*, pp. 59–63.

of self-preservation. Not only would Japan's entry into the war have been disastrous for the Russians, but the Japanese would almost certainly have seized the Siberian air bases, thus rendering them useless either to us or to the Soviets. President Roosevelt was aware of all this, and in October, 1942, publicly defended the Soviet Union against Senate criticism.

The agitation in America for Siberian bases quieted down appreciably after we had wrested the Marianas—notably Saipan, Tinian, and Guam—from Nippon's grasp and were able to use them as bases from which to launch the terrifying B29 attacks on Japan. As the Rising Sun began to wane in the Pacific, the Japanese rather than the Russians grew increasingly anxious to avoid hostilities. The United States, with less fear of interruption, continued to send lend-lease shipments to Vladivostok to strengthen the Red army for its ultimate attack upon the Japanese lines. And although Stalin on six different occasions promised the United States bases in Siberia after the U.S.S.R. had broken relations with Japan, they were never forthcoming.[14] This was partly because the Russians did not want Americans prowling around their positions, and partly because in 1945 we did not particularly need the Siberian springboard. Altogether, developments in the Far Eastern theater did not give promise of cordial co-operation during the postwar years.

---

[14] *Ibid.*, p. 259.

XXV

Forks in the Road

"I cannot forecast to you the action of Russia. It is
a riddle wrapped in a mystery inside an enigma; but perhaps there is a key. That key is Russian national interest."—Winston Churchill, 1939

I

ASIDE from the major grievances already discussed, a series
of painful misunderstandings between America and Russia persisted throughout much of World War II, and
contributed materially to the rift that began to widen ominously
once the common foe was destroyed.

Lend-lease shipments were a never-failing bone of contention
during the conflict, as well as after. The United States agreed to
make certain deliveries, and then for various reasons, including
bottlenecks in production and difficulties of shipment, failed at
first to send the expected quotas. The Russians, who had exaggerated notions of our productive power, arrived at the natural but
disagreeable conclusion that we were deliberately holding back,
much as in the case of the second front, and for essentially the
same brutal reasons. When the projected factories finally began
to belch smoke, the flood of lend-lease material sent to the
U.S.S.R. was enormous: altogether over $11,000,000,000 worth,
and including thousands of trucks, automobiles, and airplanes. Although this contribution was only a fraction of Russia's total

munitions pile, it contained many critical items of which the Soviets were desperately short, and without which they might either have succumbed or have been delayed by years in driving the invader from their soil.

The chief complaint of the American public was Russian ingratitude for what amounted to a gigantic gift. The supplies came from the taxpayers' wallet; they were delivered over circuitous and hazardous routes, with appalling loss of ships and lives on the Murmansk run; and they were diverted from what we needed to equip our own armies for the Pacific war and the second front.

The average American was certain that he was providing the bulk of Russia's military equipment, and at least in 1943 he fondly believed that he was not only winning the war but making a greater contribution to victory than the Soviets themselves.[1] He therefore rather expected the Russian people and officials to burst forth in paeans of gratitude. Although the Moscow government expressed its appreciation of lend-lease in moderate terms, it was at pains to withhold from its people the extent to which they were beholden to the distrusted capitalistic giant. The jeep was widely regarded in the Soviet Union as a remarkable Russian invention. Ambassador Standley in 1943 publicly complained of Soviet concealment,[2] and shortly thereafter the Moscow radio broadcast a full statement of American assistance.

Human beings and national states alike normally show little enthusiasm for their dependence on others. The United States in 1783 probably would not have won its independence without the aid of France, yet our history textbooks seldom accord adequate recognition of that debt. The Russians themselves felt that our lend-lease was even less than they deserved. As in 1917, we could not send men to Europe, so we sent munitions with which the Russians killed the common enemy while being killed. Were not

---

[1] Jerome S. Bruner, *Mandate from the People* (New York, 1944), p. 32.

[2] See R. E. Sherwood, *Roosevelt and Hopkins* (New York, 1948), pp. 705–706. The Soviet "line" after the war was that American lend-lease had been negligible in quantity and inferior in quality (New York *Times*, Feb. 26, 1948; Dec. 12, 1949, quoting Russian sources).

irreplaceable Russian lives more important than replaceable lend-lease equipment? Besides, we were not making an unselfish contribution. The master lend-lease agreement with Moscow stated bluntly that the aid was granted because Russia's war "against aggression is vital to the defense of the United States of America." The Russian Communist press went further and accused American capitalistic "sharks" of waxing rich while manufacturing lend-lease equipment for the hard-pressed Soviets.

In later years it became fashionable among certain American critics to say that Roosevelt should have extorted binding pledges from Moscow as to its future behavior before denuding our resources for the unappreciative Soviets. Possibly such pledges might have done something to check the Communist surge into eastern Europe. But in 1941 and 1942, particularly, the U.S.S.R. was in desperate shape, and time was of the essence. Prolonged discussions over what should be yielded under duress might have resulted in fatal delays. The Soviets, moreover, have shown a disconcerting tendency to disregard binding agreements, or to interpret them along the lines of their own peculiar interests, especially in those areas where they can exercise dominating power.

2

Another fertile source of friction with Moscow was our traffic with "fascist beasts" in neutral countries. For the purpose of speedily winning the war, Washington maintained dubious relations with the Vichyites of France and with the Francoites of Spain. These dealings may or may not have been wise, but they could at least be defended on the ground of expediency. The same could likewise be said of our negotiations with certain Fascist-tainted groups in Italy. We also dealt tenderly with anti-Communist Argentina, largely because we needed her meat and grain for the Allied cause. Moscow spokesmen could no more see the need for expediency in these matters than many of our own people could see the wisdom of continued Russian relations with Japan. We likewise incurred the Kremlin's displeasure by declining to goad Turkey into the war; the Russian objective was to divert some fifteen German divisions and open the Dardanelles for lend-lease shipments which we were having to send by round-about routes. Although Washington had sound reasons for its decisions, our obduracy in all these theaters merely confirmed the Communist dictatorship in its belief that the United States was basically a land of "filthy fascists."

Even more annoying in some respects to the Soviet leaders was our reluctance to declare war on Finland. The unfortunate Finns, seeking to regain the territory recently seized by Stalin, joined hands with Hitler in his attack on the U.S.S.R., and on the day of Pearl Harbor were hammering at the defenses of Leningrad on Soviet soil. Our people perceived that the Finns, caught between the two titans, were keeping bad company, but we appreciated their desire to take advantage of Russia's plight. We retained for them the admiration that had been built up by their heroic resistance to the Red invader; and besides they paid their debts. The British, who were more realistic and who perhaps did not relish being "shown up" by debt-paying Finland, declared war on the Finns. But we refused to go further than break diplomatic relations, which we belatedly did in June, 1944. The Moscow officials, who have never distinguished themselves for a penetrating understanding of American public opinion, could not appreciate our reluctance. If, as we claimed, we were out to crush naziism, why did we not declare war on a nation which was fighting on the side of the Nazis? Suspicions of American motives were further deepened.

Poland was an even more serious apple of discord. The anti-Communist Polish government-in-exile, marooned in London and composed of what Moscow branded as "reactionaries" and "adventurists," insisted that when Germany was crushed the boundaries of Poland be restored to their pre-Hitlerian limits. But the Soviets, not wishing to return the eastern portion of Poland that they had seized in 1939, and not wishing to have an unfriendly "fascist" neighbor on their flank, vigorously opposed the pretensions of the London group. The Kremlin set up its own hand-picked Polish government at Lublin, and then suddenly broke relations with the London faction. More than that, although their armies were only a short distance away, the Russians made no real effort to succor General Bór in Warsaw when, in 1944, he abortively rose against the Germans under orders from the London Poles. The story as told by Ambassador Lane indicates that the Soviets incited the Poles to rise and then permitted 250,000 of them to perish, in the hope of discrediting the London regime and removing patriot foes.[3]

The American people, and especially Polish-Americans, believed that the Kremlin, in unilaterally hand-picking the Communist-tainted Lublin regime, was violating the Atlantic Charter, to which Moscow had thrice subscribed. The Roosevelt administration consistently if weakly supported the London exiles, much to the dissatisfaction of the Soviets, pending the establishment of a government conforming to the democratic principles outlined in the Atlantic Charter. The Moscow *Pravda* in 1944 flatly accused reactionary Polish groups of using the United States "for their own dirty blackmailing machinations."

3

The unvarnished truth is that, despite all the fine talk about alliance and co-operation, the Soviet Union and the western democracies waged two separate wars. There never was a supreme command, as under Marshal Foch in 1918. Within broad limits each fought the common enemy in its own way. We were quasi allies, rather than allies.

The failure to achieve a fuller measure of co-operation was not due to lack of effort on the part of the western democracies, including the United States. We would give the Russian officials detailed information about weapons and military plans; little if anything came back from the Vast Land of Silences. We would

---

[3] Arthur B. Lane, *I Saw Poland Betrayed* (Indianapolis, 1948), chap. iii. The Soviets put difficulties in the way of American succor by air.

permit large numbers of Soviet experts to come freely to the
United States and examine our plans and war plants. A handful
of American observers were permitted to visit Russia, but only
after exasperating delays (four to eight weeks were required to

THE THREE MUSKETEERS . . .

(By Reg Manning in the Arizona *Republic*, 1943, by permission.)

secure visas for important persons on military missions), to say
nothing of restrictions on means of transportation and freedom of
movement. Foreign officials trying to help the Soviets were
treated like spies; when the British Military Mission in Russia was
disbanded at the end of the war, its office was found to be infested
with well-concealed N.K.V.D. dictaphones.[4] So secretive were

[4] John R. Deane, *The Strange Alliance* (New York, 1947), p. 154.

the Russians about their military needs, perhaps fearing that some of this information would reach the enemy, that Washington was handicapped in providing them under lend-lease with the supplies they most lacked. When Harry Hopkins in 1941 asked the Soviet General Yakovlev the weight of Russia's heaviest tank, the reply was, "It is a good tank." [5]

Other annoyances developed. There was the traditional bureaucratic delay in Russia resulting from fear of making decisions without reference to the highest authority, especially in the case of foreigners. "Approval in principle" was often a polite way of saying "no." The lie was liberally used to cover up deficiencies. Agreements were freely broken by Moscow under a specious interpretation, and on the pretext that one is released from all obligations if one can find the other signatory guilty of the slightest infraction. But in all fairness it must be recorded that the Soviets were right with embarrassing frequency—according to the strict letter of the law.

Several specific instances are illuminating. On American initiative and in the face of Russian resistance, shuttle-bombing facilities were finally established at Poltava in the Ukraine, thereby enabling American planes based in England or Italy to increase their radius of attack on German cities. There was a great deal of friction, some of it produced by the exuberant misbehavior of United States soldiers, and, according to General Deane, the Americans "were literally forced out" of the station when its limited usefulness came to an end. During the siege of Stalingrad, when the Soviet Union was in desperate straits, we offered to send heavy bombers to Russian bases in the Caucasus. Moscow replied that it would accept the bombers but not the highly trained American personnel, which meant that there was little point in sending the aircraft. Generally speaking, the only foreign-flown airplanes permitted to fly over the U.S.S.R. were those bearing top-level dignitaries. At times it almost seemed as though the Russians would rather lose the war than admit western

[5] Sherwood, *Roosevelt and Hopkins,* p. 330.

observers. During the later stages of the struggle, when American forces accidentally shot down some Soviet planes, the Russians angrily accused us of having done this deliberately. Here as elsewhere they were quick to attribute the worst possible motives.

4

Many of the traits that we Americans found annoying had been developed under Czars and intensified by the hostility of the western world under Commissars. But the events of World War II created other suspicions, such as those arising from the delayed second front. American observers also received the impression that the Soviets were thinking of the "inevitable" clash between communism and capitalism. The current war was but a campaign in the struggle. Why arm a potential enemy with one's secrets? Why permit his military observers to circulate freely, sizing up one's terrain for future invasion? Why permit his people to come among your own and implant subversive ideas, if not by word of mouth at least by expensive equipment, which the Russians did not have in abundance but which the effete capitalists did? [6]

General Deane, who was the chief American liaison officer in Russia, records that whenever steps were taken toward co-operation, they were almost invariably initiated by the western Allies. Hitler had two last-ditch hopes. One was the possibility of a secret weapon; the other was the possibility of a split between the Soviets and their allies. The split finally came too late to help him, but as one looks back upon the hair-trigger friction of the war years, one wonders why it did not come sooner.

The American people, perhaps fortunately, were not then privy to all these pullings and haulings behind the scenes. We were vaguely aware that the men in the Kremlin were difficult to deal with, but we were of a mind to overlook their peculiarities.

---

[6] President Roosevelt's daughter Anna, who accompanied him to Yalta in 1945, on one occasion gave some chocolate bars to a group of Russian children. A Soviet official handed them back with the admonition, "They have enough food. We do not wish the American lady to think that they lack" (Elliott Roosevelt, *As He Saw It* [New York, 1946], p. 243).

We were deeply grateful for the smashing blows of the Soviets against our enemy, and we were suffused with wishful thinking as to Russia's role in the new world order then being planned.

Various public opinion polls showed that during the high point of good feeling, on the eve of the San Francisco Conference in 1945, somewhat more than a majority of our people trusted Stalin to co-operate with us after the war.[7] A great majority were tolerantly willing to regard Russia, after all her sacrifices, as an equal in the making of the peace. The poll takers, on the other hand, never found a majority agreeable to a hard-and-fast military alliance with the Soviet Union, though during the war years we favored such an entanglement with both China and Britain.

5

The aloof Soviets revealed no eagerness to take part in Allied conferences, whether major or minor. They even rejected an invitation in 1944 to attend the Chicago aviation conference on the pretext that "fascist" countries like Switzerland would be represented. So bad was the atmosphere in 1943 that the aged and ailing Secretary of State Hull, without vaccination or immunization, boarded an airplane for the first time in his life and flew to Moscow, where he succeeded in producing an upswing in cordiality. President Roosevelt, after repeated efforts to bring about a meeting, twice risked his life in crossing the Atlantic to confer with Stalin at Teheran and then at Yalta.[8]

The standoffishness of our Slavic ally merely confirmed the worst suspicions of a host of Americans. But fair-minded observers perceived that Soviet unco-operativeness often stemmed from a desire to avoid provoking Japan. This was notably true of the Cairo conference, which was primarily concerned with

---

[7] *Public Opinion Quarterly*, IX, 103 (Spring, 1945).

[8] The battleship carrying Roosevelt across the Atlantic to Teheran was almost struck accidentally by a torpedo, and his plane flying to Yalta was almost forced down in the mountains by ice. Admiral Leahy was convinced that Stalin could not leave the direction of the Soviet armies (W. D. Leahy, *I Was There* [New York, 1950], pp. 196, 296, 303).

prosecuting the war against the Nipponese and which, insofar as it related to the Far East, could not be attended by "neutral" Russia. Stalin, moreover, was absorbed with directing the defense of the U.S.S.R., and later the gigantic offensives that the Red army finally mounted. But a noisy and growing group of Americans felt, not altogether without reason, that the nonattendance or halfhearted participation of the Soviets sprang from a determination to pursue their own aims unilaterally, without regard for the common cause.

In February, 1945, Roosevelt, Churchill, and Stalin met at Yalta, a beautiful but Nazi-ravaged resort on the shores of the Crimea. This was the last gathering of the Big Three attended by the fast-failing Roosevelt, and in some ways it marked the high tide of inter-Allied co-operation. The conferees agreed on the destruction and shackling of Germany, as well as on a voting formula for the big powers at the forthcoming San Francisco Conference. The decisions that aroused the most violent outcry at the time concerned Poland. Stalin pledged himself to support a more broadly based democratic government than that provided by either the Lublin or London factions. The new Poland was to be shorn of approximately the formerly Russian-owned eastern third, while compensating territory was to be torn from the side of Germany on the west.

These arrangements stirred up a veritable hornets' nest of criticism. The London Poles, as well as the Catholic and Polish groups in America, condemned the Yalta "betrayal." Poland, they charged, had been saved from her enemies only to be crucified by her friends. Congressman Lesinski of Michigan and Congressman O'Konski of Wisconsin assailed the "crime of Crimea" as a "stab in the back" for Poland and as a "second Munich." A secret agreement at Yalta, which leaked out prematurely the next month and caused strong reactions in the United States, stipulated that both the U.S.S.R. and the United States, as an offset to the six votes of the British Commonwealth, might seek three votes in the Assembly of the projected world organization. Washington promptly renounced any such pretension, but Russia ultimately secured one vote for herself and an additional vote for the Ukraine and White Russia.

A highly significant secret agreement at Yalta, detailing the conditions under which Russia would enter the war against Japan, was not made officially public until exactly a year later.[9] The obvious reason for secrecy was a desire not to provoke Japan until Hitler had been disposed of and the Soviets could shift their troops to Siberia. Stalin promised to enter the war "in two or three months" after the surrender of Germany, but he demanded and secured a stiff price. The *status quo* in Communist-dominated Outer Mongolia (once under China's suzerainty) was to be preserved; the former rights of Russia, lost in the Russo-Japanese War, were to be restored. These included the return to Russia of the southern part of the island of Sakhalin; the internationalization of the Manchurian port of Dairen (the pre-eminent rights of Russia at this port to be safeguarded); and the restoration to Russia of the lease of Port Arthur as a naval base. Provision was also made for a joint operation of the Manchuria railroads by both Chinese and Russians, with China retaining sovereignty and the pre-eminent interests of the Soviet Union being safeguarded. President Roosevelt undertook to persuade the Chinese Nationalist government to accept these terms, some of which ran directly counter to the pledges that he and Churchill had made to Chiang Kai-shek at Cairo in 1943. In addition, Russia was to secure the Japanese-owned Kuril Islands, which, American alarmists were quick to note, might be used as bases for bombing the United States.

The terms of the secret agreement gradually leaked out, after both Germany and Japan had been crushed, and when American confidence in Stalin's co-operativeness was evaporating. The Soviets, who were adepts at moving in once their boot was in the door, had seemingly returned to Manchuria on essentially the same basis—in some respects even stronger—than they had been

---

[9] *Department of State Bulletin,* XIV, 282 (Feb. 24, 1946).

when John Hay had tried to jockey them out. The wheel had come full circle, and as far as Manchuria was concerned the Open Door was completely unhinged.[10]

6

The San Francisco Conference, which met in the spring of 1945 with high hopes, marked a turning point in Soviet relations with the United States. Thereafter American public confidence in Stalin's willingness to co-operate in world organization began to spiral sharply downward.

The Moscow government, which revealed little interest in the new world league, chose a relatively obscure delegation. Only after a special appeal from the White House did Stalin consent to nominate Foreign Minister Molotov.

The Russian delegation, which arrived in San Francisco with a conspicuously strong bodyguard, created a disagreeable impression from the outset. Molotov championed the interests of the Soviet Union with belligerency. He insisted that the chairmanship of the Conference, instead of being held by the host nation (the United States), rotate among the Big Four. He urged representation for the new Polish government, which had been set up under Russian sponsorship. He vehemently but unsuccessfully demanded that "fascist" Argentina, which had not declared war on the Axis, be excluded from the Conference. He secured for the U.S.S.R., pursuant to the Yalta deal, three votes in the Assembly. He cavalierly brushed aside the rights of the small states, arguing that the big powers, which had borne the brunt of the fighting, should have the lion's share in running the postwar world. He vainly attempted to secure a veto over even discussion in the Security Council. He fought vigorously for the rights of colonial peoples, of whom the Soviet Union had none and of whom the leading Allied powers had many, notably Britain and France.

---

[10] The pact made by Moscow with Communist China in 1950, if it can be taken at face value, indicated a withdrawal, but during the preceding five years American anti-Soviet attitudes had crystallized.

All this does not mean that there was not a large area of agreement between the Soviet Union and the United States at San Francisco, but the aggressive tactics of Molotov made sensational headlines. In many respects the small states, elbowing for a place, caused more of an uproar. The United States delegation, with an eye to approval by the Senate, was no less insistent than the Soviets on the general veto in the Security Council. But the net effect was to reinvigorate suspicions regarding Moscow which had been lulled by the war, and to implant doubts as to Russian co-operativeness in the future.

7

On August 8, 1945, three months to the day after the surrender of Germany, and in complete fulfillment of Stalin's pledge at Yalta, Russia declared war on Japan (effective August 9) and forthwith began to crush the emaciated Kwantung army in Manchuria. Six days later Japan surrendered and the Pacific war was over. By this narrow margin the Soviet Union almost failed to purchase a ticket at the prospective peace conference with Japan. We now know that the Russians were aware of Japanese peace feelers, and that they had been advised of the atomic bomb. The epochal detonation at Hiroshima came only two days before the Soviet declaration of war.[11]

For several years an influential body of Americans had been annoyed because the Russians would not enter the Pacific combat. When the Soviet-German conflict ended, many of these critics believed that Moscow should at once declare war. We did not fully appreciate the difficulties of transferring huge forces and supplies a distance of some 8,000 miles from the European front to eastern Siberia. Stalin no doubt could have attacked sooner, with less preparation and possibly less success, had he felt under

---

[11] Yet it should be noted that Stalin had told Hopkins in Moscow on May 28, 1945, several months after Yalta and more than six weeks before the first atomic bomb was exploded in New Mexico, that the Soviet army would be ready to attack Manchuria by August 8, the very day of the declaration of war (Sherwood, *Roosevelt and Hopkins*, p. 902).

extreme compulsion to do so. But he presumably was not loath to let the Americans weaken themselves by incurring some serious casualties in fighting the Japanese. When the U.S.S.R. finally declared war, there was general rejoicing in the United States. We were faced with an invasion of Japan, which might cost hundreds of thousands of lives, and Russian participation would presumably save American boys by pinning down troops in Manchuria and in shortening the struggle.

But when it quickly became evident that Japan, dazed by atomic bombs, probably would have surrendered without Soviet intervention, our bitterness over Stalin's nonparticipation gave way to dissatisfaction over his participation. This feeling of annoyance increased when we heard that our Slavic allies were taking complete credit at home for having knocked out Japan; what the Yankees had not been able to do in over three years the Russians had done in only six days.[12] The dissatisfaction intensified when we finally learned that at Yalta we had paid a high price to bribe Stalin into a war from which he could not have been kept at any price. With the wisdom of hindsight, a multitude of Americans, especially those of anti-New Deal persuasion, clamored that the slippery Stalin had sold the sickly Roosevelt, advised by the sickly Harry Hopkins, a gigantic gold brick.[13]

But what was the situation in February, 1945, when the Big Three conferred on the Crimea? Germany was far from finished, as we were reminded by the recent and bloody breakthrough culminating in the Battle of the Bulge. Frightful additional casualties were expected in the assault on the Japanese homeland. Even when Japan was crushed, the self-sufficing Japanese Kwantung

---

[12] At a Christmas Eve dinner in Moscow, in 1945, Secretary of State Byrnes saw a moving picture of the Japanese surrender ceremony. The principal participants seemed to be Russians and Japanese; General MacArthur was in the background; and there was no indication that the scene was on an American battleship, the *Missouri* (J. F. Byrnes, *Speaking Frankly* [New York, 1947], p. 213).

[13] For the semiofficial view that the real trouble lay not in the Yalta arrangements but in the failure of the Russians to live up to them, see Edward R. Stettinius, Jr., *Roosevelt and the Russians* (Garden City, N.Y., 1949), p. 303.

army in Manchuria could presumably carry on for years, and it would have to be mopped up by American boys, with further staggering losses. There was no assurance at the time of the Yalta Conference that the atomic bomb would work, or work as devastatingly as it did, or produce the effects that were produced.

Stalin was in a position to drive a hard bargain at Yalta—and he did. But the fact is that he retreated from his maximum demands, and set a formal limit, for whatever it might be worth, on his current designs in eastern Asia. His bargaining position would have been a good deal stronger if he had remained on the sidelines as the overshadowing power in the Far East, while we exhausted ourselves hammering down the gates of Japan. But the American people, unaware of all these possibilities, developed a suspicion of Soviet gains at Yalta that augured ill for amity in the postwar years.

XXVI

The Shadow of the

Hammer and Sickle.

"What is Russia up to now? It is, of course, the supreme conundrum of our time."—Senator Arthur H. Vandenberg, 1946

1

THE most alarming development of recent years is that the wartime coalition of the United Nations collapsed, and the world was thrown back anew into the international anarchy of the Hitlerian era. The roseate dream of One World proved to be only a mirage.

Bickering among allies, once the cement of a common foe has dissolved, is an old story. It developed after World War I; it developed after World War II. In 1945 and after, we actually generated considerable friction with Britain over Palestine and with France over Germany, to mention only two disputes. But the rift with the U.S.S.R. went alarmingly beyond the ordinary misunderstandings of wartime associates.

When the conflict crashed to a close in Europe, we still cherished a substantial reservoir of good will for the stout-hearted Russians, who had saved our skins while saving their own. If the Kremlin had chosen to conciliate rather than alienate us, we no doubt would have been willing to contribute generously in technicians, materials, and money to the rehabilitation of war-ravaged Russia.

But within a few months our worst fears were aroused, and the reservoir of good will cracked wide open. Numerous public opinion polls showed that before the summer of 1946, and even earlier in some cases, the American people had by strong or over-whelming majorities reached the following disquieting conclusions:

1. Russia could not be trusted to co-operate effectively in the new world organization.
2. The foreign policies of the Soviet Union could not meet with our approval.
3. The dominance of Russia over her satellite neighbors was prompted by aggressive rather than defensive designs.
4. The Soviet Union was not a peace-loving nation.
5. Another world holocaust was probable within twenty-five or so years.
6. Russia was most likely to start it.
7. A "get tough" policy was needed to halt the Soviets.[1]

A small but vocal minority of Americans, preponderantly isolationists, were complaining that we should never have entered World War II; that the U.S.S.R. could have squeezed through without us; and that an exhausted Russia was preferable to the Communist threat that now confronted us.

Just as the Japanese unified the United States by their electrifying attack on Pearl Harbor, so the Russians—less spectacularly but hardly less effectively—united the Americans against them by their crude and blustering tactics. The American people were in a mood to be lulled to sleep, and by arousing them to prospective dangers the Soviet leaders thwarted their own ostensible ends. Stalin and Molotov were the real fathers of the huge and costly postwar preparedness program in the United States. Possibly their long-range strategy was to bankrupt the bastion of capitalism and soften it up for world revolution.

---

[1] Conclusions based on an analysis of all the national public opinion polls for these years, the skeletonized results of which appear in *Public Opinion Quarterly*.

"I'M HERE TO STAY, TOO"

(From the Washington *Post*, 1947, by permission.)

2

The myth has somehow gained currency that, if Roosevelt had not been stricken in the hour of victory, co-operation between Russia and America would have been brought to the high level of which he had dreamed.

This view is held by many admirers of the late President, and is also voiced by Communists and other Soviet apologists, especially those who seek an excuse for deteriorating relations. But whatever the views of the Soviet spokesmen, the Russian masses, knowing vaguely of Roosevelt's friendliness and openhanded generosity with lend-lease largesse, held—and perhaps still hold—their benefactor in considerable esteem.

The proof is convincing—as detailed in the published postwar revelations of James F. Byrnes, Henry L. Stimson, and Harry L. Hopkins—that Roosevelt died knowing or strongly suspecting that his bold bid for conciliation had failed. The sharp shift in Soviet policy was clearly discernible by mid-March, 1945, about two weeks before the enfeebled and disillusioned President made his final trip to Warm Springs.

In March, 1945, the western Allies were negotiating for the surrender of the German army in Italy. Stalin, evidently fearing that certain German divisions would be released for action against the Red army, dispatched a scorching telegram to Roosevelt, reflecting on American truthfulness and good faith. Although the affair was finally patched up, the President was deeply hurt by the man whom he had familiarly called "Uncle Joe."

Roosevelt himself sent a sharp telegram to Stalin when he learned that the Russians were releasing captured American prisoners in out-of-the-way places, contrary to the Yalta agreement. We assumed, whether correctly or not, that the Soviet rulers did not want our officers to see their Communist infiltration in Poland and elsewhere.[2]

Roosevelt likewise found the voracious designs of the Soviet-backed Yugoslavs on Italy's Trieste "wholly unjustified and deeply disquieting"—to quote Secretary Stimson.

---

[2] John R. Deane, *The Strange Alliance* (New York, 1947), p. 190. Admiral W. D. Leahy comes to the same conclusions and notes that the Soviets refused to permit American relief planes to land in Poland (*I Was There* [New York, 1950], p. 329). For the Stalin-Roosevelt interchange of telegrams, see *ibid.*, pp. 330–336.

By mid-March, 1945, the Soviets were clearly taking over Romania in violation of Stalin's pledges at Yalta.

Most distressing of all was unmistakable evidence that the Soviets, also in defiance of the Yalta pact, were setting up in Poland a prefabricated Communist government. Unless there was a freely constituted Polish regime, the heart would be cut out of the Yalta agreement, which would then turn out to be a cruel hoax.

On April 1, 1945, Roosevelt dispatched a vigorous telegram to Stalin remonstrating against Soviet usurpations in both Romania and Poland. The response being unsatisfactory, the President instructed the State Department to prepare a reply jointly with the British Foreign Office. Before the message could be sent he died, weary and sick at heart.[3]

3

Why did the Kremlin so rudely slap aside the proffered hand of co-operation and fellowship?

The Soviets had never allied themselves with the western democracies in spirit, and when the fighting stopped there was a natural tendency for the Russian mind to return to—or remain in—the old grooves of antiwestern distrust. Secretary Hull concluded that Moscow started to launch out on its independent course as early as 1944, when it scented final victory and felt less dependent upon the democracies for aid. About the same time, and presumably for the same reason, Soviet spokesmen began to stress once more the orthodox Communist ideals of internationalism and world revolution, quite in contrast to their emphasis on nationalism during the wartime crisis.

This disquieting development was entirely natural. Communism, which openly proclaims warfare on capitalism, could not

---

[3] See J. F. Byrnes, *Speaking Frankly* (New York, 1947), pp. 54–55; R. E. Sherwood, *Roosevelt and Hopkins* (New York, 1948), pp. 875–876; H. L. Stimson and McGeorge Bundy, *On Active Service* (New York, 1947), p. 609.

trust the democratic world, and Moscow's policy was no doubt permeated by anticapitalistic fears. Soviet misgivings were further fed by the irresponsible utterances of certain American newspapers and political leaders, including the prominent American legislator in Italy who in 1945 asked a group of American soldiers if they did not want to keep going right on to Moscow. The cloistered occupants of the Kremlin, having risen to precarious power with the cry of capitalistic encirclement, would be less indispensable and hence less secure if that encirclement should end. To co-operate would kill a substantial part of their reason for existence. Not only was it to their personal advantage to harp on western aggression, whether they really feared it or not, but an outside bogey would prove useful in quieting disunity at home and in arousing an already exhausted people to greater sacrifices.

The Soviet leaders at first were inclined to belittle the atomic bomb, but gradually they began to promote a fear psychosis among their people. Rich and powerful Uncle Sam had this horrible new weapon, loaded and ticking, and the Russians did not have it in 1945, and did not get it, according to our information, until four years later. The alarm of large segments of the Russian people over the so-called "rattling of the atom bomb" was unquestionably real, especially when no less a figure than ex-Governor George H. Earle of Pennsylvania, among others, could proclaim in 1946 that we should attack the Russians with the bomb "while we have it and before they get it." [4]

To Americans, Soviet charges of aggression seemed ludicrous. With unprecedented haste and with a juvenile disregard of power realities, we had disbanded the fresh and potent mechanized army that had cracked Hitler's famed west wall. As for the atom bomb, Governor Earle's fulminations represented the views of an inconsequential minority. All we wanted was peace and a return to prewar days.

Soviet fears of capitalistic aggression were further deepened by our attitude toward Moscow's dealings with its weaker neighbors,

[4] San Francisco *Chronicle*, March 24, 1946.

notably Poland, whose democratic status had presumably been guaranteed at Yalta. The protests of the western Allies against Soviet encroachments merely confirmed the Kremlin's suspicions, and provided the Russians with justification for building up anti-capitalistic puppets in neighboring countries before the democracies could foster anti-Communist regimes.

The leaders of Communist Russia harbored additional grievances. They professed to be angered by our open support of "fascist" Argentina at the San Francisco Conference. They were disconcerted by our abrupt and seemingly brutal termination of lend-lease, even though our cancellation was dictated by the terms of the law, and even though we continued for nearly two years to fulfill many of our commitments. They were angered by our vigorous support of France for a place on the reparations commission—a France that had left its allies in the lurch by hoisting the white flag of surrender five years before the end of the war. They were affronted by our inept handling of their request for a huge loan, which the State Department announced in 1946 had been "misplaced." [5] But by this time so many things had gone wrong that American opinion, as nation-wide polls revealed, would not have tolerated substantial grants to rebuild the nation that was looming up as our most formidable potential foe.[6]

4

The war-hating Americans were especially disturbed by the inability of the Soviet Union to agree with the western world on terms of peace for the fallen Axis foe. A series of meetings of the foreign ministers of the major powers, after prolonged wrangling, resulted by late 1946 in the drawing up of treaties for Hungary, Italy, Romania, Bulgaria, and Finland. But no agreement could be reached on Germany, Austria, or Japan.

The Austrian problem was peculiarly vexatious. We regarded the Austrians as a people liberated from the shackles of Hitler; the

---

[5] New York *Times*, March 2, 1946.
[6] *Public Opinion Quarterly*, IX, 533 (Winter, 1945–1946).

Soviets regarded them as willing accomplices of Hitler. We labored to protect Austrian assets and to rehabilitate an independent government. The Russians made off with assets for much-needed reparations, and undertook to thwart our efforts to create a democratically based regime. They also succeeded in defeating all our efforts to extend American principles of free navigation to the Danube. Painful clashes between tommy-gun-equipped Soviet soldiers and Americans added to the tension, as was true also in Berlin.

The prospect seemed even darker in Germany, which had been chopped up into four zones under the administration of Russia, Britain, France, and the United States respectively. Contrary to the Potsdam agreement of 1945, the Soviets seized reparations from current production;[7] supported the temporary western boundary of Poland as a finality; blocked Allied efforts to treat Germany as an economic entity; and sought to communize Germany by propaganda, by the discriminatory distribution of food, and by other police-state methods. The Russians also retained hundreds of thousands of German prisoners of war, contrary to agreement, and deported or lured away German technicians, thus securing the know-how for making the latest-type submarines and other lethal weapons. (The United States by less arbitrary methods did substantially the same thing when it could.) The Soviets further opposed urgently needed currency reform, hounded displaced persons who had anti-Communist leanings, and, while seeking a hand in the joint control of the Ruhr, loudly accused the western powers of trying to revive Hitlerian cartels.

Secretaries of State Byrnes and Marshall, departing sharply from American tradition, vainly attempted to obtain Russian adherence to a twenty-five- to forty-year treaty designed to keep Germany disarmed.[8] The very fact that public opinion in the

---

[7] In mid-1948 the State Department reported thirty-seven violations of agreements with the United States by the Soviets, chiefly the Yalta and Potsdam pacts (*Senate Reports*, 80 Cong., 2 sess., No. 1440).

[8] Byrnes, *Speaking Frankly*, pp. 125, 171, 174, 176.

United States did not flare up violently against this forsaking of sacred principles is in itself eloquent testimony to the growing fear of the Soviet Union. The deadlock finally became so paralyzing that the three western Allies—Britain, France, and the United States—had no alternatives but to abandon their respective zones, leaving Germany with its enormous war potential to fall into the hands of Communist Russia, or to create an amputated new Germany around the three western zones. Following Secretary Byrnes' uncompromising speech at Stuttgart, Germany (September, 1946), serving notice that we were there to stay, determined steps were taken in the direction of establishing a western Germany, to the accompaniment of charges from Moscow that the Allies had broken the Potsdam pact. The ghost of Hitler must have laughed ghoulishly to see the democratic west building up Germany against Communist Russia.

The disheartening conviction gradually deepened among our citizenry that the Kremlin did not want agreement—except on its own terms. Delay and deadlock would produce further chaos in western Europe; and chaos is the natural seedbed of communism. When people become desperate enough, they will try almost anything. Starvation knows no ideology. Nor were the Soviet officials enthusiastic about reviving the German standard of living. The inhabitants of adjoining Communist countries might ask dangerous questions if their capitalistic neighbors enjoyed more consumers' goods, superior sanitary facilities, and other modern conveniences. Common misery would make for more willing Communists.

The Soviets of course had their own point of view regarding the four-power revival of central Europe. Their constant complaint—and one seemingly justified by events—was that the western bloc was trying to outvote them in conference and thus promote capitalism. They were right, in the sense that any rebuilding of Germany and Austria on pre-Hitlerian lines was antipathetic to communism. In pursuance of their obstructionism the Russian delegates, especially Foreign Minister Molotov, were past masters at wearing down their adversaries by extravagant demands, browbeating tactics, insulting charges, and the constant iteration of irrelevant or repetitious arguments pending further instructions from the Kremlin. Delay was a secret weapon of the Soviets. The French, with their well-founded terror of a revived Germany, were at times even more unreasonable than Russia, especially during the formative six months following the overthrow of Hitler, but at least they preserved the amenities.

5

Soviet distrust and obstruction transformed the United Nations organization, which had been begotten in San Francisco with high hopes, into a verbal cockpit.

Outnumbered by the capitalistic world, the Russians with their three votes gathered their satellites around them in a solid bloc to resist western proposals. The Soviet delegation brought deadlock and futility to the Security Council by the intemperate and routine use of the veto. From the American point of view this was negation gone to seed; from the Soviet point of view it was the legitimate exercise of the "principle of unanimity."

The Washington government, with what it regarded as unheard-of generosity, offered to share the "secret" of the atomic bomb if an adequate method of international control could be worked out by the United Nations. But the Soviets, demanding that we outlaw the bomb and destroy all stock piles even before a discussion of arms reduction could take place, spurned our plan. They countered with sweeping proposals for disarmament, reminiscent of those of the 1920's, which would clearly be unacceptable to a world made apprehensive by Communist tactics. The Russians could then pose as the true friends of peace against the designs of the "warmongering" west, while their scientists worked feverishly to unlock the atom.

In the face of repeated Soviet vetoes, all schemes for atomic control finally had to be suspended in 1948. The chief stumbling block was the unwillingness of Moscow freely to admit international inspectors, without whom there could be no effective control. The Russians, whether under Czars or Commissars, have never welcomed prying foreigners.

Within the United Nations organization the Soviet delegates further antagonized the American public. They did not welcome investigations of Communist-supported guerrilla activity in Greece. They pressed for the ostracism of Franco's Spain, which our people at first favored. But Spain, as a potential dike against the Russians, rose in respectability with the democratic nations as the Communist menace became more threatening. The vicious circle was again at work. The Russians, having driven us toward Franco, found in our action proof of their charges that we were essentially "reactionary." The Soviets also vigorously opposed the admission of new "fascist" members into the United Nations, such as Eire and Portugal.

Underscoring the split between the Communist and non-Communist world, the Russians persistently declined to join many of the organizations set up by the United Nations, except those few from which they derived direct benefit. They even withdrew from the World Health Organization in 1949. Under the Czars the Russians had shown relatively little interest in such cooperative ventures, especially in the economic world; under the Communists, who operate what is in effect an enormous cartel of their own, there was even less enthusiasm.

The conclusion gradually forced itself upon many thoughtful Americans that the Russians had not joined the United Nations in good faith, but for the purpose of shaping it or deadlocking it in such a way as to safeguard Soviet interests. Moscow may well have had in mind exploiting the organization as an espionage center and a global sounding board for Communist propaganda. Certainly the shockingly violent charges of Andrei Y. Vishinsky against American "warmongering," beginning in 1947, supported this interpretation and also accelerated the "new diplomacy," which was characterized by the language of the fishwife rather than that of Lord Chesterfield.

6

Disquieting though all this friction with the Soviet Union was, nothing so actively aroused the American masses as the gradual lowering of what Winston Churchill called the "iron curtain."

Within a short time after the Russian "liberator" had reached the countries of eastern Europe and the Balkans, Moscow had taken over. The misbehavior of the Red army, and the resultant disillusionment of the people, may have prompted the Kremlin to accelerate the communizing process.[9]

Romania and Poland, despite the unequivocal pledges at Yalta, were the first to go. Yugoslavia fell under the domination of Tito, a lesser Stalin, who at first subserviently sided with the Soviet bloc against the western democracies. Backed by Russia, Tito tried to seize Trieste; scorned our pleas not to execute his pro-Ally rival, General Mikhailovitch (Moscow denounced Washington for interfering in the case); and in 1946 shot down one of our transport planes, some of which had persisted in passing over his territory, with a loss of five lives. An outraged United States forced Tito to make such reparation as was possible, all the while suspecting that he would not have been so bold as to slap such a great power without at least the silent backing of Moscow. Two years later, in 1948, Tito regained the headlines when he refused to jump at the crack of the Kremlin's whip, and the United States, delighted to see a gap widening in the iron curtain, encouraged him in his spectacular deviation from the Stalinist "line."

Soviet darkness likewise descended upon Albania, Bulgaria (an earlier objective of Czarist ambitions), and Hungary, despite repeated protests from the banks of the Potomac. A free Czechoslovakia survived until 1948, when the Communist ax fell. Simul-

---

[9] A contemporary witticism was that Russian communism suffered two great setbacks during the war years: when Europe saw the Red army, and when the Red army saw Europe. Posters were put up in Russia warning, "Do not believe all returned soldiers" (Walter B. Smith, *My Three Years in Moscow* [Philadelphia, 1950], p. 287).

taneously Finland was forced more closely into the Soviet orbit through a defensive treaty of alliance with the U.S.S.R.

The success of the Moscow Communists was usually facilitated by the coercive presence of the Red army. The standard formula was for the local Communists to secure those ministries that controlled propaganda, education, justice, and the police. With this giant boot in the door, the rest was easy. In no single one of the iron-curtain countries where there was a free election did the Communists win a majority of the votes cast, though the presence of splinter parties often made a majority difficult to obtain. In the case of ill-starred Poland, when the "free and unfettered" election was finally held early in 1947—an election that was a fraudulent farce—the American ambassador accepted the estimate that 60 per cent of the Poles favored the opposition Peasant Party.[10]

The Soviets in addition put the screws on their neighbors to the north and south. Norway tremblingly rejected a request for strategic bases on her Spitsbergen islands, no doubt with encouragement from the western democracies. In 1946 oil-rich Iran— the Persia of Russo-British nineteenth-century rivalry—was belatedly and reluctantly evacuated by the Red army, under strong pressure from world opinion and the United Nations, but not until the Russian delegate Gromyko had dramatically stalked out of the Security Council, and not until the Soviets had planted their puppets in Azerbaijan, an Iranian province. The Iranians, with American encouragement, finally wiped out this dangerous fifth column. But Russia was to be heard from again. Potential Iranian bases were too near her vitals, and she was under powerful compulsion to secure the priceless black gold of Iran for herself, while denying it to the war machines of her capitalistic enemies.

While Iran was conspicuously in the world's eye, the Soviets, either in their press or officially, were waging a war of nerves against Turkey. They demanded a return of the Black Sea provinces of Kars and Ardahan (transferred by the Bolsheviks in

[10] Arthur B. Lane, *I Saw Poland Betrayed* (Indianapolis, 1948), p. 287.

1921), and joint control of the Dardanelles. The Turks stood fast, keeping their armies mobilized, while the United States provided moral support by dispatching warships to Turkish and Greek waters, to the acute dissatisfaction of the Soviet press. The Greek regime also needed bolstering, menaced as it was by Communist guerrillas succored from Yugoslavia, Bulgaria, and Albania.

7

In the Far East the pattern of Soviet absorption was essentially the same. The Red armies delayed evacuation of Manchuria until the Communists could secure a toehold, and then permitted them to appropriate huge quantities of "abandoned" Japanese arms. Before leaving, Soviet troops stripped the factories of Manchuria, which sustained the bulk of Chinese manufacturing, presumably to prevent the machines from falling to the Nationalists of Chiang Kai-shek.

Nationalist resistance in Manchuria collapsed during 1948, and the Communists drove inexorably southward. Although the Communist party in China had been created by Moscow in the 1920's, and although it was led to a considerable extent by Moscow-trained or Moscow-inspired leaders, Soviet aid to the Chinese Communists was indirect rather than direct. The unconcealed efforts of the United States to bolster up the collapsing Nationalist regime with hundreds of millions of dollars and shiploads of supplies went far beyond anything done openly by the Russian Communists in China. Soviet spokesmen complained bitterly that the Americans were seeking aerial or military bases in China from which to bomb or otherwise attack Russian installations, and the same charges—some of them fantastic—were repeated endlessly regarding our alleged designs on Japan, Korea, Greece, Turkey, Portugal, Spain, France, Italy, Iceland, Iran, North Africa, Greenland, and other strategic spots.

The "free" Manchurian port of Dairen, now in the iron grip of the Soviets, was definitely not free. Outer Mongolia, as arranged at Yalta, gravitated completely within the Soviet orbit. Nationalist or other disruptive movements were being fomented by Moscow or Moscow-trained Communists in French Indo-China, in British Malaya, in Dutch Indonesia, in Burma, in Siam, in India, and in the Philippines. The chameleonlike Russian Communists were not averse to using local nationalist movements as temporary tools for promoting their world revolutionary aims. With similar inconsistency, they have not hesitated to demand rights for "colonial" peoples abroad which their own people would not dare to seek at home.[11]

In Korea north of the 38th parallel, the Soviets propped up a Communist clique and trained a Communist army, which seemed quite capable of absorbing South Korea whenever the American troops should withdraw, as they did in 1949. The Russians had only to make a minority Communist; the Americans had to make a strong majority democratic—and keep it that way.

Only in Japan did the United States clearly hold the whip hand. Under the military rule of General Douglas MacArthur, who repaid Moscow for its unilateralism elsewhere with some of his own, the Soviets were unable to hamstring American policy, though protesting vociferously. They may have found some solace in retaining hundreds of thousands of Japanese prisoners of war, presumably for Communist indoctrination but clearly in violation of their plighted word.

8

The schemes of the Soviets to dominate their smaller neighbors could be defended with more plausibility than their efforts to dominate noncontiguous areas. Moscow argued with considerable force that the U.S.S.R. had to have friendly states on its flanks, just as the Americans had to have friendly governments in those countries that commanded the Panama Canal lifeline.

---

[11] After opposing colonialism, the Soviet Union used its forty-second and forty-third vetoes in the Security Council of the United Nations to block a resolution congratulating the Dutch and Indonesians on arranging for a free Indonesia (New York *Times*, Dec. 14, 1949).

The opinion was rather generally held in the United States that no one could quarrel with the desire of the war-racked Russians to have well-disposed neighbors. But there is a world of difference between a friendly neighbor and a vassal state whose liberties have been subverted, whose parliamentary institutions (where they existed) have been swept aside, whose sovereignty has been extinguished, and whose foreign policy is dictated by the Kremlin.

And where does defense end and aggression begin? If one must have a "friendly state" (say Poland) on one's flank, one must also have a "friendly state" (say Germany) on Poland's flank, and one must have a "friendly state" (say France) on Germany's flank. If this line of reasoning were pursued relentlessly, there would be only Communist states, and the Marxian dream of global conquest would come true. The situation had become so ominous by the middle of 1946 that approximately half our people were prepared to say that the Soviet aim was not local defense but world domination.[12]

The Communists labored desperately in the favorable chaos of the postwar period to win ascendancy in France and Italy, both of which countries harbored enough underprivilege to provide fertile soil for agitators. In 1947 and early 1948 it seemed like touch and go in both France and Italy, with Soviet Russia pouring out "political wheat" from her short supplies, and with the United States countering somewhat haphazardly from its capacious storehouses. The grim fact was that if Italy and France succumbed to the Communists, Soviet power would sweep to the English Channel, and all Europe would fall under the Hammer and Sickle. The western democracies, notably Britain and America, would then be thrown back where they had been in the dismal days of Dunkirk in 1940, only in some respects their plight would be worse. If anything was to be done, it had to be done quickly.

---

[12] *Public Opinion Quarterly*, X, 265 (Summer, 1946).

XXVII

The Cold War

"I believe that it must be the policy of the United States to support free peoples who are resisting attempted subjugation by armed minorities or by outside pressures."—Harry S. Truman, 1947

I

BY EARLY 1947 the tactics of the Kremlin had so alarmed the American people, as numerous public opinion polls reveal, that formidable popular support could be confidently expected for a get-tough-with-Russia policy. The stage was set for the Washington government to seize the diplomatic initiative in the cold war against communism.

The overburdened British were about to withdraw their large-scale support from Greece, with the strong probability that this strategic peninsula, which commands the eastern Mediterranean and the Suez Canal, would fall into the clutch of communism. Into the breach stepped President Truman, who, in a reverberating message to Congress (March 12, 1947), urged the United States to support free peoples in their efforts to escape Communist engulfment, and specifically recommended an initial appropriation of $400,000,000 for military and economic aid to both Greece and Turkey. The plight of Turkey was hardly less precarious than that of Greece, and its strategic importance no less vital.

Public reactions in America were on the whole strongly favorable to supporting the cause of freedom against communism,[1] and the necessary appropriations passed Congress by heavy majorities. There was a strong undertone of opposition from hidebound isolationists, from those frugal citizens who saw no end to the outpouring of dollars, from those timid souls who did not want to provoke the U.S.S.R., and from those zealous internationalists who felt that the United Nations should not have been bypassed. The obvious reason for a unilateral course was that Moscow would undoubtedly have delayed any effective group action.

The American people, as the historic champions of liberal movements the world over, did not relish the role of shoring up a reactionary monarchy in Greece. But in this critical hour we were prepared to put security above democracy, in the hope that democracy would come later. The Senate made the decision less difficult, and the affront to the United Nations less painful, by carrying through an amendment which stated that whenever the United Nations was prepared to take over the burden, the United States would lay it down.[2]

News commentators in America who knew their history were quick to point out parallels between the Truman Doctrine of 1947 and the Monroe Doctrine of 1823. The Monroe Doctrine was inspired largely by the Russian menace; the Truman Doctrine almost solely by the Soviet menace. In 1823 Monroe made it clear that we would not intervene to support the Greek revolutionists against their Turkish overlords, and would expect the European powers to reciprocate by keeping their hands off this hemisphere. In 1947 Truman made it clear that we would go into Greece for the purpose of bolstering the existing regime against Communist revolutionists, and in this way defend at long range both our hemisphere and our way of life. The Truman Doctrine on the surface seemed to be a complete reversal of the Monroe Doctrine;

[1] National Opinion Research Center, *Opinion News*, April 15, 1947.
[2] *United States Statutes at Large*, vol. LXI, pt. I, pp. 103–105.

actually both policies were prompted by self-defense. In 1823 our defense line had been the Gulf of Mexico; by 1947 it had become the Gulf of Corinth.

Turkey and Greece were but small sectors on the far-flung front between communism and the rest of the world. Chaos was still king in much of western Europe, where Communist-inspired sabotage and strikes were cripplingly effective. Something drastic would have to be done if the democratic dikes were not to collapse.

2

The spark was provided by Secretary of State Marshall in his epochal speech at Harvard University, on June 5, 1947. He rather broadly indicated that if the nations of Europe—this was later interpreted to include Britain and Russia—would get together and carefully outline their needs for economic rehabilitation, the United States would support them so far as practicable. The basic assumption was that an economically prosperous Europe, which was essential to our own economy, would reject the creeping paralysis of communism.

Foreign Minister Molotov journeyed to Paris to discuss the Marshall Plan with representatives of France and Britain, but in the end walked out. A week or so later another conference convened in Paris, attended by hopeful delegates from the sixteen Marshall Plan countries, but boycotted by the U.S.S.R. and eight satellites. Czechoslovakia, which had not yet been taken over by the Communists, had promptly accepted and then had suffered the humiliation of having to withdraw under pressure from the Kremlin.

A major mystery is why the Soviets did not accept the Marshall proposal, and then snarl it up with their filibustering tactics. Congress by 1947 almost certainly would not have appropriated funds for a scheme that would result in heavy direct benefits to the Soviet Union. Perhaps the Politburo reasoned that it could best serve Soviet ends, particularly with the satellite states, by causing the boundaries to be drawn more sharply between the Communist and non-Communist world.

A partial answer by Moscow to the Marshall Plan was the so-called Molotov Plan, by which the satellites of Russia were knit more closely into the Soviet economic system. Another answer was the creation of the Cominform (Communist Information Bureau), which in effect was a revival of the old Comintern and which embraced the iron-curtain countries, plus the Communist parties of Italy and France. The Communist "line" was that the "dollar imperialists" of Washington, by cooking up the Marshall Plan, had forced the world to split into two camps. The truth is that Secretary Marshall brought out into the open a split that was obvious to all who had eyes to see—a split that had been deliberately chosen and fostered by the Kremlin. The Communist "line" was that the American "dollar imperialists" were trying to ram capitalism down the gullets of nations that did not want it. The truth is that the Marshall Plan was designed to set up conditions of economic vitality under which the people could exercise a free choice—free from the compulsive chaos fomented by communism. Prosperous nations that have known freedom do not willingly choose Marxist-Stalinist chains.

3

After passing emergency aid to keep France and Italy afloat, Congress debated at length early in 1948 the implications of the Marshall Plan. In effect the United States was proposing to appropriate a maximum of some seventeen billion dollars over a period of four and one quarter years. This seemed like an enormous sum to tax-burdened Americans, some of whom were inclined to brand the whole scheme "Operation Rathole." But to more far-visioned citizens the outlay seemed minor when compared with the cost of the war into which we seemed to be slithering. As the richest of the nations and as one that had come through the war with relatively little physical destruction, we had something of a moral obligation to unfortunate allies abroad; as an industrial giant, we could not deny that our prosperity was in

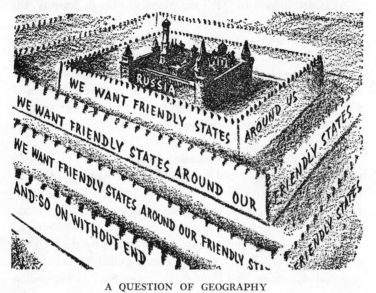

A QUESTION OF GEOGRAPHY

(From the Milwaukee *Journal*, 1948, by permission.)

considerable measure dependent upon prosperous overseas customers; and as the leader of the western democracies, we were under strong obligation to help hold the fort against communism. Without the stimulus of Soviet aggression, the aid-to-Europe program almost certainly would never have been proposed, much less accepted.

The Communist coup in Czechoslovakia, in February, 1948, helped spur the languishing Marshall Plan appropriation through Congress. The little Czech democracy, by far the most advanced of eastern Europe, had a host of friends in America, and its cruel fate had somewhat the same galvanizing effect abroad as Hitler's final rape of the mutilated republic nine years earlier. American eyes were further unglued when Jan G. Masaryk, the foreign minister who was popular in the United States, committed suicide

339

by falling from a window under circumstances that suggested foul play.[3]

As if determined to speed the Marshall Plan on its way, the Kremlin, not content with scooping in Czechoslovakia, further aroused the American people by forcing the hapless Finns into a distasteful alliance. Faced with these alarming object lessons, both the Senate and House overwhelmingly passed an initial appropriation of $6,098,000,000 for the relief of the European countries and China. Thus was the United States committed for four years to a species of lend-lease, this time not against fascism but against communism.

Marshall Plan succor was made available just in time to help tip the scales in the crucial Italian election of April, 1948, when the Communists threatened to wrest control from the non-Communists. Confronted with the actual fleshpots of "degenerate capitalism" and the hollow promises of communism, encouraged by American counterpropaganda, and bolstered by the presence of American warships, the Italian masses marched to the polls and returned surprising anti-Communist majorities. A resounding victory was chalked up for the western democracies in the cold war.

4

Serious difficulties had meanwhile been developing between the Soviets and the western Allies over supply routes through the Russian zone to the Allied sectors in Berlin. Symptomatic of this heightening tension were the drive in Congress for a tremendous air force and the final passage of a peacetime conscription law in June, 1948. Before the month ran out the Allies were forced to begin their costly and hazardous airlift to relieve the blockaded Berliners. Almost simultaneously, and obviously for retaliatory purposes, the United States dispatched a fleet of sixty giant bombers to bases in Britain. The western Allies likewise established a damaging counterblockade against the Russian zone of

[3] New York *Times*, March 11, 1948.

Germany. The extraordinary success of "Operation Vittles" in Berlin, despite Soviet obstacles and menaces, not only demonstrated impressive aerial power but bespoke the determination of both the western Allies and the beleaguered Berliners to hold on at all costs. In May, 1949, after nearly a year of face-losing failure, the Russians agreed to lift the blockade, and another victory for the democracies was chalked up.

The east-west struggle was also projected into the presidential campaign of 1948. Henry Wallace headed a Progressive ticket, with crazy-quilt support from various disaffected groups, including the American Communists. The latter applauded the intemperate charge of Wallace that the United States rather than Soviet Russia was the aggressor, that Wall Street-ridden America was out to "enslave the world," and that Washington was beset with fears that peace would "break out." Wallace's own inept efforts to serve as a self-appointed negotiator with Stalin had little effect other than to provide Communist propagandists with further excuses for assailing the warlike intentions of the United States. The Soviet press played up Wallace's utterances as representative of the real sentiments of the American people, and the Kremlin was probably encouraged to continue its stiffened attitude in Berlin and elsewhere by this evidence of serious disunity in America.[4] The unexpectedly small vote for Wallace, and the astounding triumph for Truman, who had taken the lead in promoting a get-tough-with-Russia policy, may have had a sobering effect on the Politburo.

In the closing months of 1948 additional sensations heightened the tempo of the ideological clash. War-weary Nationalist China, which America had backed half-heartedly and blunderingly, fell to pieces at the seams, and a momentous triumph was registered for the Communists when their armies swept to the gates of Nanking and Chiang Kai-shek was forced to bow out as president. A new Red Scare, whipped up in 1947 by the House Committee on Un-American activities, rocked the nation. Startling evidence as

---

[4] Walter B. Smith, *My Three Years in Moscow* (Philadelphia, 1950), p. 158.

to Soviet spy plots was unearthed, and faith in the integrity of the State Department was shaken when Alger Hiss, a former highly placed official, was inferentially found guilty of having passed on secret documents to Moscow. Firsthand evidence of Soviet brutality was brought dramatically home to Americans in August, 1948, when Mrs. Oksana Kasenkina, a Russian school teacher, dived to the pavement from the third story of the Soviet consulate in New York City rather than suffer further detention.[5] This episode apparently confirmed the revelations set forth by Russian refugees, notably in Victor A. Kravchenko's best-selling *I Chose Freedom* (New York, 1946).

5

By early 1949 it was evident that the sickly countries receiving aid under the Marshall Plan were beginning to respond favorably to the golden injections from America. Stalin's "peace offensive," launched deviously through a newspaperman and designed to bring Truman and Stalin together within the iron curtain, was rebuffed by Washington. The problems of the east-west split concerned not only the United States but the nations of western Europe as well. Besides, the machinery had already been set up to smooth out all these differences—machinery that had been effectively sabotaged by the Soviets.

In 1948 the democracies of western Europe, forced together by the Communist threat and inspirited by the Marshall Plan, had taken the first definite steps toward a defensive alliance. The United States, as their chief underwriter, was inevitably drawn toward them, and the world was not surprised by the announcement from Washington, in March, 1949, that we were about to sign the proposed pact.

The next month in Washington, with appropriate ceremony,

---

[5] See her own story in *Leap to Freedom* (Philadelphia, 1949). Such disclosures were further highlighted by the trial in New York of Valentin A. Gubitchev as a Soviet spy. This Russian engineer, attached to the United Nations staff, was found guilty in March, 1950, but was permitted to return to the Soviet Union.

the foreign ministers of twelve western nations, including the United States, affixed their signatures to the treaty. Almost simultaneously it was announced that Britain, France, and the United States had come to an agreement for the new government of western Germany, which ultimately would be eligible for membership in the Atlantic alliance. The action regarding Germany, while leaving open the door to union with the Soviet Zone, was in effect a separate peace, and as such further underscored the rift between east and west. The Russians retaliated by setting up a Communist regime in eastern Germany.

The American people welcomed the Atlantic pact, if not with enthusiasm, at least with an appreciation of its implications.[6] After our disillusioning experience in 1917 and 1941, there was little likelihood that we could stay out of a World War III. Perhaps the best way to prevent it was to serve notice on potential aggressors that we would be in it at the outset, rather than wait for our prospective allies to be picked off by the piecemeal tactics of Hitler. From the point of view of the western world, and contrary to the Communist cry, the treaty was not aggressive; produced by Communist aggression, it was designed to halt that aggression. It was not necessarily, as the Communists claimed, a deathblow to the deadlocked United Nations, but a regional defense pact clearly within the letter if not the spirit of the original charter. Even while the treaty was being negotiated, Communist leaders in the principal western nations, as if to contradict their own charges of aggression, served notice that in the event of a shooting war they would welcome invading Red armies.[7] The Communist *Daily Worker* in New York branded the Atlantic pact as "International Murder, Inc."

The epochal Atlantic Treaty was approved by the United States Senate, on July 21, 1949, by the lopsided vote of 82 to 13, and with surprisingly little opposition. More difficulty was encountered, especially in the House, over a huge arms appropria-

[6] *Public Opinion Quarterly*, XIII, 549 (Fall, 1949).
[7] For the views of American Communists, see New York *Times*, March 3, 1949.

tion for the new western allies. Finally, in September, 1949, Congress approved President Truman's recommendation in slightly reduced form, and voted $1,314,010,000 for the anti-Communist nations, chiefly our European partners.

The seriousness of the tension was dramatically high-lighted when President Truman, after having previously announced in September, 1949, that the Russians had recently exploded an atomic bomb, declared on January 31, 1950, that the United States would attempt to manufacture the even more dreaded hydrogen bomb. America was determined at all costs to defend her democratic institutions against Communist aggression.

The dark uncertainties of the future were rendered more gloomy by the open trafficking of the victorious Chinese Communists with the Kremlin. After protracted negotiations in Moscow, a disquieting Chinese-Soviet treaty was announced to the outside world on February 15, 1950. The Soviets not only promised to grant economic assistance worth $300,000,000 in the next five years, but agreed to withdraw from Port Arthur and Dairen.[8] Even though American commentators doubted that the Russians would keep their promises, and expressed the belief that there were secret protocols which were less favorable to China, the conclusion could hardly be escaped that the Russians were attempting to build up China—or at least to use her—as a formidable military ally.

The Far Eastern powder keg exploded at dawn, June 25, 1950, when the North Korean Communist army, trained and equipped by the Russians, suddenly launched a powerful all-out attack on the Republic of Korea, whose army had been trained and equipped by Americans, and whose government was sponsored by the United Nations. The circumstantial evidence is strong that the assault had been ordered by the Kremlin, which hitherto had been content with subversion and infiltration, but which now for the first time was flagrantly committed to armed aggression.

The Security Council of the United Nations met hastily at

---

[8] *Ibid.,* Feb. 15, 1950.

:cess, New York, to deal with a crisis that threatened its
ife. The Soviet delegate refused to attend, in pursuance of a
cott in protest against the continued presence of Nationalist
,hina, and without the usual Russian veto the Security Council
promptly and unanimously passed a resolution which branded
North Korea the aggressor, demanded a withdrawal of the invader, and called upon the member nations "to render every
assistance" to the United Nations in halting the invader.

The spotlight then shifted to Washington, for the United States
was the only power in a position to exert any appreciable strength.
American opinion overwhelmingly favored a strong stand; our
people were united against the Soviet Union by this wanton
attack. The feeling was general that the more territory the Communists grabbed the stronger they would be at the time of the
final showdown; that there must be no more Munichs; and that
a halt must be called to Soviet aggression, whatever the cost. On
June 27, 1950, only two days after the appeal of the United
Nations, President Truman gave orders for American air and sea
forces, later joined by ground forces, to repel the North Koreans.
Reversing his hands-off-Formosa policy, he announced that we
would not permit a Communist invasion of that strategic island.
Several hours after Truman's fateful decision, the Security
Council endorsed his action by voting formal military sanctions,
with the Russian delegate again absent.

The Moscow propaganda machine blared that South Korea
was the aggressor, and that the action of the United Nations was
illegal, because the Soviet Union and Communist China had not
been represented on the Security Council. But aggression had
been met with force, not appeasement, and if the men in the
Kremlin wanted to start World War III, it could begin in the
rain-drenched valleys of Korea.

Reviewing the torrential events of the years since 1945, the informed observer could readily perceive that Communist tactics
had within a few months caused the American people to modify
substantially their way of life, and to change drastically their

345

most basic foreign policies. The once-unilateral Monroe Doctrine, already shared with the Latin-American republics in 1940 to counter the threat of Hitler to this hemisphere, was further altered to meet the menace of Stalin to Greece and Turkey. The Truman Doctrine and the Marshall Plan were painful departures from our time-honored and long-cherished policies of isolation and noninvolvement. The Atlantic pact was an almost incredible reversal of the nonentanglement tradition, stemming back to the troublesome treaty of 1778 with France.

The intervention in Korea, most incredible of all, showed that the American people, in a crisis of this nature, were willing to take the war-declaring power out of the hands of Congress and put it into the hands of the President and the United Nations, and to send their boys to battlefields at the far ends of the earth, under the blue and white flag of the newly revitalized United Nations.

These portentous new policies and departures were not products of American tradition or of basic American desires. They were made in Russia and were authored by the men in the Kremlin.

XXVIII

A Long View

I

LOOKING back over the panorama of nearly two centuries
of Russian-American relations, the observer notes that
there were protracted periods of friendship and protracted periods of friction. In the days of the Czars the concept
of friendliness was on the whole dominant, despite its selfish base
—at least until the 1880's. But even during the heyday of the
friendship era there was vastly more ill feeling than the official
documents reveal. This was primarily because the American public, which did not write the diplomatic notes, reacted bitterly to
the despotic practices of the Russian government.

Why did the United States get along reasonably well—at times
conspicuously well—with Czarist Russia, in spite of the ideological gulf that yawned between the two great nations? The answer
is relatively simple. There were common foes, notably Britain;
there were common problems, such as freedom of the seas.
Neither nation was vibrantly aggressive, though Pan-Slavism and
Manifest Destiny provided something of a spark, in limited areas
and for limited periods. Each nation sprawled over an enormous
land mass; each saw relatively little of the other at close range; and

347

each could expand without impinging upon the domain of the other. But in the late nineteenth century, when the twin imperialisms—Russian and American—began to clash in the Far East, the traditional friendship went largely by the boards. There was of course some deception in official Russian intercourse, after the manner of monarchs everywhere, but there was no concerted effort in the nineteenth century on the part of the Russians to foment anti-American feeling through a systematic campaign of falsification and vituperation.

All this, or at least most of it, was changed under the Communist dispensation.

American attitudes toward Communist Russia, from 1917 to 1941, ran through cycles of hysteria, ignorance, indifference, and wishful thinking. During the war years, from 1941 to 1945, we tried to clasp our standoffish ally to our bosoms, but there was no warmth of response. Then came the era of disillusionment since 1945, when our eyes were opened to the nature of Russian communism. Our people learned—or at least a multitude of them did —a number of disagreeable truths about the Soviet Union.

First of all, the men in the Kremlin evidently did not want our friendship. Determined to create a Communist world and conditioned to a conspiratorial atmosphere, they deliberately turned their backs on us.

Second, the rift between Russia and America did not spring from any ordinary misunderstanding that could be readily ironed out by a personal meeting between Stalin and the President of the United States. The differences were too deep and too fundamental.

Third, the Communist party of Russia was not a political party at all in the American sense, but the spearhead of a world revolutionary movement that had its center in the U.S.S.R.

Fourth, Washington and Moscow could find no easy key with which to solve their common problems. The Soviet leaders were unable to view mutual difficulties through the spectacles of Anglo-Saxons or even western Europeans. With their Oriental-

Byzantine-Muscovite background, they have never really known the essence of democratic institutions, of the give and take of open debate, and of compromise and adjustment. The problem of negotiation with Russia was difficult enough under the Czars; now there has been erected the additional barrier of a fanatical neo-Marxist ideology.

Fifth, the pledges and agreements of the Russian Communists, like those of the Nazis, could not be trusted. Treaties have proved useful to the Kremlin as instruments for binding the hands of other countries, and freeing the Soviets to pursue their own world-girdling objectives.

Finally, the American public, at least by 1947, concluded that a head-on clash between the American democratic system and the Soviet socialist system was inevitable, unless the Moscow directorate was prepared to deviate sharply and sincerely from the objective of world revolution.

2

The historical record fortunately is studded with experiences that can well be borne in mind as one approaches the problem of Soviet Russia—the most frightening one of our times.

First, the Russian as an individual is still largely and basically the child of his ancestors. Not even the iron hand of Communism has been able to remold his genes. Traits noted in Russians of the nineteenth century by American observers have also been noted in Soviets of the twentieth century. Most commonly mentioned have been antiforeignism, secretiveness, suspicion, duplicity, evasiveness, procrastination, crudeness, callousness, ruthlessness, and brutality. Also observed have been resignation to absolutism; dependence on bureaucrats and centralized authority; toleration of censorship and the secret police; the Oriental attributes of patience and docility ("scratch a Russian and you will find a Tartar"); the tendency toward expansion and imperialism; and the missionary impulse of Pan-Slavism and communism. An awareness of these traits may enable us to approach the Russian problem—at best a complex and explosive one—with deeper understanding.

Second, whatever the Soviet rulers may say and do, the masses of neither Russia nor the United States want to fight each other. The men of the Kremlin, like Hitler, presumably do not welcome war, provided they can achieve their aims by bloodless victories.

Third, most of the traditional sentiment in Russia for the United States has clearly melted away under the hot blasts of poisoned air from the Soviet propaganda machine. But some residue presumably remains, especially among the fast-disappearing older generation.[1]

Fourth, despite the dismal record of Russian nonco-operation in the years after 1945, the Soviets made certain concessions or apparent concessions which indicated that the future was not completely hopeless. They continued to ship to us large quantities of manganese and chrome, so essential for our steel industry. They came to an agreement in 1948 regarding the return of some thirty lend-lease ships, though leaving other lend-lease accounts unsettled. They consented to our taking over the former mandated islands of Japan in the Pacific, though not until President Truman had served notice that we would keep them anyhow, and not until Secretary Byrnes had hinted that the Russians had better be reasonable if they expected us to support their title to Sakhalin and the Kurils.[2] They went along with us, and in some respects were ahead of us, in setting up an independent Israel, though probably with the intent of muddying the troubled waters of the Middle East to their own advantage. They did accept the United Nations Charter, and this new organization has done some notable work, particularly in the direction of social and economic welfare, even without Soviet co-operation. They did withdraw their disconcerting demand for a mandate over Tripolitania, though

[1] Baron Rosen in 1922 reminisced that after school in his boyhood town he would occasionally steal away to the American consulate and "take off my cap to the flag that represented to my boyish mind an emblem, of what, I could not exactly define, but which I felt deeply" (Baron Rosen, *Forty Years of Diplomacy* [New York, 1922], I, 67).

[2] J. F. Byrnes, *Speaking Frankly* (New York, 1947), p. 221.

this presumably was advanced merely as a bargaining lever. They did consent to peace treaties with Italy, Hungary, Romania, Bulgaria, and Finland, and in so doing made what they regarded as important concessions. They did ratify the Italian pact with surprising speed, though probably to get western troops out of the peninsula and leave the Italian Communists with a freer hand.

Fifth—and this seems to be the logical deduction from the instances just cited—the Soviets can and will co-operate when they perceive that it is to their own interests to do so. Self-interest is the one line of argument—perhaps the only line of argument—that has proved persuasive, and future western negotiators will do well to remember this fact.

Sixth, it has become abundantly clear that the only language that the Soviets really respect is the language of force. Stalin is supposed to have referred sneeringly to the Pope by saying, "How many divisions does he have?" The Sphinx of the Kremlin may never have made this remark, but the expression is thoroughly in character.[3]

Seventh, the Communist leadership has drastically changed its program and parts of its basic philosophy before, and since this is true, there is a possibility that it may do so again, this time in the direction of reasonableness and co-operation with the western world. The abandonment of global revolution actually would scarcely involve a greater break with pure Marxism than the Communist dictators of Russia have already made. The ideal of world revolution may in fact prove much less alluring to them if it becomes evident, should war break out, that there will not be any world left to revolutionize.

3

What constructive program can be properly outlined for American citizens hoping to grope their way through the frightening maze of postwar difficulties?

First, we should try to inform ourselves as fully as we can

---

[3] Byrnes denies that Stalin made this remark at Yalta (*ibid.*, p. 28). Admiral W. D. Leahy thinks it was at Potsdam (*I Was There* [New York, 1950], p. 408).

about the Soviet Union. If we do so, we can help shape more intelligently, and support more purposefully, the policies enunciated by our government in Washington. Fortunately, we have developed a body of experts, notably at the Slavic study centers of our great universities, who are equipped to deal objectively with Russian materials.

AN IMPOSSIBLE TRAIL?

(From the St. Louis *Post-Dispatch*, 1950, by permission.)

Second, in spite of manifest difficulties, we should actively encourage a program of informing the leaders and peoples of the

U.S.S.R. about ourselves and the democratic way of life. The
masses of Russia have long been buoyed up by the conviction,
implanted by the propaganda of the Soviet rulers, that though
conditions may be bad in Russia, they are worse in other countries, where laborers are "enslaved" by "monopoly capitalism." A
Russian song popular in the years after 1945 ran:

> I know of no other land
> Where man breathes as freely as here.[4]

The determined efforts of the Soviet rulers to withhold information from the rank and file is proof that they fear what will happen
should the light of truth ever penetrate the iron curtain. Not only
are the Russian masses deceived, but there is abundant evidence
that the Communist leaders are dangerously ignorant of conditions in the western world, or have fallen victim to Communist
self-deception.[5]

Third, we must "sell" democracy vigorously, even militantly.
We must recapture in this century much of the zeal that we had
for our democratic ideals in the nineteenth century, when we regarded ourselves—and were so regarded—as the natural enemies
of dictators and despots everywhere. Imperfect products are
difficult to export, and if our democracy is to prove attractive to
foreign peoples, we must make it work more effectively here at
home.

Fourth, since force is apparently the only language that the
Soviet leaders respect and since Soviet power instinctively seeks

---

[4] *Public Opinion Quarterly*, XI, 17 (Spring, 1947). Anne O'Hare McCormick
was asked by a child in a Moscow school "why the Americans kept their workers locked in dark cellars" (W. B. Smith, *My Three Years in Moscow* [Phila-
delphia, 1950], p. 113).

[5] Stalin told Ambassador Harriman in 1941 that he did not know much about
American public opinion, and he seemed to attach little importance to it. Stalin
also remarked to Roosevelt at Teheran that the way to overcome our moral objections to Soviet absorption of the Baltic states was to subject the American
people to a barrage of propaganda (R. E. Sherwood, *Roosevelt and Hopkins*
[New York, 1948], pp. 388, 861). Hopkins explained to Stalin on one occasion
that war materials were being delayed by strikes. Stalin replied, "Strikes? Don't
you have police?" (Smith, *My Three Years in Moscow*, p. 123).

vacuums, we would be courting both war and disaster if we were to permit our armed forces to fall provocatively behind those of the U.S.S.R. This does not mean that the door should not be kept wide open for a multilateral—not a unilateral—reduction of armaments.

Fifth, we should remember that patience is needed in dealing with the Soviets, who themselves have the Oriental-Byzantine patience of the Czarist Russians. Perhaps the Soviet system will overextend itself; perhaps Titoism or other deviations will get out of hand; perhaps fatal disunity will develop; perhaps there will be civil war over the succession to Stalin. An armed clash between Russia and the democratic world may or may not be inevitable, but in looking back over the vistas of history it is comforting to note how many "inevitable" wars—for example, the "inevitable" Anglo-Russian war of the late nineteenth century—never occurred. Crises sometimes work themselves out peacefully if one does not rush into them with clumsy hands. The following passage is taken from a popular American magazine:

It is a gloomy moment in history. Not for many years—not in the lifetime of most men who read this paper—has there been so much grave and deep apprehension; never has the future seemed so incalculable as at this time. In our own country . . . thousands of our poorest fellow-citizens are turned out against the approaching winter without employment, and without the prospect of it. In France the political caldron seethes and bubbles with uncertainty; Russia hangs as usual, like a cloud, dark and silent upon the horizon of Europe; while all the energies, resources, and influences of the British Empire are sorely tried. . . .

It is a solemn moment, and no man can feel an indifference—which, happily, no man pretends to feel—in the issue of events.

Of our own troubles no man can see the end.

The journal is *Harper's Weekly* magazine. The date is nearly one hundred years ago—October 10, 1857.[6]

In the current crisis one may extract some assurance from the

---

[6] I, 642.

fact that Czarism was about as antipathetic ideologically to democracy as is present-day Stalinism. Czarism in the nineteenth century was a menace not only to Europe but at times to us. Although the menace is now much more insidious and formidable, we are vastly stronger. In the nineteenth century the two nations succeeded, in spite of their antagonisms, in getting along reasonably well in the same world, although it was a larger world and although Pan-Slavism was a far cry from hemispheric revolution. Perhaps we can continue to tolerate each other, and possibly work out some kind of adjustment if—and this is a big "if"—we can only keep our heads clear, our nerves steady, and our powder dry. But we can hardly hope to achieve an enduring peace unless the present techniques and ultimate aims of Russian communism are substantially modified.

Bibliography

THE best coverage of the diplomatic aspects of the subject
to 1824 is John C. Hildt, *Early Diplomatic Negotiations
of the United States with Russia* (Baltimore, 1906); the
best coverage of diplomatic relations for the later years to 1867
is Benjamin P. Thomas, *Russo-American Relations, 1815–1867*
(Baltimore, 1930). A more general and highly readable survey of
Russian-American relations is Foster R. Dulles, *The Road to
Teheran: The Story of Russia and America, 1781–1943* (Princeton, 1944), which is based on published materials.

An excellent specialized bibliography appears in Anna M.
Babey, *Americans in Russia, 1776–1917: A Study of the Ameri-
can Travelers in Russia from the American Revolution to the
Russian Revolution* (New York, 1938). Broader in coverage is
Samuel F. Bemis and Grace G. Griffin, *Guide to the Diplomatic
History of the United States, 1775–1921* (Washington, 1935).
More general readings are listed in the present author's *A Diplo-
matic History of the American People* (4th ed., New York, 1950).

The present book rests in substantial part on the unpublished
records of the Department of State in the National Archives, from
1809 to 1906, when they break down into subject matter files,
and the most important of these were examined to 1916. Some
scattered materials of the 1930's were likewise made available. The
books by Hildt and Thomas develop diplomacy until 1867 on a

357

much larger scale than is undertaken here, and for this reason little attempt has been made to go behind their analyses of the purely diplomatic correspondence. But for the years following 1867 a considerable amount of new material has been extracted from the Department of State Archives and is here presented for the first time.

This study is less concerned with diplomacy than with American public opinion regarding it. A systematic survey has been made of the congressional debates and of the various documents published by Congress. Complete or substantially complete files of the following magazines, among others, have been canvassed: *The American Review of Reviews, The Century Magazine, Current Opinion, De Bow's Review, The Democratic Review, Fortune, Harper's Monthly Magazine, Harper's Weekly, The Independent, The Literary Digest, The Living Age, The Nation* (New York), *The New Republic, Niles' Weekly Register, The North American Review, The Outlook,* and *Public Opinion.* Many useful articles appear in specialized journals like *The Public Opinion Quarterly* and *The Russian Review.* For obvious reasons little attention has been paid to British newspapers and journals, except when articles from them were reprinted in American journals.

This is a pioneer work, and there are many phases of it that will repay intensive cultivation by other students. An attempt to analyze minutely the reactions of our daily newspapers toward Russia from 1781 to the present is a task beyond the powers of any one person, and for those periods when nothing of consequence was happening, singularly unrewarding. The present writer has concentrated on the newspapers for specific topics, notably the Civil War and the purchase of Alaska, but in order to cover general press reactions with any degree of adequacy he has found it necessary to rely heavily upon the monographic studies of other scholars and upon reprint magazines like *Public Opinion* and *The Literary Digest.* All significant American public opinion polls from their inception in 1935 to the present have been studied, and some of the conclusions drawn from them appear in the present author's *The Man in the Street* (New York, 1948). A detailed press opinion study by William E. Nagengast, *Russia through American Eyes, 1781–1871,* is being completed as a doctoral dissertation at Columbia University.

Two unpublished studies were graciously made available by their authors. Professor Richard W. Burkhardt, of Syracuse University, has prepared "The Soviet Union in American Textbooks," and Michael Cherniavsky, "The History of Soviet Opinion of the United States, 1936–1946, as Expressed in Russian Newspapers, Journals, Books and other Sources" (master's thesis, University of California, 1948). Professor Burkhardt has summarized his findings in "Report on a Test of Information about the Soviet Union in American Secondary Schools," *American Slavic and East European Review,* V (1946), 1–28.

The titles listed below are in general those most revealing of American attitudes toward Russia, official and public. They constitute a list for further reading, while indicating the principal published materials upon which this study rests.

Chapter I. The Legend of the Cordial Catherine

Samuel F. Bemis, *The Diplomacy of the American Revolution* (New York, 1935); C. F. Carusi and C. D. Kojouharoff, "The First Armed Neutrality," *National University Law Review,* IX (1929), 3–69; W. P. Cresson, *Francis Dana: A Puritan Diplomat at the Court of Catherine the Great* (New York, 1930); Roger Dow, "Prostor: A Geopolitical Study of Russia and the United States," *Russian Review,* I (1941), 6–19; F. A. Golder, "Catherine II and the American Revolution," *American Historical Review,* XXI (1915), 92–96; Miecislaus Haiman, *The Fall of Poland in Contemporary American Opinion* (Chicago, 1935); J. C. Hildt, *Early Diplomatic Negotiations of the United States with Russia* (Baltimore, 1906); Francis P. Renaut, *Les relations diplomatiques entre la Russie et les Etats-Unis, 1776–1825* (Paris, 1923); Francis Wharton, ed., *The Revolutionary Diplomatic Correspondence of the United States* (6 vols., Washington, 1889).

Chapter II. The Era of the Amiable Alexander

Charles F. Adams, ed., *Memoirs of John Quincy Adams* (12 vols., Philadelphia, 1874–1877), vol. II; Samuel F. Bemis, *John Quincy Adams and the Foundations of American Foreign Policy* (New York, 1949); Elizabeth Donnan, ed., "Papers of James A. Bayard, 1796–1815," *Annual Report of the American Historical Association for the Year 1913* (Washington, 1915), vol. II; F. A. Golder, "The Russian Offer of Mediation in the War of 1812," *Political Science Quarterly*, XXXI (1916), 380–391; William E. Nagengast, "Moscow, the Stalingrad of 1812: American Reaction toward Napoleon's Retreat from Russia," *Russian Review*, VIII (1949), 302–315; F. A. Updyke, *The Diplomacy of the War of 1812* (Baltimore, 1915).

Chapter III. A Muscovite Menace

C. F. Adams, ed., *Memoirs of John Quincy Adams* (12 vols., Philadelphia, 1874–1877), vol. II; "Correspondence of the Russian Ministers in Washington, 1818–1825," *American Historical Review*, XVIII (1913), 309–345, 537–562; Samuel F. Bemis, *John Quincy Adams and the Foundations of American Foreign Policy* (New York, 1949); A. G. Mazour, "The Russian-American and Anglo-Russian Conventions, 1824–1825: An Interpretation," *Pacific Historical Review*, XIV (1945), 303–310; Dexter Perkins, *The Monroe Doctrine, 1823–1826* (Cambridge, Mass., 1927); *Proceedings of the Alaskan Boundary Tribunal* (7 vols., Washington, 1904); J. Fred Rippy, *Joel R. Poinsett, Versatile American* (Durham, N.C., 1935); E. H. Tatum, Jr., *The United States and Europe, 1815–1823* (Berkeley, Calif., 1936); Arthur P. Whitaker, *The United States and the Independence of Latin America, 1800–1830* (Baltimore, 1941).

Chapter IV. Rifts in the Friendship

W. C. Bruce, *John Randolph of Roanoke, 1773–1833* (2 vols., New York, 1922); Arthur P. Coleman, *A New England City and the November Uprising; A Study of Editorial Opinion in New Haven, Conn., concerning the Polish Insurrection of 1830–1831* (Chicago, 1939); H. A. Garland, *The Life of John Randolph of Roanoke* (New York, 1850); David Hecht, *Russian Radicals Look to America, 1825–1894* (Cambridge, Mass., 1947).

Chapter V. The Calm of Despotism

G. T. Curtis, *Life of James Buchanan* (2 vols., New York, 1883); G. W. Curtis, ed., *The Correspondence of John Lothrop Motley* (2 vols., New York, 1889); Susan Dallas, ed., *Diary of George Mifflin Dallas: While United States Minister to Russia 1837 to 1839, and to England 1856 to 1861* (Philadelphia, 1892); John S. Maxwell, *The Czar, His Court and His People* (New York, 1848); J. B., Moore, ed., *The Works of James Buchanan* (12 vols., Philadelphia, 1908–1911), vol. II.

Chapter VI. Ferment in the Fifties

M. E. Curti, "Austria and the United States, 1848–1852," *Smith College Studies in History*, XI (1926), no. 3; J. G. Gazley, *American Opinion of German Unification, 1848–1871* (New York, 1926); F. A. Golder, "Russian-American Relations during the Crimean War," *American Historical Review*, XXXI (1926), 462–476; A. J. May, *Contemporary American Opinion of the Mid-Century Revolutions in Central Europe* (Philadelphia, 1927); J. W. Oliver, "Louis Kossuth's Appeal to the Middle West—1852," *Mississippi Valley Historical Review*, XIV (1928), 481–495; A. D. White, *Autobiography of Andrew Dickson White* (2 vols., New York, 1905).

Chapter VII. Fires of Civil Conflict

E. D. Adams, *Great Britain and the American Civil War* (2 vols., London, 1925); Félix Aucaigne, *L'alliance russo-américaine* (2ᵉ éd., Paris, 1863); H. E. Blinn, "Seward and the Polish Rebellion of 1863," *American Historical Review*, XLV (1940), 828–833; J. M. Callahan, "Russo-American Relations during the American Civil War," *West Virginia University Studies in American History*, Series 1, No. 1 (Morgantown, West Va., 1908); C. M. Clay, *The Life of Cassius Marcellus Clay* (Cincinnati, Ohio, 1886); Marion M. Coleman, "Eugene Schuyler: Diplomat Extraordinary from the United States to Russia, 1867–1876," *Russian Review*, VII (1947), 33–48; Roger Dow, "Seichas: A Comparison of Pre-Reform Russia and the Ante-Bellum South," *Russian Review*, VII (1947), 3–15; F. A. Golder, "The American Civil War through the Eyes of a Russian Diplomat," *American Historical Review*, XXVI (1921) 454–463; Marie Hansen-Taylor and H. E. Scudder, *Life and Letters of Bayard Taylor* (2 vols., 3rd ed., Boston, 1885); Albert Parry, "John B. Turchin: Russian General in the American Civil War," *Russian Review*, I (1942), 44–60; James R. Robertson, *A Kentuckian at the Court of the Tsars* [Cassius M. Clay], (Berea College, Ky., 1935); Joseph Schafer, ed., *Memoirs of Jeremiah Curtin* (Madison, Wis., 1940).

Chapter VIII. The Russian Fleet Myth

E. A. Adamov, "Russia and the United States at the Time of the Civil War," *Journal of Modern History*, II (1930), 586–602; Boston City Council, *Complimentary Banquet Given by the City Council of Boston to Rear-Admiral Lessoffsky* [sic] *and the Officers of the Russian Fleet, at the Revere House, June 7, 1864* (Boston, 1864); A. P. Coleman and M. M. Coleman, *The Polish Insurrection of 1863 in the Light of New York Editorial Opinion* (Williamsport, Penn., 1934); C. A. de Arnaud, *The Union, and Its Ally, Russia* (Washington, 1890); F. A. Golder, "The Russian Fleet and the Civil War," *American Historical Review*, XX (1915), 801–812; William E. Nagengast, "The Visit of the Russian Fleet to the United States: Were Americans Deceived?" *Russian Review*, VIII (1949), 46–55. The writer concludes on the basis of a few handpicked editorials that the American people *knew* all the time why the fleets had come. The present author has prepared an article entitled "The Russian Fleet Myth Re-examined," which challenges Mr. Nagengast's conclusions, and which will appear in a forthcoming issue of the *Mississippi Valley Historical Review*. The Nagengast thesis is presented somewhat more briefly and moderately in Earl S. Pomeroy, "The Myth after the Russian Fleet, 1863," *New York History*, XXXI (1950), 169–176.

Chapter IX. The Purchase of Alaska

T. A. Bailey, "Why the United States Purchased Alaska," *Pacific Historical Review*, III (1934), 39–49; James M. Callahan, "The Alaska Purchase and Americo-Canadian Relations," *West Virginia University Studies in American History*, Series 1, Nos. 2 and 3 (Morgantown, West Va., 1908); J. D. Champlin, Jr., *Narrative of the Mission to Russia, in 1866, of the Hon. Gustavus Vasa Fox, Assistant-Secretary of the Navy. From the Journal and Notes of J. F. Loubat* (New York, 1879; Foster R. Dulles, *America in the Pacific* (Boston, 1932); Victor

J. Farrar, *The Annexation of Russian America to the United States* (Washington, 1937); R. H. Luthin, "The Sale of Alaska," *Slavonic Review*, XVI (1937), 168–182; A. G. Mazour, "The Prelude to Russia's Departure from America," *Pacific Historical Review*, X (1941), 311–319; Hunter Miller, "Russian Opinion on the Cession of Alaska," *American Historical Review*, XLVIII (1943), 521–531; Virginia H. Reid, *The Purchase of Alaska: Contemporary Opinion* (Long Beach, Calif., 1940); Stuart R. Tompkins, *Alaska: Promyshlennik and Sourdough* (Norman, Okla., 1945).

Chapter X. *Cracks in the Ancient Friendship*

Constantine de Catacazy, *Un incident diplomatique* (Paris, 1872); William H. Egle, ed., *Andrew Gregg Curtin: His Life and Services* (Philadelphia, 1895); Wickham Hoffman, *Leisure Hours in Russia* (London, 1883); Allan Nevins, *Hamilton Fish: The Inner History of the Grant Administration* (New York, 1937); Albert Parry, "A Grand Duke Comes to America," *American Mercury*, LXVII, 334–341 (Sept., 1948); L. I. Strakhovsky, "Russia's Privateering Projects of 1878," *Journal of Modern History*, VII (1935), 22–40; Mark Twain, *The Innocents Abroad or the New Pilgrims' Progress* (2 vols., New York, 1901).

Chapter XI. *Pogroms and Prisons*

Cyrus Adler and A. M. Margalith, *With Firmness in the Right; American Diplomatic Action Affecting Jews, 1840–1945* (New York, 1946); A. C. Coolidge, *The United States as a World Power* (New York, 1918); Jerome Davis, *The Russian Immigrant* (New York, 1922); William W. Ellsworth, *A Golden Age of Authors* [Kennan] (Boston, 1919); J. W. Foster, *Diplomatic Memoirs* (2 vols., Boston, 1909); Thomas Hunt, *The Life of William H. Hunt* (Brattleboro, Vt., 1922); George Kennan, *Siberia and the Exile System* (2 vols., New York, 1891); Lewis A. Leonard, *Life of Alphonso Taft* (New York, 1920); Ralph M. McKenzie, *Jew Baiting in Russia and Her Alleged Friendship for the United States: A Brief History of Russia's Relations with America* (Washington, 1903); O. S. Straus, *Under Four Administrations* (Boston, 1922).

Chapter XII. *Despotism at Home and Dominance Abroad*

Chapter XIII. Malnutrition and Extradition

Henry Adams, *The Education of Henry Adams* (Boston, 1918); William C. Edgar, *The Russian Famine of 1891 and 1892* (Minneapolis, 1893); W. C. Ford, ed., *Letters of Henry Adams, 1858–1891* (Boston, 1930); W. C. Ford, ed., *Letters of Henry Adams, 1892–1918* (Boston, 1938); J. W. Foster, *Diplomatic Memoirs* (2 vols., Boston, 1909); Royal A. Gettmann, *Turgenev in England and America* (Urbana, Ill., 1941); Isabel F. Hapgood, *Russian Rambles* (Boston, 1895); William L. Phelps, *Essays on Russian Novelists* (New York, 1911); W. M. Salter, *America's Compact with Despotism in Russia* (Philadelphia, 1893); A. D. White, *Autobiography of Andrew Dickson White* (2 vols., New York, 1905).

Chapter XIV. The Sunset of the Century

A. L. P. Dennis, *Adventures in American Diplomacy, 1896–1906* (New York, 1928); J. K. Eyre, Jr., "Russia and the American Acquisition of the Philippines," *Mississippi Valley Historical Review*, XXVIII (1942), 539–562; Orestes Ferrara, *The Last Spanish War* (New York, 1937); F. W. Holls, *The Peace Conference at The Hague* (New York, 1900); A. D. White, *Autobiography of Andrew Dickson White* (2 vols., New York, 1905); Harvey Wish, "Getting Along with the Romanovs," *South Atlantic Quarterly*, XLVIII (1949), 341–359; E. H. Zabriskie, *American-Russian Rivalry in the Far East: A Study in Diplomacy and Power Politics, 1895–1914* (Philadelphia, 1946).

Chapter XV. A Parting of the Ways

Cyrus Adler, ed., *The Voice of America on Kishineff* (Philadelphia, 1904); Cyrus Adler and A. M. Margalith, *With Firmness in the Right* (New York, 1946); A. J. Beveridge, *The Russian Advance* (New York, 1903); Claude G. Bowers, *Beveridge and the Progressive Era* (New York, 1932); Tyler Dennett, *John Hay* (New York, 1933); A. L. P. Dennis, *Adventures in American Diplomacy, 1896–1906* (New York, 1928); A. W. Griswold, *The Far Eastern Policy of the United States* (New York, 1938); O. S. Straus, *Under Four Administrations* (Boston, 1922); O. S. Straus, "The United States and Russia: Their Historical Relations," *North American Review*, CLXXXI

(Aug., 1905), 237–250; W. R. Thayer, *The Life and Letters of John Hay* (2 vols., Boston, 1908); E. H. Zabriskie, *American-Russian Rivalry in the Far East* (Philadelphia, 1946).

Chapter XVI. The Russo-Japanese Debacle
Chapter XVII. Berated Are the Peacemakers

Cyrus Adler, *Jacob H. Schiff: His Life and Letters* (2 vols., London, 1928); J. B. Bishop, *Theodore Roosevelt and His Time* (2 vols., New York, 1920); Tyler Dennett, *Roosevelt and the Russo-Japanese War* (Garden City, N.Y., 1925); S. L. Gulick, *The White Peril in the Far East* (New York, 1905); F. H. Harrington, *God, Mammon, and the Japanese: Dr. Horace N. Allen and Korean-American Relations, 1884–1905* (Madison, Wis., 1944); A. S. Hershey, *The International Law and Diplomacy of the Russo-Japanese War* (New York, 1906); M. A. De Wolfe Howe, *George von Lengerke Meyer: His Life and Public Services* (New York, 1920); Henry F. Pringle, *Theodore Roosevelt* (New York, 1931); Baron Rosen, *Forty Years of Diplomacy* (New York, 1922); W. B. Thorson, "American Public Opinion and the Portsmouth Peace Conference," *American Historical Review*, LIII (1948), 439–464; W. B. Thorson, "Pacific Northwest Opinion on the Russo-Japanese War of 1904–1905," *Pacific Northwest Quarterly*, XXV (1944), 305–322; Sergei Witte, *The Memoirs of Count Witte* (Garden City, N.Y., 1921); E. H. Zabriskie, *American-Russian Rivalry in the Far East* (Philadelphia, 1946).

Chapter XVIII. Battling for Principle

T. A. Bailey, "The North Pacific Sealing Convention of 1911," *Pacific Historical Review*, IV (1935), 1–14; A. L. P. Dennis, *Adventures in American Diplomacy, 1896–1906* (New York, 1928); B. P. Egert, *The Conflict between the United States and Russia* (St. Petersburg, 1912); David R. Francis, *Russia from the American Embassy* (New York, 1921); J. V. Hogan, "Russian-American Commercial Relations," *Political Science Quarterly*, XXVII (1912), 631–647; Baron Rosen, *Forty Years of Diplomacy* (New York, 1922); W. Morgan Shuster, *The Strangling of Persia* (New York, 1912). There is a voluminous State Department file in the National Archives on the

Pouren case (No. 10901), on the Rudewitz case (No. 16649), on the abrogation controversy (No. 711.612), and on the Knox Manchurian proposal (No. 5315). All of these have been used in the present study.

Chapter XIX. Days That Shook the World
Chapter XX. The Red Specter of Bolshevism

F. L. Allen, *Only Yesterday* (New York, 1931); A. L. P. Dennis, *The Foreign Policies of Soviet Russia* (New York, 1924); D. R. Francis, *Russia from the American Embassy* (New York, 1921); W. S. Graves, *America's Siberian Adventure, 1918–1920* (New York, 1931); P. C. Jessup, *Elihu Root* (2 vols., New York, 1938); Meno Lovenstein, *American Opinion of Soviet Russia* (Washington, 1941); Dimitri von Mohrenschildt, "The Early American Observers of the Russian Revolution, 1917–1921," *Russian Review,* III (1943), 64–74; G. S. Moyer, *Attitude of the United States towards the Recognition of Soviet Russia* (Philadelphia, 1926); F. L. Schuman, *American Policy toward Russia since 1917* (New York, 1928); L. I. Strakhovsky, *Intervention at Archangel* (Princeton, 1944); L. I. Strakhovsky, *The Origins of American Intervention in North Russia, 1918* (Princeton, 1937); Pauline Tompkins, *American-Russian Relations in the Far East* (New York, 1949); John A. White, *The Siberian Intervention* (Princeton, 1950).

Chapter XXI. Reds Become Pinker
Chapter XXII. The Right Hand of Recognition

See works of Lovenstein, Moyer, and Schuman listed above. Also Harold H. Fisher, *The Famine in Soviet Russia, 1919–1923* (New York, 1927); M. W. Graham, "Russian-American Relations, 1917–1933: An Interpretation," *American Political Science Review,* XXVIII (1934), 387–409; S. N. Harper, *The Russia I Believe In* (Chicago, 1945); J. G. Hodgson, *The Recognition of Soviet Russia* (New York, 1925); Cordell Hull, *The Memoirs of Cordell Hull* (2 vols., New York, 1948); C. O. Johnson, *Borah of Idaho* (New York, 1936); Pauline Tompkins, *American-Russian Relations in the Far East* (New York, 1949); Sumner Welles, *The Time for Decision* (New York, 1944).

366

Chapter XXIII. A Descent Into the Abyss

L. F. Budenz, *This Is My Story* (New York, 1947); J. F. Byrnes, *Speaking Frankly* (New York, 1947); J. E. Davies, *Mission to Moscow* (New York, 1941); Cordell Hull, *The Memoirs of Cordell Hull* (2 vols., New York, 1948); R. E. Sherwood, *Roosevelt and Hopkins: An Intimate History* (New York, 1948); Pauline Tompkins, *American-Russian Relations in the Far East* (New York, 1949).

Chapter XXIV. The Strange Alliance
Chapter XXV. Forks in the Road

See books of Byrnes, Hull, Sherwood, and Tompkins listed above. Also J. R. Deane, *The Strange Alliance* (New York, 1947); D. D. Eisenhower, *Crusade in Europe* (Garden City, N.Y., 1948); H. H. Fisher, *America and Russia in the World Community* (Claremont, Calif., 1946); Frances Perkins, *The Roosevelt I Knew* (New York, 1946); Eleanor Roosevelt, *This I Remember* (New York, 1949); Elliott Roosevelt, *As He Saw It* (New York, 1946); P. A. Sorokin, *Russia and the United States* (New York, 1944); Edward R. Stettinius, Jr., *Roosevelt and the Russians: The Yalta Conference* (Garden City, N.Y., 1949); H. L. Stimson and McGeorge Bundy, *On Active Service in Peace and War* (New York, 1948); W. L. White, *Report on the Russians* (New York, 1945).

Chapter XXVI. The Shadow of the Hammer and Sickle
Chapter XXVII. The Cold War
Chapter XXVIII. A Long View

See books by Byrnes, Hull, Sherwood, and Tompkins listed above. Also, anonymous (presumably George F. Kennan), "The Sources of Soviet Conduct," *Foreign Affairs*, XXV, 566–582 (July, 1947); anonymous, "Stalin on Revolution," *ibid.*, XXVII, 175–214 (Jan., 1949); William C. Bullitt, *The Great Globe Itself* (New York, 1946); John C. Campbell *et al.*, *The United States in World Affairs, 1945–1947* (New York, 1947); John C. Campbell *et al.*, *The United States in World Affairs, 1947–1948* (New York, 1948); W. H. Chamberlin, *The European Cockpit* (New York, 1947); Lucius D. Clay, *Decision in Germany* (Garden City, N.Y., 1950); Vera M. Dean, *The United States and Russia* (Cambridge, Mass., 1948); John Fischer, *Why They Behave Like Russians* (New York, 1947); Frank Howley, *Berlin Command* (New York, 1950); Oksana Kasenkina, *Leap to Freedom* (Philadelphia, 1949); Arthur B. Lane, *I Saw Poland Betrayed* (Indianapolis, 1948); W. D. Leahy, *I Was There* (New York, 1950); Walter Lippmann, *The Cold War* (New York, 1947); Edgar A. Mowrer, *The Nightmare of American Foreign Policy* (New York, 1948); F. L. Schuman, *Soviet Politics at Home and Abroad* (New York, 1947); Walter B. Smith, *My Three Years in Moscow* (Philadelphia, 1950); *The United States and the Soviet Union: Some Quaker Proposals for Peace* (New Haven, 1949); Sumner Welles, *Where Are We Heading?* (New York, 1946).

Index

Adams, Henry, 149, 176, 177-178
Adams, John, 8
Adams, John Quincy, 1, 7, 14-16, 26-27, 32, 46
Adrianople, 17, 38
Afghanistan, 116-117, 143, 223
Alabama, 71, 86, 119
Alaska, 12, 29-33, 51, 91, 95-107, 127
Alexander I, 1, 12-21, 33, 35
Alexander II, 75-76, 92, 96-97, 115, 119
Alexander III, 132, 144
Alexis, Grand Duke, 108-111, 112-115, 118
Alliance, Russo-American, 19, 26, 82, 87, 91-92, 99, 288-303, 312
American Federation of Labor, 209, 266
American Legion, 266
American Relief Administration, 254-256
American Society of the Friends of Russian Freedom, 128
American system, 37
Amtorg Trading Corporation, 259
Anarchists, 134, 137, 143
Anglo-Russian entente, 223, 225
Antietam, 79
Archangel, 241
Argentina, 306, 315, 325
Armed Neutrality, 4-5, 66
Armenia, 117, 205
Atheism, 235, 264, 268, 277
Atlantic Charter, 308
Atlantic Treaty (1949), 343

Atomic bomb, 316, 318, 324, 328-329, 344
Austria, 25, 26, 30, 71, 117, 326
Azeff, Yevgeni, 213-214
Azerbaijan, 331

Baku, 205
Balkans, 38, 117, 147, 225, 285
Baltic states, 115, 169
Bases (bombing), 302-303, 310
Beilis, Mendel, 223n
Bergh, Henry, 96n
Berkman, Alexander, 143, 248
Berlin, 117, 326, 340-341
Bessarabia, 117, 179, 284
Bigelow, Poultney, 139
Black Sea, 38, 53, 116
Blaine, James G., 92-93, 151
Bloody Sunday, 206
Bobrikov, Governor General, 170
Bodisco, Alexander A., 65
Boer War, 162
Bolsheviks, 234-273
Bór, General, 308
Borah, Senator W. E., 270
Bosnia, 225
Botkine, Pierre, 133-134
Breshkovsky, Catherine, 207, 232n
Brest-Litovsk, 239
Bribery, 7-8, 131. *See also* Corruption *and* Graft
Britain. *See* Great Britain
British Columbia, 101-102, 104
Brown, Neill S., 59, 61-63

INDEX

Bryan, William J., 137, 153
Buchanan, James, 42, 47-50, 214
Bukovina, 284
Bulgaria, 55, 117, 148, 285, 330
Bureaucracy (Russian), 131, 138-139, 199, 310
Butchkavitch, Monsignor, 264
Butler, B. F., 87, 105
Byrnes, James F., 317n, 322, 326, 350

Cairo conference, 312-313
California, 28, 31, 225
Cameron, Simon, 96
Campbell, G. W., 46
Canada, 101-102
Canning, George, 32
Cassini, Count, 162, 180, 196, 201, 204
Catacazy, Constantine de, 65, 110-115, 118
Catherine II, 3-11, 20-21
Catholics. See Roman Catholics
Caucasus, 38, 40
Censorship (Russian), 47-48, 52, 60, 130-131, 139-140, 199
Chemulpo Bay, 196
Chesapeake, 14
Chiang Kai-shek, 314, 332, 341
Chicago aviation conference, 312-313
Chichester, Captain, 161
China, 148, 164, 176-179, 181, 257, 279, 315n, 332, 341, 344, 345
Chinese Eastern Railway, 172, 224, 258
Churchill, Winston, 246, 300, 313, 330, 347
Cimbria, 119
Circassians, 53
Civil War (U.S.), 70-94
Clarendon, Lord, 63
Clay, Cassius M., 45, 76, 95, 96, 106-107, 113n
Clay, Henry, 37
Clay, Launey, 96
Cleveland, Grover, 160
Cody, "Buffalo Bill," 109-110
Colby, Bainbridge, 249
Cold war, 335-346
Collective security, 277
Collins, P. M., 103n
Colonialism, 315, 333
Cominform, 338
Comintern, 246, 250, 263, 276n, 296. See also Communist Third International
Commerce, Russian-American, 7, 12-

14, 15, 36-37, 49-50, 69, 71, 172-173, 174-175, 221, 230, 259-261, 265, 268-269, 275
Commercial treaty of 1832, 50, 214-223
Communist Party (U.S.), 238, 263, 267, 276, 291, 296, 341
Communist Political Association, 296
Communist Third International, 246, 263, 275, 291. See also Comintern and World revolution
Confiscations (Bolshevik), 267
Congress of Berlin, 117
Congressional resolutions, 216-222
Constantinople, 38, 117
Constellation, 153
Contraband (1904-1905), 197
Coolidge, Calvin, 257
Corruption, 199-200. See also Bribery
Counterclaims (Russian), 266-267, 272
Cox, S. S., 122, 123-124
Crimean War, 63-65, 66, 76
Cummings, A. J., 125
Curtin, Jeremiah, 92, 99
Czechoslovakia, 279, 293, 330, 337, 339
Czolgosz, L. F., 143

Dairen, 314, 332, 344
Dallas, George M., 51
Dana, Francis, 6, 16, 46
Danube, 54-55, 326
Dardanelles, 31, 38, 116, 285, 307, 332
Darrow, Clarence S., 212
Dashkov, Andrei, 24
Davies, Joseph E., 296
Deane, General J. R., 289, 300, 310
Debts, problem of, 234, 244, 249, 256, 272-273
Decembrist revolt, 35, 37
Declaration of Paris, 69
Declaration of the United Nations, 289
Degaiev, Russian terrorist, 130-131
Department of State (U.S.): and 1821 ukase, 30-31; and pogroms, 124-125, 180-183; and seals, 155; and life insurance companies, 159; and proposed protest, 191; and Pouren, 209, 210; and Jews, 215; and treaty abrogation, 219; and extradition, 222; and Russia in 1945, 323; and Russian loan, 325; lists Russian violations, 326n
Depression (U.S.), 259-260, 266
Dewey, Admiral George, 161
Dillon, E. J., 247

Disarmament, 195, 257-258, 277, 328, 353-354
Dostoevsky, F. M., 137
Dukhobors, 138
Duma, 206, 220-221
Dungan, Irvine, 125

Earle, George H., 324
Education (Russian), 52-53, 292
Emancipation proclamation, 79
Embargo (1807–1809), 36-37
England. See Great Britain
English Society of the Friends of Russian Freedom, 128
Esthonia, 280, 284
Ethiopia, 144, 277-278, 293
Expansion (Russian), 39, 53-54, 62, 143-149
Extradition, 156-159, 209-212

Famine relief, 150-160, 253-256
Fascism, 277, 306
Field, Cyrus, 103n, 127
Finland, 169-171, 192, 205, 231, 280, 282-283, 307, 330, 340
Finnish immigration, 170-171
Fish, Representative Hamilton, 266, 273
Fish, Secretary Hamilton, 112, 118-119
Five-Year Plans, 258-261, 291
Fleets, Russian, 88 ff., 119, 165
Florida, 34
Formosa, 345
Fort Ross, 28
Fox, G. V., 97-99, 108
France, 3-4, 5, 26, 63-66, 71-72, 91, 144-146, 283-284, 300, 319, 328, 334, 338
Francis, David R., 222, 233
Franco, Francisco, 278
Franco-German War, 116
Franco-Russian entente, 144-145
Franklin, Benjamin, 7n
Frederick the Great, 3n, 8
Free love, 247
Free Russia, 128
Freedom of the seas, 29, 66, 196, 347
Freedom of worship, 272
Freneau, Philip, 11-12
Frick, Henry C., 143
Friends of Russian Freedom, 210
Friendship (Russo-American), 1-2, 15, 28-31, 34, 42-43, 47, 70, 73-74, 84 ff., 102, 104, 107, 111, 115, 120, 126, 132-133, 134, 152-153, 160-166, 183-184, 191-192, 195, 205, 219-222, 224-225, 293, 347-355
Frost, George A., 127
Furs, 12, 29-30, 31

Gapon, Father, 206
Garfield, James A., 120
Genoa Conference, 256, 266
George III, 3, 4
Germany, 261, 326, 327, 343. See also Prussia
Gettysburg, 83
Gogol, N. V., 137
Gold standard, 173
Golder, Dr. F. A., 86
Goldfogle, Henry M., 183, 216
Goldman, Emma, 143, 248, 266
Gompers, Samuel, 209
Good Neighbor Policy, 270
Gorchakov, Prince M. A., 77, 99, 106
Gorky, Maxim, 187, 253
Graft (Russian), 61, 66, 131, 138, 230. See also Bribery
Grant, U. S., 65, 109, 112-115, 116, 118
Great Britain, 2, 6, 14, 26, 31, 63-66, 70, 78-80, 99-100, 117n, 119, 146-147, 161-162, 178, 193, 223, 266, 307, 319
Greece, 30, 34, 329, 332, 335
Greek Orthodox Church, 16, 48, 53, 121-122, 134, 138, 186-187, 233, 263, 267-268, 292
Greeley, Horace, 75-76
Gresham, W. Q., 160
Gromyko, A. A., 331
Gubitchev, V. A., 342n

Hague, The, 168-169, 195
Hague Disarmament Conference, 168-169, 195
Hale, Senator J. P., 57
Hapgood, Isabel F., 137
Harding, Warren G., 251, 254
Hawaii, 159-160
Hay, John, 144, 176-179, 180, 188
Haymarket Riot, 134, 143
Hearst press, 180-181, 235, 278-279
Hemp, 37
Hirohito, Emperor, 277
Hiroshima, 316
Hiss, Alger, 342
Hitler, Adolf, 13, 261, 270, 277, 302
Holmes, O. W., 97-98, 108, 111
Holy Alliance, 25-27
Hoover, Herbert, 254, 259, 261, 266, 283

Hopkins, Harry, 310, 317, 322, 353n
House Committee on Un-American
  Activities, 277, 341-342
Howe, Julia Ward, 128, 211
Hughes, Charles E., 251
Hull, Cordell, 272-273, 312, 323
Hungary, 55, 57, 330
Hyde, Charles C., 212
Hydrogen bomb, 344

Ignorance of Russia, 289-293
Immigration (Russian), 56, 182
Imperialism (Russian), 225-226
Inalienable citizenship, 214-216, 223
India, 116-117, 145-147, 333
Indians (American), 29, 51
Industrial Revolution, 172-173
Intervention: in United States, 77-94;
  in Russia, 240-246; in Korea, 344-346
Iran, 331
Irish, 73
Iron curtain, 330
Isolationism (U.S.), 5, 8, 294-295, 320,
  346. See also Nonentanglement
Italy, 176, 235, 266, 334, 338, 340

Jackson, Andrew, 42, 49
Japan, 176, 178, 185-188, 188-190, 224-
  225, 243, 261, 270, 279, 285, 301, 314,
  316-317, 326, 333
Jeannette, 144n
Jefferson, Thomas, 12, 58
Jews, 121-126, 134, 179-181, 209-212,
  214-216, 217-218, 229, 294
Johnson, Andrew, 97, 102
Johnson Act, 274

Kalinin, M. I., 272-273
Kasenkina, Mrs. O., 342
Kellogg, Frank B., 257, 258
Kellogg-Briand Pact, 258, 271
Kennan, George, 126-135, 137, 157, 189,
  235
Kennan, George F., 59n, 126n
Kipling, Rudyard, 147, 161-162
Kishinev, 179-182
Knight Commander, 197
Knox, P. C., 224
Kolchak, Admiral, 241, 243
Korea, 146, 178, 185, 186, 190, 196, 333,
  344-345
Kosciuszko, Thaddeus, 9-10, 39
Koslov, Consul, 24-25
Kossuth, Louis, 57, 58, 62

Koszta, Martin, 59
Kravchenko, V. A., 342
Kropotkin, P. A., 131
Kulaks, 258
Kuril Islands, 314
Kuropatkin, General, 199
Kwantung army, 316-318

Lafayette, General, 3, 40, 63
Laibach, 27, 29
Lamsdorff, Count, 201, 202
Lane, Arthur B., 308
Lane, Franklin K., 91
Latvia, 280, 284
League of Nations, 257, 276, 283
League of Neutrals, 5
Legends. See Myths
Lend-lease, 287, 292, 294-295, 300, 304-
  306, 325, 340
Lenin, Nicolai, 234, 236, 245, 257
Leningrad, 45, 233n, 307
Lessovsky, Admiral, 82-84, 97
Life insurance companies, 159
Lincoln, Abraham, 71, 75-76, 79, 95
Literacy, 292
Literature (Russian), 92, 136-138
Lithuania, 52, 280, 284
Litvinov, Maxim, 257, 272, 277
Loan (to Russia), 234, 325
Lodge, Henry Cabot, 217
Lowell, James R., 128
Lublin, 308, 313, 315
Lynchings, 124-125, 181

MacArthur, General Douglas, 317n,
  333
McKinley, President William, 143, 162
McLeod Affair, 50
Madison, James, 16-20
Malby, G. R., 219
Manchuria, 146-147, 164, 166, 176, 177,
  178, 179, 185, 186, 190, 223, 224, 261,
  314-315, 316n, 332
Manganese, 350
Manifest Destiny, 50, 100-102, 102-104,
  347
Markham, Edwin, 208
Marshall, General George C., 326, 337
Marshall Plan, 337-340, 346
Martens, L. C. A. K., 248
Maryland Steel Company, 172
Masaryk, Jan G., 339-340
Massachusetts Peace Society, 26, 27
Maximilian, Archduke, 71, 78-79, 90-91

Mediation, 16-18, 34, 77-94
Memphis, 110
Mennonites, 138
Merv, 143
Mexico, 55, 71, 75, 90-91
Meyer, George von Lengerke, 201, 202, 204-205
Mikhailovitch, General, 330
Milwaukee, 109
Mission to Moscow, 296
Missionaries (American), 159, 176, 189
Moldavia, 38
Molotov, V. M., 284, 315, 327-328, 337, 338
Monroe, James, 33
Monroe Doctrine, 8, 32-33, 336, 346
Morrill tariff, 76
Motley, John L., 51, 111
Munich conference, 279-280
Murmansk, 241, 305
Mussolini, Benito, 277
Myths (about Russia), 3-4, 18-21, 33, 38, 152-153

Naples, 27, 29
Napoleon I, 13, 16
Napoleon III, 63, 71-72, 78-79, 90-91
Negroes (American), 21, 215, 293
Netherlands, 5-6
Neutrality, 276, 278, 285, 302, 303
New Deal, 261, 267
New Economic Policy, 252
New England, 19, 26, 27
New York, 81 ff.
Nicholas I, 35, 49
Nicholas II, 166-169, 204 ff., 231, 244
Nihilists, 136
Niles, Hezekiah, 20-21
Nonentanglement policy (U.S.), 27, 40, 74-75, 85, 346. See also Isolationism
North Pacific Convention of 1911, 255
Norway, 331

O'Brien, William S., 64
Open Door, 174-179, 190, 200, 224
Oregon, 29-30, 50-51
Orr, James L., 46
Orth, G. S., 81
Outer Mongolia, 227, 314, 332

Pacific bases, 350
Paderewski, I. J., 169

Palestine, 319, 350
Palmer, A. M., 247-248
Pamir Ridge, 146
Pan-Slavism, 55, 347, 355
Panama Canal, 333
Panama Pacific International Exposition, 222
Paris Peace Conference, 246
Paris Tribunal, 155
Paternalism (Russian), 131
Pearl Harbor, 294-295
Pearson, Drew, 299-301
Pendleton, J. O., 150, 152
Perkins claim, 105-106, 112
Permanent Court of Arbitration, 169, 187
Perry, M. C., 189
Persia, 23, 37, 53, 116-117, 146-147, 178, 225, 331
Peter the Great, 55, 60
Petrograd, 233n
Philadelphia, 12
Philippines, 161, 163, 164, 200, 205, 285, 333
Platov (the Cossack), 20
Plehve, V. K. von, 206
Pobyedonostsev, Constantine, 138
Pogroms, 121-126, 192, 278-279
Poland, 8, 10, 35-44, 56-57, 73-75, 86, 115-116, 121-126, 169-170, 192, 205, 229, 231, 244, 280-281, 307-308, 313, 322, 330
Police (secret), 7, 141, 156-157
Polish Aid Committee, 73
Political Refugees Defense League, 210
Poltava, 310
Popov, Rear Admiral, 83, 86, 97
Port Arthur, 146, 166, 186, 192, 314, 344
Portsmouth Treaty, 198-207
Portugal, 27, 329
Pouren, Jan J., 209-212
Prisoners of war: American, 322; retained by Russia, 326, 333
Prisons (Russian), 126, 128-129
Private property (Russian), 291-292
Privateers, 69, 77
Prohibition (Russian), 229
Propaganda (Communist), 263-264, 267, 272, 276, 326, 329, 345
Provisional government (Russian), 232-236
Prussia, 25, 26, 72-73. See also Germany
Pulaski, Casimir, 39
Purge trials, 138, 278

Quadruple Alliance, 25-26

Randolph, John, 46
Rapallo treaty, 256
Rasputin, 230
Recognition: of United States, 6-7, 13, 14; of Russia, 232, 261-273
Red Scare, 247-248
Red Terror, 245
Religious liberty, 204
Remington, Frederic, 139
Reparations, 251, 326
Reuter's, 77
Robert College, 148
Robins, Raymond, 213
Roman Catholics, 73, 115, 138, 264, 293-294
Romania, 284, 323, 330
Romanzoff, Count, 18n
Roosevelt, Anna, 311n
Roosevelt, Franklin D., 261 ff., 271, 295, 317, 322-323
Roosevelt, Theodore, 182-183, 185, 190, 198, 201, 204, 216
Root, Elihu, 213, 233
Rosen, Baron, 204, 350n
Rosenstraus, Herman, 122
Rothschilds, the, 126
Rozhdestvensky, Admiral, 193, 196
Rudewitz, Christian, 212-213
Russian-American Company, 29, 99, 101
Russian army, 22-24, 330n, 331
Russian expansion, 147-149
Russian Famine Relief Commission, 151
Russian fleets, 81-94, 92-93
Russian navy, 33, 99-100
Russian revolutionists, 141-143
Russo-German War, 285-286
Russo-Japanese War, 183 ff.

St. Louis, 109
St. Petersburg, 45-46
Sakhalin, 202-203, 314
San Francisco, and Russian fleet, 81 ff.
San Francisco Conference, 313, 315-316
Sarajevo, 227
Sardinia, 63
Sazonov, S. D., 220
Schiff, Jacob H., 204, 229
Schuyler, Eugene, 92, 136
Seals, 101, 102, 154-156, 225
Sebastopol, 64-65, 116
Second front, 298-300

Secret protocol (1939), 280-281
Secret treaties (Czarist), 234, 236
Secretiveness (Russian), 51, 60-61
Security Council, 316, 328, 331, 333n, 344-345. See also United Nations
Separate peace, 299
Serbia, 225
Serfs, 51-52, 75, 79
Seward, W. H., 57, 91, 102
Shuster, W. Morgan, 226
Shuttle bombing, 310
Siberia, 28, 36, 56, 100, 102, 126, 156, 243, 252
Sienkiewicz, Henry, 169
Singer Sewing Machine Company, 188
Slavery: in Russia, 21; in United States, 57, 64, 71
Smith, Alfred E., 271
Socialism, 247, 252
Socialists (American), 120
Society for the Abrogation of the Russian Extradition Treaty, 158-159
South Carolina, 43, 49
South Manchurian Railway, 224
Soviet-German Pact, 280
Spain, 5, 15, 27, 28-29, 163, 278-279, 329
Spanish-American republics, 27, 31-32, 34
Spanish-American War, 161-165
Spargo, John, 247
Spies (trial of British), 260-261. See Spying
Spitsbergen, 331
Spying (Russian), 47-48, 51, 60, 309
Stalin, Joseph, 13, 22, 234, 257, 261, 278, 279, 312n, 313, 316n, 320-323, 342, 354
Stalingrad, 310
Standley, Admiral W. H., 305
Stepniak, S. M., 131
Stereotypes, 15, 20, 42, 198-200, 208, 247-248, 292-293
Stimson, Henry L., 258, 271, 322
Stoeckl, Edouard de, 65, 102-105
Stoessel, General A. M., 192
Straus, Oscar S., 184
Stuttgart, 327
Suez Canal, 335
Sumner, Senator Charles, 73, 87, 104

Tabriz, 226
Taft, William H., 211, 217-222
Tariff of 1828, 37
Tariff war, 173-175
Tariffs, 60, 66, 173-175

Taylor, Bayard, 96, 137n
Taylor, M. C., 297
Teheran Conference, 312
Tennyson, Alfred, Lord, 67
Thompson, Lydia, 109
Tibet, 146, 178, 223
Tilsit, 13
Tito, Marshal, 330
Tochman, 56
Togo, Admiral, 190, 194
Tolstoy, Alexis, 92n
Tolstoy, Leo, 136-137, 138
Townsend, Senator C. E., 242
Trans-Siberian railroad, 185, 243, 302
Treason trials, 260-261
Treaty of 1824, 31
Treaty of 1832, 50, 214-223
Treaty of Washington, 112
Trent affair, 77
Trieste, 322, 330
Troppau, 27
Trotsky, Leon, 234, 236, 238, 257, 258
Truman, Harry S., 335-336, 341, 345
Truman Doctrine, 336, 346
Tschaikovsky, P. I., 150
Tsushima, 194, 199
Turchin, John B., 72
Turgenev, I. S., 92n, 136
Turkey, 6, 23, 30, 37, 53, 117, 146, 178, 307, 332, 335

Ukase of 1821, 29-33
Union of American Hebrew Congregations, 122
United Nations, 315, 328, 336, 343, 344-345, 350. *See also* Security Council
Universities (Russian), 142, 205-206
Ural Mountains, 291-292

Vatican, 297
Veto (in U.N.), 316, 328-329

Vicksburg, 84
Vishinsky, A. Y., 261, 329
Vladivostok, 197, 285
Vodka, 51-52
Votes (in U.N.), 313-314

Walachia, 38
Wallace, Henry A., 341
Wallbridge, General Hiram, 85
War debts, 266, 307. *See also* Debts
War of 1812, 3, 16, 37
War of Independence, 2
Warsaw, 39, 56, 308
Washington, George, 26, 35-36, 85
Washington Disarmament Conference, 252
Welles, Gideon, 84
Welles, Sumner, 284
White, Andrew D., 64, 66, 137n, 139, 140, 155, 215
White, William L., 298
White Terror, 246
Whites, 240-246
Wilson, Woodrow, 218, 222, 223, 228, 232
Wisconsin, 56
Witte, Sergei, 173, 202
Women's suffrage, 171
Work camps, 260
World Health Organization, 329
World revolution, 238, 246, 249-250, 251, 277, 291, 323, 334
World War I, 23, 228-238
World War II, 24, 280 ff.
Wrangel, General, 241

Yakovlev, General, 310
Yalta, 311n, 312, 313-314
Yellow Peril, 186, 187, 200
Yugoslavs, 322, 330

Date Due